The Enemy at His Pleasure

THE ENEMY

AT HIS

PLEASURE

————

*A Journey Through the Jewish Pale of
Settlement During World War I*

S. ANSKY

Edited and Translated by

JOACHIM NEUGROSCHEL

METROPOLITAN BOOKS

Henry Holt and Company · New York

Metropolitan Books
Henry Holt and Company, LLC
Publishers since 1866
115 West 18th Street
New York, New York 10011

Metropolitan Books™ is a registered
trademark of Henry Holt and Company, LLC.

Originally published in Warsaw in 1925 under the title
Khurbn Galitsiye, in S. Ansky: *Gezameite Shriftn.*

Library of Congress Cataloging-in-Publication Data
An-Ski, S., 1863–1920.
  The enemy at his pleasure : a journey through the Jewish pale
of settlement during World War I/S. Ansky ; edited and translated
by Joachim Neugroschel.—1st ed.
     p.   cm.
ISBN 0-8050-5944-X (hc.)
1. Jews—Persecutions—Poland. 2. Jews—Persecutions—Russia.
3. World War, 1914–1918—Jews—Poland. 4. World War, 1914–1918—
Jews—Russia. 5. Poland—Ethnic relations. 6. Russia—Ethnic relations.
7. An-Ski, S., 1863–1920. I. Title.

DS135.P6 A63 2002
940.3'089'9230438—dc21

                                              2002028823

First Edition 2003

Designed by Victoria Hartman

Printed in the United States of America

1   3   5   7   9   10   8   6   4   2

Beware of terrible times . . . the earth
opening for a crowd of corpses.
Expect famine, earthquakes, plagues,
and heavens darkened by eclipses.

But our land will not be divided
by the enemy at his pleasure . . .

—From "July 1914," by Anna Akhmatova
Translated by Stanley Kunitz and Max Hayward

Introduction

Historians of the twentieth century in Europe may well decide to name it the age of slaughter. In terms of civilian deaths, the twentieth century surpassed even the excess of the Thirty Years' War of 1618–1648, which had claimed two-thirds of Germany's population of eighteen million. While modern technology was certainly responsible for the wide-scale killing of noncombatants—which far outnumbered the soldiers who died in war—what was unique to the twentieth century was the effort to wipe out entire and specific populations—Jews, in particular, by the Nazis, and also Gypsies and homosexuals.

In total, some hundred million Europeans were killed in twentieth-century warfare. The United States and Latin America also played a role, but Europe carried the day, not only with regard to sheer numbers but also in terms of the varieties of despotism: dynastic autocrats, revolutionaries, dictators, and even elected tyrants controlled and installed the fatal regimes of czarist Russia, the Soviet Union, Fascist Italy, Spain, and Nazi Germany.

A comprehensive record of this modern carnage is hampered by significant gaps in the history. One such omission is a full accounting of the crimes committed against Jews during World War I, specifically a campaign of brutalization by the Russian army that involved wholesale expulsions and massacres (despite the presence of half a million Jews serving in the czar's army). Approximately 600,000 Jews were deported from their homes; the deportations were especially vicious near the front lines;[1] and

---

1. John D. Klier and Shlomo Lambroza: *Pogroms,* Cambridge University Press, Cambridge, 1992, pp. 291–292.

according to historians' anecdotal estimates, perhaps as many as 100,000 to 200,000 Jewish civilians in Russia and in the Russian-occupied zones of the Austrian-Hungarian Empire were killed.

At the outbreak of World War I, most Jews in czarist Russia were still governed by a set of residential and commercial prohibitions that confined their lives to the Pale of Settlement, a strictly defined region decreed by Catherine the Great in the 1790s. The census of 1897 indicated that some five million Jews lived in the Pale, which then included all of Russian Poland, Lithuania, Belorussia, most of the Ukraine, the Crimea, and Bessarabia. Only 200,000 lived elsewhere in Russia. Jews had few civil rights. A string of antisemitic pogroms during the 1880s and 1890s had heralded a period of utter disillusionment for many who expected to see some relaxation of the prohibitions imposed on them as the new century approached. Instead, economic, religious, and cultural activities (especially in connection with Yiddish) were subjected to ever more rigid controls. As a result, millions of Jews fled Russia for Western Europe and America prior to the war.

Any remaining hopes that the twentieth century would deliver on the promise of the Enlightenment were dashed by the Kishinev pogrom in 1903: 45 dead, nearly 600 injured, 1,500 homes burned, and 600 stores looted. Damage was estimated at three million rubles.[2] Although pogroms persisted until 1906 and sporadically thereafter, the riot in Kishinev stood out, particularly to observers in the United States and Western Europe, as a symbol of the czar's repressions, generating protests, articles, pamphlets, books, and a degree of universal dismay. In the years that followed, attention turned away from the fate of Russia's Jews, perhaps partly resulting from the czar's alliance with France and Great Britain and almost certainly, once the Great War began, from the overwhelming general devastation of the fighting.

The Jewish tragedy taking place on the Eastern Front was essentially "kept separate from world events,"[3] as one historian noted, although a few writers did speak up: leftists like Maxim Gorky and John Reed, as

---

2. Ibid., p. 200.
3. David Roskies: *Against the Apocalypse,* Harvard University Press, Cambridge, Massachusetts, 1985, p. 92.

well as Jews like Herman Bernstein, L. Levinson, Zvi Cohn, Simon Dubnow, and Sholem Asch.[4] And there were also visionary poems by Yiddish poets such as Zishe Landau and H. Leivick. Clearly, some observers were aware that a historic "phenomenon" was occurring, but there was almost no focused documentation or analysis.

In Victor Trivas's 1931 German film *No Man's Land,* a few soldiers from different armies, friends and foes, accidentally wind up in the same trench, where they worked out a mode of cooperation and communication. They manage to converse in their various languages, but one soldier, a Jew from the Pale of Settlement, can only gesticulate, having lost the power of speech. He is referred to simply as the "unknown soldier." While Trivas shows the general experience of the Jews in the Pale, depicting their expulsion from a small town, in the unknown soldier the director created the truest personification of those victims of the Russian army during the Great War. In light of this memory hole, S. Ansky's detailed recollections of his experiences on the Eastern Front are of the greatest importance: they constitute our most direct and specific descriptions of that period.

S. Ansky (1863–1920), Yiddish and Russian writer, now best known for his play *The Dybbuk,* was no stranger to the Pale of Settlement or to the Russian-occupied area of Austria-Hungary. Born Shloyme Zanvel ben-Aaron Rappaport in Vitebsk (now in Lithuania), Ansky rejected Jewish Orthodoxy at an early age, embracing socialism with the ferocity characteristic of his pious forebears. By age seventeen he was running a commune on the edge of Vitebsk for boys who like him had fled the rigidity of a yeshiva education.

A revolutionary dedicated to spreading the socialist word, Ansky was determined to learn about the Russian peasantry and working class, and so he left the Pale in 1887, at age twenty-four, taking work as a miner near Yekaterinoslav in southern Russia. There he acquired the name Semyon Akimovich, discarded the Yiddish of his childhood, and rejected his past, declaring it "bourgeois" and "decadent." Three years later, Ansky appeared in St. Petersburg, determined to infiltrate the

---

4. Ibid., p. 325, notes 45–52, p. 325, note 56.

intelligentsia. He began to write, publishing accounts of his time as a miner and signing his work as S. Ansky (a name he invented, he explained, in honor of his mother, Anna). The czar's police eventually caught up with Ansky's illegal socialist activities and forced him into exile, which led to six years spent in Paris and Switzerland, where, in 1901, he helped found the Russian Social Revolutionary Party.

Ansky underwent a transformation upon his return to St. Petersburg in 1905, dramatically taking up Jewish and Yiddish culture. The pogroms were partly responsible for this change, as was Y. L. Peretz, the Yiddish and Hebrew writer, who proved to Ansky that Yiddish could be written as modern European literature. What began with Yiddish writing developed into full-time devotion to the Jewish institutions that abounded in St. Petersburg: the Jewish Literary Society; *Evreski Mir,* the Russian-Jewish monthly, of which Ansky was the literary editor; the Society for Jewish Folk Music. He even took up the cause of Yiddish as a national Jewish language. This engagement led to lectures and travels in the Pale, teachings on Jewish folklore, Yiddish culture—and revolution.

This sympathy and familiarity with the folklore, fully on display in *The Dybbuk,* made Ansky a natural leader for an ethnographic expedition, organized by the Jewish Ethnographic Society and financed by Baron Vladimir Ginsbourg, designed to preserve and record the artifacts—songs, stories, pictures, superstitions, customs—of a culture in decline. Having flourished in the Pale more or less unimpeded for several centuries, Jewish culture was by 1911, the year of Ansky's first expedition, threatened by the joined forces of emigration, persecution, and modernity.

The expeditions continued until 1914, stopped only by the outbreak of war. But by this time Ansky knew the Pale, its people and geography, intimately, and when much of "his" territory was overrun or cut off by the fighting, he was well able to envision the devastation that invading—and antisemitic—armies would bring to small communities already much afflicted by poverty, discrimination, and isolation. His expedition experience had taught him some other crucial lessons, among them the arts of fund-raising, lobbying, and winning influential backers. Alarming reports of massacres and mass deportations came quickly, prompting Ansky and other concerned Jews with influence in political and military circles to act. Wheedling, begging favors, pounding on tables, pulling strings—all of which Ansky describes here in excruciating detail—paid off in the form of an organized relief operation set up under the auspices of official, nonsectarian Russian welfare and medical institutions. But Ansky's mission was clear and explicit: to bring material help to Jews trapped on the front lines, enlist the authorities in their protection if possible, and let the world know what was happening.

Thus in the spring of 1915, Ansky went back to the Pale, this time on the coattails of the Russian army. He traveled the Eastern Front—every bit as bloody as the better-documented trench warfare on the Western Front—intermittently until the outbreak of the Russian revolution, following the fortunes of his country's military forces: when they were pushed back from the front, so was he. However, Jews in the Pale and in Galicia—the Austrian region occupied by Russia—suffered the alternating presence of not one but two conquering and retreating armies: the habitually antisemitic czar's troops on the one side (who rarely cared that many of the Jews they encountered were in fact Russian), and the Germans and Austrians on the other. Moreover, the army in retreat was often far more brutal than the army advancing.

Ansky provides an extraordinary catalogue of barbarism: commonplace rape and looting; expulsions of whole villages and towns; scorched-earth withdrawals; humiliations, lynchings, kidnappings, torture, massacres. And not just once or twice: one shtetl on Ansky's route was conquered and reconquered no fewer than fourteen times. In countless meetings with community leaders and representatives, he heard account after account of starvation and homelessness; indeed, he witnessed the complete breakdown of civilized life. Ravaged by war, the towns he visited were wastelands of rubble, famine, hollowed-out, half-collapsed buildings, people missing limbs, tribes of orphans. While other populations certainly suffered from the fighting (especially the ethnic Germans, who had settled in the region generations earlier), the Jews, according to Ansky's portrait, were exquisitely vulnerable; subject to routine persecution during peacetime, the particular conditions of war made this open season on Jews for all comers—soldiers, peasants, Cossacks, neighbors.

Ansky's contributions were perforce limited, dwarfed by the scale of the peril. He went from one place to another, distributing rubles, arranging for supplies of food and access to medical treatment. Beyond money, though, Ansky was probably most effective (and most in demand) in the timeless Jewish practice of intercession. Over and over, local Jews would beg him to plead their case with the regional commanders—to modify curfews, release hostages, rescind expulsion orders, put an end to the looting and the killing, even allow the baking of matzohs. The Jews well understood the historic dimensions of Ansky's position, and of their own: He heard about a lavish dinner prepared by one community leader for the local army officer and his adjutants. While serving the food, the host reportedly told his guests the story of Queen Esther, a Jew, and her husband, the ruler of Persia—how Esther plied the king with entertainments in the hope of influencing him to save her people.

As well as physical privation, Jews were the victims of an additional form of harassment, reported at length by Ansky: gossip, rumor, and libel, all of which amounted to a propaganda campaign. Stories abounded of Jews aiding the enemy, hiding German soldiers, developing special telephones for communicating secrets to the enemy, building devilish machines able to blow up Moscow in one stroke. And the old libels resurfaced: that Jews were murdering Christian children for use in their rituals. Ansky heard these rumors at all levels of Polish and Russian society—illiterate peasants, St. Petersburg intellectuals, citified hotel chambermaids, high-level officers and politicians. Often he heard the same story repeated in towns separated by hundreds of miles: for example, that one Cossack massacre was provoked by a Jewish girl who fired at the soldiers from her window. The persistence of this centuries-old, primitive mechanism of persecution, particularly on the eve of high-tech warfare, is perhaps one of the most poignant aspects of Ansky's findings.

When not traveling, Ansky was knocking on the doors of Jewish benefactors for contributions, buying supplies, pleading with army personnel for travel permits and space for freight, lobbying political and welfare figures for some relief to the Jewish plight. It is hard to imagine a better-qualified, more fitting man for the moment or the task. Very few, if any, of Ansky's contemporaries were at once as deeply Russian and profoundly Jewish as he was. Ansky's experience was remarkable, perhaps unique: He was a traditional Jew from the Pale, a Russian worker, a key political insider, an influential and widely published Russian writer (his collected Russian writings ran to five volumes), and a Yiddish specialist. He did his relief work wearing a Russian army uniform, and Jews in the Pale were astounded to find him speaking Yiddish. His friends included such Russians as Count Alexei Tolstoy and Alexander Kerensky, who would lead the first government after the czar's 1917 abdication, and such Jews as Simon Dubnow, the great historian, and Y. L. Peretz. At the same time he felt a deep affinity with the poor and the refugees, taking pains to note down the names even of people he met once and would never see again.

The duality that made Ansky so right for his relief work—perhaps it might be called ambivalence—also marked him with the affliction of the assimilated modern Jew: he was never quite at home either in the secular Russian world or among traditional Jews. This discomfort was evident in his writing, indeed in these memoirs themselves. The first literary fruits of his war travels were Russian journals that were later used as a basis for this retrospective account, written in Yiddish but in the Russified Yiddish of the assimilated intellectual. There are only occasional biblical and Talmudic references, and the Hebrew-Aramaic component is almost entirely missing (although Ansky was able to incorporate this skillfully and intricately in such works as *The Dybbuk*). And while the different speakers quoted in the book demonstrate a variety of Yiddish vocabularies, Ansky himself relies heavily on German as a source of words and even follows German pronunciation. Ambivalence lurks in his other work as well. The subtitle of *The Dybbuk* is "Between Two Worlds." And in his satirical mini-epic *Ashmedai*, Lilith, queen of the demon world, eventually returns to her Jewish roots but is punished for her straying by never being fully accepted by either the Jews or the demons. Then again, in his humorous nonfiction *Letters from Beyond*, Ansky pokes fun at Russian Jews who try to live with a foot in each world—secular and religious.

Nonetheless, in these memoirs—the title of the original Yiddish is *The Destruction of Galicia*—Ansky's identification is unequivocal: he is a Jew in a position of privilege speaking for his people. Perhaps for this reason, and also given his knowledge of Russian military and institutional antisemitism, Ansky was quick to dismiss the rumors of Jewish assistance to Russia's enemy (on a mythical level, he also gives certain credence to some fantastical Jewish tales of last-minute salvation and vengeance). Strangely, he never allows for even the slightest possibility that Jews might have wanted to help Germany and Austria. But who could have blamed them? Jews enjoyed civil rights in both monarchies, while czarist Russia regarded them as domestic traitors. And the Austrians were the most decent army of occupation, in Ansky's assessment. The Germans were somewhat less decent, but still far more so than the Russians, the Cossack regiments, and the Poles.

Ansky's record of Jewish experience in the Pale during the war raises the question: Was this the first act in the horror that would culminate in World War II? We can find no clear uninterrupted line that stretches from the Russian persecutions to the Nazi regime. While multiple anti-Jewish traditions existed in both Russia and Germany, regardless of the political system in place, there was no consistent structure of discrimination. The legal and popular status and definition of Jews varied greatly. Russians, for example, seldom defined Jews as a race, and despite some hurdles, those who converted to Christianity were more or less accepted into the Russian fold. German antisemitism, on the other hand, relied on a biological definition of Jews inspired by the French writer Gobineau. While the church, in all its variations, had always been hostile to Jews, especially in Germany, Austria, and Eastern Europe, Christian attitudes and behavior were never uniform and at no period could one predict or predetermine the response of the local population. Perhaps the constant is that bystanders—indeed, accomplices—were on hand to aid and implement a policy of persecution and many of these were in positions of governmental or military power.

If there is any visible direct link between the different experiences in the Pale during the First and Second World Wars, it is to be found in the most surprising of realms: in 1939, as Poland (once largely part of the Pale of Settlement) was carved up between Hitler's Germany and Stalinist Russia, some Jews chose to live under Nazi rule. They or their parents recalled the bestiality of the Russian army, and weighed it against the more humane treatment received from the Germans only twenty-five years earlier.

When the czar fell in 1917, Ansky was taken by surprise, even though he had anticipated a seismic shift for several years, traveling, as he had been, with angry, hungry soldiers. He returned to Russia to throw his weight behind the Social Democrats and his friend Kerensky, even taking a seat in the Duma. Not surprisingly, Ansky opposed the Bolshevik revolution that occurred a few months later, ultimately distancing himself from politics, for a while resuming relief work during the bloody civil war that followed the revolution. He also devoted himself to giving this account of the years 1914 to 1917, which he was able to complete, but he did not live to see either the end of the civil war or his war memoirs published. Ansky died of illness in 1920; *The Destruction of Galicia* was published posthumously in Yiddish.

—Joachim Neugroschel

The Enemy at His Pleasure

VOLUME ONE

I

The world war broke out in 1914 after a brief moment of half-genuine, half-bogus Jewish patriotism for Russia. Rabbis had even embraced V. M. Purishkevitsh, cofounder of the antisemitic Union of the Russian People. And Jews in St. Petersburg had actually knelt down at the monument to the worst Jew-baiter, Czar Alexander III, and recited the prayer for the dead. But with the war dark storm clouds gathered over the Jews of Russian Poland, Russia, and Galicia (the official name for Austrian-ruled Poland), bringing the most dreadful accusations and persecutions. The years of horror began in Poland, with its dense and lethal antisemitic air and the Poles' bitter economic struggle against Jews. . . . Through whispered libel, slander, and denunciations, the Poles set about tarring the Jews as Russian traitors, emphasizing in the process their own devotion and loyalty. They claimed, falsely, that each time the Germans and Austrians marched into a Russian-Polish town or village, the Jews befriended them, and supplied them with food and information. The lies went further: Jews were spying for the enemy, sending secret messages, channeling millions of rubles' worth of gold—and more.

As a result, wild and fantastic stories circulated in the Russian army. Some people said that Jews had tried to smuggle a million and a half rubles in gold to the Germans by hiding the cash in an empty coffin. There was a similar tale about Jews who had stuffed gold into slaughtered geese. Also, a Jewish miller had allegedly used a telephone in his cellar to contact the Austrians, while another Jew had cut the Russian phone lines, reconnecting them to the Austrian exchange. Supposedly, Jews were using fires and light signals to send information to the enemy:

they had flashed lights from windows and had set trees and houses ablaze to reveal the Russian army's positions. In another report, Jews had put the plans for the Kronshtadt mutiny into a bottle and tossed it into the sea, so that it would float to Germans in the city of Danzig.* Then there was the Jew who had rescued Germany's Kaiser Wilhelm from Russian captivity. And a thousand other stupid, outlandish fabrications that were accepted uncritically by the officers, not to mention the rank and file. The scope of the slander is evident in a letter from a Russian soldier to his family: "The Jews are betraying us. . . . They disemboweled one Jew's carcass, stuffed it with eight million rubles' worth of gold, and carried it across to the enemy. When the war is over, we'll get even with them."

At first, the slanderers did their work quietly and furtively. But soon they took off their masks and accused the Jews openly. Prince Lubomirski† himself was not ashamed to tell the Russian writer Kondurushky that "90 percent of the Jews are traitors and 10 percent are spies." The smaller politicians and the masses were even less restrained. They said everywhere that the Jews were waiting for the Germans to arrive and helping them. German zeppelins were called Beilises‡ and Jews were nicknamed "Vilyush"—after Wilhelm, the German kaiser. Poles routinely told Russian soldiers, "May God protect you from Germans and Kikes."

In the Polish churches the priests stirred up the congregations and it was often stated quite explicitly that the goal of the incitement was to kill the Jews in Poland. One Polish journalist wrote, "We don't need our independence if the Jews stay in our country—they have defiled it."

The libel snowballed, becoming more and more ugly, spreading through the army and all over Russia. These lies encouraged a powerful anger toward the Jews, even among people who had always been free of antisemitism.

The rumors found particularly fertile soil among the troops on the front line and especially the officers and commanders, who got their

---

*The Kronshtadt port was the site of several anti-czarist actions.
†Prince Zdzislaw Lubomirski was a leading member of Poland's governing body, the Regent Council.
‡Mendel Beilis, a Jew from Kiev, was tried on ritual murder charges in 1913 and acquitted; the case was notorious.

ideas about Jews from *Novoye Vremya* and other newspapers that supported the Black Hundreds.* Indeed, the officers' corps was thoroughly permeated with profound hatred for Jews. The former supreme commander in chief, Grand Prince Nikolay Nikolayevitsh, was an old lunatic who did little else but rant and rave at everyone around him and slap them as well. A Jew-baiter like the rest of the imperial family, he had fallen under the sway of Boleslaw Januszkiewicz, a general and a virulent Polish antisemite. Januszkiewicz made it his life's goal to be rid of the Jews, and he pursued his mission with a vengeance.

From the generals down to the lowest ensign, the officers knew how the czar, his family, the general staff, and Januszkiewicz felt about Jews; and so they worked to outdo one another in their antisemitism. The conscripts were less negative but hearing the venom of their superiors and reading about Jewish treason day after day they too came to suspect and hate Jews.

By tightening the noose, the Poles hoped not only to achieve the goal of ridding themselves of Jews but also to exploit the idea of Jewish treason to cover up their own sin of Austrian leanings. Most Poles living under the czar were pro-Austrian, which they expressed by forming underground anti-Russian societies. The same may be said of the czarist army. The real traitors, like Colonel Miasoyedov, who had the highest rank in the army, needed to blame someone for their treason. And what better scapegoat than the Jews? They were used for this purpose as much as possible. It was no coincidence that when Jews were tried for espionage, the accusers and the witnesses were usually unmasked as spies themselves.

Nor were the traitors the only ones who had a need for Jewish treason. Every commander and every colonel who made a mistake had found a way to justify his crime, his incompetence, his carelessness. He could make everything kosher by blaming his failures on a Jewish spy. The officers, who accepted lies against Jews without question or investigation, were quick to settle accounts with the accused. In Radom, nine Jews were hanged for "welcoming Germans in a friendly way"; in Zamosc, seven for the same wrongdoing; in Krasnik, four Jews, including the local rabbi and the government-appointed rabbi. There were similar incidents in

---

*A right-wing vigilante group. Its rallying cry was *"Bey zhidov,"* Beat the Jews!

numerous towns and shtetls. On the roads one often saw Jews strung up in trees or shot for treason—and always with no inquiry and no trial.

The persecution reached mammoth proportions. No concrete indictment, no proof of espionage or welcoming the Germans was needed to arrest, banish, or hang a Jew. Being a *Jew* sufficed. And since all Jews were traitors, why bother looking for individual offenses? And why punish or kill one Jew at a time? Mass violence was launched. When the Russian army passed through many towns and villages, especially when there were Cossacks, bloody pogroms took place. The soldiers torched and demolished whole neighborhoods, looted the Jewish homes and shops, killed dozens of people for no reason, took revenge on the rest, inflicted the worst humiliation on them, raped women, injured children. One Cossack boasted that he had grabbed a boy and ripped off both his sidelocks, along with some skin. A Russian officer talked about seeing Cossacks "playing" with a Jewish two-year-old: one of them tossed the child aloft, and the others caught him on their swords. After that, it was easy to believe the German newspapers, when they wrote that the Cossacks hacked off people's arms and legs and buried victims alive.

I happened to get hold of a letter written by an ordinary Russian soldier, who described what he had seen: "It all depends, of course, but I feel a little sorry for the Jews. Imagine, the soldiers whip them, hitting them with sticks seventy-five times, countless times, they shoot them, perhaps even innocent people. It's like calling to a chicken to give you its neck—you tear the head off, and the chicken scurries away. The Jews are like that too."

The rotten, criminal elements in the army did terrible things to Jews, giving in to vile and shameful urges. For political purposes, the atrocities were repeated, in different ways and on a larger scale, by the officers: the supreme commanders of the different armies, including Nikolay Nikolayevitsh. On the assumption that every Jew was a spy, they began by expelling Jews from the towns closest to the front: at first it was just individuals, then whole communities. In many places Jews and ethnic Germans were deported together. This process spread farther and farther with each passing day. Ultimately all the Jews—a total of over two hundred thousand—were deported from Kovno and Grodno provinces.

Thus began one of the darkest periods in Jewish history. Over a quarter million Jews found themselves trapped on the battlefield; the economic upheaval caused by the war ruined thousands of families; and hundreds of towns and villages were destroyed in the savage cross fire. Tens of thousands fled the horrors of the war, hundreds of thousands were deported, driven out, left homeless. . . .

The people were ruined by a catastrophe, which was made all the more devastating by the utter disorganization of Russian and Polish Jews, who were caught in a state of total chaos. Nevertheless, by exerting its strength, Jewish society managed to respond to the catastrophe on a material level, finding the wherewithal to resettle and prevent the starvation of about one million refugees. Politically, however, our leaders were unable to gain any concessions or help by lobbying the Russian government. They tried everyone—but always came up against a brick wall. They also turned to England and France, as the community's leaders had done before. But these two democratic countries regarded Nicholas II as an ally and his subjects as an inexhaustible source of cannon fodder, so they bowed to Russian reactionism and turned a deaf ear to our cries.

Nor did it help to implore Russia's liberal intelligentsia, which was enjoying a romance with the Poles and beginning to believe every anti-Jewish lie. Liberals tried to explain the treason of which Jews were accused, blaming it on the czarist government's persecution. Russian intellectuals had one response to complaints from Jews: "Keep quiet, hold your tongues, the army's anger against you is so intense that drawing attention to yourselves will only make things worse."

Some Jewish leaders tried ingratiating themselves with the cabinet ministers who were the leading, most despicable pogromists. Naturally, these efforts got them nowhere. And the situation grew worse and worse.

2

Right after the outbreak of hostilities, the Russian army overran Galicia. Within two or three months it swept all the way to Prague in the west and Hungary in the south. There were vague, murky reports that the

Russians, especially the Cossacks and Circassians, were savaging the Jewish population in these occupied areas. In Brody, the troops, provoked by a stray shot, burned down a huge portion of the city, pillaged homes, and massacred several Jews. They also razed Austrian Husiatyn and Belz. In Lwow, a pogrom claimed a large number of victims. Similar rumors were heard about dozens of other towns, and in the conquered region the Jews, economically ruined and cut off from both Austria and Russia, were starving to death.

The worst thing about the news was that it arrived sporadically in the form of obscure and ambiguous rumors: a letter from the front line that had somehow managed to elude the censor, a story heard from a Jewish soldier who had been wounded and evacuated, and so forth. All other channels of information were blocked. Ordinary citizens could not get in or out of Galicia. Chance letters and stories conveyed shocking cries rather than systematic facts.

"My arms go numb and my eyes fill with tears," wrote one Jewish soldier, "when I think of the horrors I've seen in Galicia, when I remember the soldiers' and the Cossacks' atrocities. The Jews were killed, the women were raped in the streets, old women's breasts are slashed off, and the people are left to die in their agony."

Another wrote: "We arrived at a shtetl in Galicia. The military discovered a wine cellar, broke it open, and started to get drunk. I too joined with others and got drunk. But when I left the wine cellar and saw what was happening in the streets, what the soldiers were doing to the Jews, I quickly sobered up."

A third soldier, who was eventually driven insane by his experiences in Galicia, noted:

> Whenever the Russians come through, the Christians would put icons in their windows. If there was no icon, the house was therefore Jewish, and the soldiers could destroy it without fear of punishment. When our brigade marched through one village, a soldier spotted a house on a hill, and told our commander that it was probably the home of Jews. The officer allowed him to go and have a look. He returned with the cheerful news that Jews *were* indeed living there. The officer ordered the brigade to approach the house. They opened the door and found some twenty Jews

half dead with fear. The troops led them out, and the officer gave his order: "Slice them up! Chop them up!" I didn't stay to see what happened next. I ran and kept running until I passed out.

From these and other dismaying reports, we realized that things beyond human comprehension were going on in Galicia. A vast region of one million Jews, who only yesterday, under Austrian rule, had enjoyed human and civil rights, was trapped in a cordon of blood and iron. Severed from the rest of the world, they were at the mercy of Cossack and Russian soldiers provoked like wild beasts. It was as if an entire people were perishing.

The first urgent task was to make contact with the Galician Jews and bring them material aid. But this was no easy mission. During the early months of the war, affluent people were unwilling to organize any large-scale plan to help the victims. Hoping to make up for their inaction by donating large sums to the overall war effort, they argued that the Jews "mustn't set themselves apart" from the rest of society—that might make them look unpatriotic. With their exuberant patriotism and indifference to the plight of their people, these wealthy men refused to hear anything about the Galician Jews.

A high-level Russian official, returning from Galicia, asked one millionaire, a renowned leader in the Kiev Jewish community: "Why don't you organize some kind of relief for your Galician brothers, who are starving to death?"

The millionaire replied: "Your excellency, we do not regard the Galician Jews as our brothers; we see them as enemies, with whom we're at war."

I must add, however, that within a short time this attitude changed, even among the wealthy patriots. When the news from Galicia clearly showed the reality of the devastation, I decided to do whatever I could to get into Galicia, tour the ruined towns, confirm the scope of the crisis and the destitution, and come back to Russia with facts and figures. Then I would not plead for but *demand* help.

It was a hard plan to carry out. For three months I knocked on all sorts of doors until I was finally granted a travel pass to Galicia. Initially, I hoped to get a commercial permit allowing me to ride the freight trains shipping flour, and I would then switch to a sugar consignment. But this proved impossible. So I approached the mayor of St. Petersburg, Count Ivan Ivanovitsh Tolstoy, and asked him to assign me to any medical division leaving for Galicia.

Tolstoy, a true friend of the Jews, responded eagerly to my request. Since no medical unit was heading there, he gave me a letter addressed to S. Tchelnokov, the mayor of Moscow and chief delegate to the Russian Association of Towns. He in turn gave me a letter to Prince George Y. Lvov, chairman of the All-Russian Zemstvo Alliance.* The prince was unable to help me, but he did advise me to get Count Tolstoy to write a letter to Alexander Guchkov,† who was in Warsaw and had the power to dispatch me on a mission to Galicia. Upon returning to St. Petersburg to see Count Tolstoy, I received a wire from Moscow. Prince F. D. Dolgorukov, who was heading a detachment to Galicia, would be willing to take me along. I hurried back to Moscow—but Dolgorukov's detachment was then ordered to go to Riga instead. Another commander, Konovalov, was forming a detachment, but refused to include me. In short, everyone expressed sympathy with my task, offered to help—and sent me on to someone else.

I finally made up my mind to reach Galicia via Warsaw. With Count Tolstoy's letter to Guchkov and a recommendation from Prince Lvov to V. V. Virubov, deputy of the Warsaw section of the Zemstvos Union, I left for Warsaw on November 21, 1914.

---

*Zemstvos—local assemblies of self-government that functioned in most Russian provinces.
†Alexander Guchkov, an influential industrialist, had been instrumental in organizing relief efforts during Russia's 1904–5 conflict with Japan. A member of the Duma and leader of the progressive, reformist Octobrist Party, Guchkov was appointed chairman of the Duma Committee of Military and Naval Affairs when the war began.

3

I spent over a month in and around Warsaw, until I was allowed to enter Galicia. I did not meet Alexander Guchkov. He was in Lodz, and it was nearly impossible for a civilian to set foot there. Virubov gave me a very cold reception, and stated flat out that he could not possibly help me. He did add, however, that in the next few days a detachment of the Zemstvo Alliance would be heading toward the Galician border, under the command of General Gerasimov, who had a Jewish adjutant named Blokh. I ought to try; perhaps they would take me along. After a while he suggested that if I got nowhere with Gerasimov, I might take a job with the Warsaw office of the Zemstvo Alliance. Figuring this would help me find some way of getting to Galicia, I accepted. But then he told me that there was no opening for me, and he didn't know when one might be available. I thought Virubov was confused and unreliable; he reminded me of the Russian proverb about a person who has seven Fridays in one week— that is, he kept changing his mind. And soon he did something that confirmed this impression.

That same evening, several hours after our conversation, he showed up at my hotel room; he was preoccupied and agitated. He stood in the doorway and began talking: "You wanted to work at the alliance," he said. "I've got a job for you. Over ten thousand wounded men have just arrived. Some of them are in the train yard, out in the open. They are tired, frozen, hungry. We have absolutely no place to put them. It'll be your assignment tomorrow morning to set up a hospital for six thousand wounded. The alliance will give you whatever you need. Find an empty house, an unoccupied building. If the owner won't let you use it, requisition it in the name of the union. Get hold of doctors, orderlies, nurses. I don't care if they're all Jews. But it has to be ready tomorrow. Can you do it?"

He wanted me to build a palace overnight.

Organizing a Jewish military hospital in Warsaw for the alliance would have been an extremely significant step. While the whole enterprise sounded preposterous, and I, a stranger, had no idea where to begin, I was nevertheless determined to do whatever it would take to see the idea through. I promised Virubov I'd give him a definite answer by midnight.

I asked Y. L. Peretz, the writer, what to do, and he advised me to consult two people, Natanson, president of the Warsaw Jewish community, and Kempner, the secretary. When I contacted them, they expressed interest in the project and they introduced me to Vaysblat, chairman of the Jewish medical committee, and Farbshteyn, the secretary. The two gentlemen were offended that Virubov, who knew about the medical committee, hadn't appealed to them directly. I reported this to Virubov and wanted to bow out from my role as middleman, but he insisted that the arrangements were to go through me.

The committee began working energetically and by midnight it had a building that could hold 4,000 men. A staff had also been quickly pulled together: doctors, orderlies, nurses. When I passed all this on to Virubov, he said they now needed space for only 2,000 patients. By morning the figure had dropped to 500, and later that evening it turned out that all the wounded had been evacuated. Nevertheless, the hospital was still needed—thousands of men would be arriving soon.

Several days after that, Virubov suggested that I go to Rovno and pick up some ambulances. When I had completed my mission, he said I should set up a food distribution center at a small station three miles from Warsaw; once again, I agreed.

By the time I was done, some twelve days had passed and I had had a chance to survey the mood in Warsaw. The city was in a feverish state, still reeling from the furious German assault in October. The people were preparing for even worse attacks. Terrible battles were raging near Lodz. Day after day, some thirty or forty thousand wounded men arrived in Warsaw; the streets were teeming with ambulances, orderlies, nurses. Everyone was on the move; the roads were jammed, claustrophobic, choked by masses of people. Endless convoys drove by; automobiles dashed to and fro; artillery rumbled through; troop trains lumbered along. In the distance, we could hear the cannon booming, and from time to time German doves of steel flew through the clear sky, bringing death and destruction. The city breathed with the hot gasping of a man with a deathly disease.

By now, all the fighting on the eastern front was concentrated in Poland, bringing Warsaw with all the bloody horrors of war, the grieving and suffering, sobbing and moaning. Vast numbers of injured soldiers and refugees had come from the battlefields; many of them miserable Jewish deportees, who had left their towns and villages, driven out by terror, racism, denunciation and slander. More than any other place, Warsaw bore the evidence of the calamity that had struck the Jews of Poland. Each day brought thousands of additional refugees, most of them on foot, robbed, naked, starving, shaken, and helpless. All these wretched people headed toward Warsaw's Jewish community center, which was boiling like a kettle, overflowing with anguish. There were more than fifty thousand uprooted Jews in Warsaw. Most were given temporary shelter in various institutions. Several hundred women and children were put up at Hazomir, the Jewish literary club established and directed by Peretz.

Sick and weary, battered by the troubles, Peretz found himself at the heart of the disaster. He spent half of each day at the community center working *with* the new refugees and the second half working *for* them: collecting money, dashing to meetings, writing articles and appeals.

Right after my arrival in Warsaw, Peretz took me to Hazomir. The huge auditorium was packed wall to wall with cots, benches, and crates, with men, women, and children. Three or four children were sitting or lying on each cot. The place looked like a devastated anthill. It was filled with a deafening roar of voices. I noticed that the elderly stayed apart, off to the side, while isolated people were moving through the human torrent all alone, pensive, embittered, unaware of anybody else.

Normally a large gathering of children is a joyful event. But these children wandered through the room, looking forlorn, aimless, bereft.

Most tragic of all was the refugees' calm. No one complained; no one got excited. As Peretz, Yakov Dineson, the writer, and I entered the room, no one even noticed that strangers had arrived. The refugees looked at us blankly and said nothing. When we questioned them, they talked about the hardship they had suffered. They spoke softly, in a monotone, with stony faces. It was as if these people had lost themselves as well as all hope.

A young man told us about the destruction of his shtetl, adding in a flat, indifferent tone, "My father and brother stayed there. They've probably been killed."

"Of course they've been killed," a woman interrupted coldly. "People who came from there said they'd seen both their bodies lying in the street."

The young man took this news apathetically, as if it didn't concern him.

Another woman talked about her seventy-four-year-old uncle with the same icy detachment. He had been found in a pit with his arms and legs cut off and his tongue sliced out.

At this point, we were surrounded by dozens of people, each one with a story—dreadful accounts of blood and terror. The refugees drew appalling pictures of war and vicious Cossack atrocities. It was the same story everywhere: Cossacks had ridden in with swords and sticks, driven the Jews out of their homes and ordered them to leave town. People had trudged twenty, thirty, forty miles through the rain and mud, with their young, their old, and their sick. They had struggled on, day and night, fainting with hunger and thirst. The old and the feeble collapsed and died; frail children perished in their mothers' arms; pregnant women gave birth.

We stood in the middle of the auditorium, listening to these dismal tales. Next to me a skinny little girl of about eight with a delicate face also listened earnestly, like an adult. Her big, black eyes expressed an eternity of sadness.

4

I had heard about the Polish libel campaign but in Warsaw I got to see it at work with my own eyes. It was a thoroughly organized, methodical attack. The slander had poisoned every corner of Polish life, down into the most remote cracks. No matter where I went, I kept hearing rumors about Jewish espionage.

I was staying at the Hotel Europa, which was filled mostly with high-level Russian officers. When I entered my room, it was being straightened by an elderly Polish maid with a simple yet respectable appearance. As soon as I arrived, she began: "Oh, Excellency, you can't imagine what's going on here. You can't imagine what we've had to put up with. The Germans come flying in their diabolical machines, dropping bombs and killing dozens of innocent people! . . . The disasters we've seen, all because of the Germans and the Jews."

"How have the Jews harmed you?" I asked.

"The telephones," she said vaguely. "They tell the Germans everything. On Sunday, when the flying machines came over, the Jews sent them all sorts of signals—they told them that the biggest generals were in the church. So they started bombing it. Luckily, they missed."

The elderly maid went on, delivering a recitation that she apparently replayed for every guest she met. The bombs had killed or wounded a dozen people, she said, all of them Poles, and all because the "Jews have an ointment, which they smear on their bodies so the bombs won't hurt them."

Several hours later, I met with Virubov, who angrily snapped: "It's maddening the way the Poles behave toward Jews. Not a day passes without a scandal. We have a food center here, where Polish students work. Today six Jewish students arrived to join them, but as soon as the Poles saw the Jews, they got up and stormed out, leaving the center without a staff. And then they refused to come back until the Jews were gone."

The next day, I was visited by a Jewish woman, Miss Markovitsh, who had worked as a nurse in Lodz. When the situation there grew critical and the wounded were evacuated, she was transferred to Warsaw. Arriving late at night, she went to the first military hospital she found. She showed her papers and asked if she could spend the night. But when the woman in charge saw that the nurse was Jewish, she screamed: "You're all traitors! You send gold to Germany, you destroy our phone lines. You should be ashamed that you're a Jew!"

And she wouldn't allow the nurse to sleep there—she threw her out in the dead of night.

A few days later, I met with Shifsboyer, the delegate of a medical unit stationed in Lodz. He too was Jewish.

"Of all the ordeals we've suffered in Lodz," he told me,

the worst was the way the Poles treated us. There was no lie they wouldn't spread about us. When airplanes were flying overhead, one man standing out on his porch looked up and sneezed. The Poles reported him, claiming that his sneeze was a signal indicating where to drop the bombs, even though the planes were high up, and the man was arrested. Another time, the Poles dragged a Jew to headquarters and accused him of hiding a German pilot. A plane had crashed near the man's house and the pilot had vanished. Maybe the Jew had concealed him. And even though he argued that he hadn't even seen the plane, that the whole story was a fabrication, they jailed him. Next they went to get the fallen aircraft but they couldn't find it. And instead of concluding that the whole story was fantasy, they arrested two more Jews on suspicion of hiding the plane.

However, the worst suffering came from the Sokols, the nationalist Slavic organizations. When the Germans took Lodz a second time, the Sokols came with them and terrorized us. They stole our property, beat us, killed us, humiliated us. They forced young men to join them. We ran, we hid, and then resorted to the most persuasive kind of inducement: bribes. At first we paid them a hundred or just fifty rubles apiece. Later on, a three-kopek coin was enough. In the end, when the Germans pulled out and the Russians returned to Lodz, the Poles circulated a rumor that the Sokols were really Jewish groups in disguise. They actually called them Jewish brigades.

While setting up the food and medical center near Warsaw, I had to buy provisions. The Zemstvo Alliance gave me a list and told me which stores to shop at. I saw that these were exclusively Polish; no Jewish stores were listed. But when I was told that the alliance always patronized these stores and received discounts, I did my shopping there. I also needed several thousand pounds of cabbage. Not finding any, I went to the market and placed my order with a Jew named Vaysfleysh. The next morning I was at the alliance's warehouse to receive the purchases, and had several phone conversations, including one with Vaysfleysh. Two young Poles working in the warehouse heard me and became fairly upset. "Listen, you obviously don't know anyone here, and you don't know where to shop. We'll give you a list of the stores you can go to."

"The alliance already gave me a list," I replied.

"What do you mean?" said the second Pole. "I heard you talking to someone called Vaysfleysh, he's a Jew."

"Well, so what? I found some good cabbage at his stall."

"No, we'll give you a list of Polish stores."

I pretended to be naive. "What's the difference whether they're Polish or Jewish?"

"You're not serious. It's better to buy from a Christian—the Jews are all crooks."

"Now listen, I'm a Jew, and I assure you that the real crooks are the Polish profiteers."

I told Virubov the whole story. He was embarrassed and promised to remove the two men from the warehouse, but he never did. And no wonder. The Zemstvo Alliance was controlled by Poles, and to some extent had joined the anti-Jewish boycott.

I could soon see that the anti-Jewish agitation was happening not only in the army and among the masses, but also among intellectuals and liberal Russians in Poland, among members of the Zemstvo Alliance and the Association of Towns, and especially among the journalists. Within a few weeks I witnessed a profound change in the liberal attitude toward the Jewish question in Poland. Liberals began to show indifference toward the Jewish plight. They listened more attentively to all sorts of derogatory stories and eventually began to repeat them in their private conversations and even in their articles.

5

One day I ran into an acquaintance of mine, Moyzhel, a Russian author, who published in the Socialist journal *Ruskoye Bogatsvo*. He considered himself a great radical and a friend of the Jews. Moyzhel told me that the Polish section of the civic commission had invited him to an intimate get-together of Russian and Polish writers. Its goal was to create an association of literati in both nations. They would deal with a number of important issues, especially the acute Jewish question.

"Who's been invited?" I asked him.

"Fyodorov, Niemirovitsh-Dantshenko, Grigory Petrov, Count A. Tolstoy, Valery Bryustov, me . . ."

"And not a single Jewish writer?"

"No."

"Do you think it makes sense to discuss the Jewish question without inviting any Jewish writers?"

"Obviously not. I'll bring it up at the meeting."

Several nights later, I bumped into him just as he was coming from the meeting. He told me it had been more of a social event. They would talk about the Jewish question next time.

"Did you bring up the issue of inviting Jewish authors?"

"No . . . I couldn't manage. . . . But I did something better. When they were drawing up a list of invitees, I suggested you, since you write for Russian newspapers. And they agreed. I said you were Jewish, of course."

When I reported this to Peretz, Noyekh Prilutsky (another writer) and several community leaders, we decided that I should propose asking a few representatives of the Jewish press to future gatherings. And if my motion were voted down, I should protest and walk out.

But I wasn't given the chance to protest. I was simply not invited.

Grigory Petrov, a priest who had left the priesthood preaching fiery radicalism, had published several articles defending the Jews. A few weeks later I asked Petrov for a favor. I wanted him to approach a high-ranking Russian officer and bring up the predicament of eight Jews in Suchostow who had been libeled, arrested, and sentenced to hang. He responded with a typically long-winded lecture, which I noted verbatim:

> It's a terrible story you've told, but I can't help those people; all I can do is sympathize. My heart bleeds, and I've heard so many stories like this one, and they all weigh on me. But what difference does our distress make? None! But you and Prilutsky and

Grinboym carry on, telling us these awful stories and upsetting us right when we need some peace and quiet. . . . Just two months ago, I gave Prilutsky some advice. You've got your rabbis. Haven't you got a chief rabbi? Tell him to issue an appeal to the Jews, instructing them how to act. They shouldn't watch the soldiers at work, shouldn't question them, shouldn't hide goods. There have been a few cases of Jews who have been hanged just for asking the soldiers questions. They have to understand that the army is under great pressure and doesn't have time to investigate every incident.

Even though I used to be a priest, I never realized that you Jews have some law about cordoning off your courtyards. And during a war, people can't always remember the day of the week, so not every Christian knows that it's the Sabbath and that the Jews don't do business. When the soldiers arrive in town, they find the Jewish shops closed and they think it's out of hostility to the army. You people have to explain these things, write pamphlets, make sure the information reaches the army.

And you have to admit that there are Jews involved in spying. I know of hundreds of cases. There was a sentry posted at a bridge on the Vistula and an old Jew walked by, carrying a heavy sack on his shoulder. The soldier let him through; he even pitied him for having to lug such a load. But when the next sentry stopped the Jew and tapped the sack, he felt that a person was inside. And it's true—the man was hiding a German. So the German and the Jew were both sentenced to death. I heard this from Guchkov, who thought it was unfair to shoot the German and hang the Jew; they should have hanged the German too.

"And you think that's true?" I asked. "An old man strong enough to carry an adult on his back and bold enough to smuggle a German across a bridge guarded by sentries?"

"Who knows—?"

"I know," I broke in. "I heard the same story from Moyzhel. But he said it happened on the Dvina River, and when they opened the sack they found not only a German but also 2,500 silver thalers. Moyzhel even knows the German's name, Otto Bauer! Can't you see that this old man carrying a German on his back was made up for a reason?"

"Maybe so. But if it *is* a fabrication, then someone should write about it and clear the whole thing up. You can't imagine how hostile the soldiers are toward the Jews. I heard another story of a Jewish village near the front line. The commander was told that a redheaded Jew and a woman had been driving a cow toward the German trenches. The commander ordered his men to seize the Jew and bring him back. The soldiers went into town, grabbed the first redheaded Jew they found, and brought him to the commander. It turned out that the Jew didn't own a cow and hadn't left his house all day. The commander ordered the soldiers to string him up anyway, and they did. Do you understand what's happening? And your newspapers just make it worse. A couple of days ago I read an editorial—it was something about a holiday and the Maccabees! I was really upset, and so was the officer traveling with me. What's going on? Is Russia so full of Jews that we're celebrating Jewish holidays now?"

I think it useful to quote another conversation I had around the same time with Vasily Alekseyevitsh Maklakov, of the Constitutional Democratic Party. He was also the attorney who defended Beilis, and he offered to help me obtain a travel pass to Galicia. "Your mission is not easy," he said. "The Galician Jews are extremely hostile toward the Russians. They're all involved in spying." He went on. "I'm not saying that Jews are the only ones. The Ruthenians are also against us—but they're scattered all over the place. The Poles are pro-Russian at the moment, so the only people antagonistic to us are Jews. And if truth be told, it's not only the military, the local population in Galicia is angry because of the way Jews exploit them. Just imagine, in Galicia the Jews are landowners."

"Only Jews?" I asked. "Aren't there any Polish landowners?"

"Of course! But people are used to the Poles, and the Jews are very insolent. Just imagine, Count Bobrinsky, the governor-general, received a delegation complaining that the peasants refused to kiss their hands! Now that's arrogance!"

"Vasily Alekseyevitsh, who did you hear that from—a lunatic?"

"It's a fact. An isolated incident, certainly—but a fact just the same! True, all sorts of lies are made up about Jews. But in Lwow, Jews shot at our soldiers—there's no doubt about it."

And this was how one of the finest Russian intellectuals reacted to the idiotic lies spread by certain Polish groups. What, then, could we expect of ordinary people?

6

The Jews, frightened and cowed, had no way of fighting either the persecution or the lies. And so they wove their sighs and tears into legends, as they had done in the past, from which they drew comfort and courage. One rumor maintained that the local rebbe was writing a long saga about the war, "which would surpass anything ever written. When he finishes, the redemption will come." Jews talked about the Messiah in many places; they consulted ancient texts and believed that the Messianic age was finally dawning. But more than anything, Jews told stories about the false espionage charges. As they saw it, such accusations were not outright lies but were sparked by crimes the Christians committed in order to turn the blame on the Jews. Of course, like all folktales, these were filled with optimism, with the faith that in the end truth will out.

The most widespread accusation was that Jews had telephones for conveying information to the enemy. The collective Jewish imagination reacted to this with a series of legends tied mainly to the city of Zamosc. One story was very simple: Because of a lie about a telephone, the local authorities had hanged several Jews and were about to hang some more. But then a Christian priest approached the judges and swore on the cross that the real wrongdoers were Poles. The Jews were promptly released, and sixteen Poles were hanged instead.

The next legend was more poetic: In Zamosc, some Poles had denounced the Jews for aiding the enemy and so a number of Jews were arrested. When the judges convened and were about to sentence them to death, a Russian teacher and another Russian judge knelt down before the court and begged to be heard out before the verdict was issued. The teacher and the judge swore that the Jews were innocent. "If you want to find the real culprit," they said, "come with us." The two Russians led the judges to the courtyard of one Count Zamojski and down into a deep cellar. There they found the countess on the phone with the Austrians. She was strung up immediately.

I heard the story in Minsk. In Lublin I heard a similar version, with a different ending. When the party entered Countess Zamojska's cellar, they found a large group of Jews wearing earlocks, long caftans, yarmulkes, talking on the phone to the Austrians. The Russian judges were shocked; this proved the Jews were indeed guilty. "Take them in for questioning," one judge said. But when the Jews were brought in, it turned out they were actually Poles in disguise, so that if they were caught, suspicion would fall on the Jews.

There was another story about a Pole who dressed a German spy as a Jew, left him in a pit near the interrogation office, and then denounced him. But when the authorities arrested the man, they discovered a German pass and he confessed that he wasn't Jewish.

All kinds of stories were in circulation.

Six Jews had been supplying the Russian army with oats. The instant the horses tasted the oats they keeled over. Five of the Jews were arrested, sentenced, and hanged. The sixth was arrested later, and as he was taken to the gallows the next day, he exclaimed: "Why are you in such a hurry to kill me? Before you hang me, please go to a Polish landowner named X and bring back some oats from his middle granary."

They dispatched several riders to the Pole. He received them graciously and offered them oats from all his granaries except the middle one.

They asked him, "What do you have in there?"

He replied, "Those are very bad oats."

They then forced him to open the granary. When the oats were tested, they proved to be poisoned. So the Jew was released and the Pole hanged instead.

Before the war, when I was traveling through Volhynia and Podolia, gathering folklore, I kept hearing a very popular tale about a bride and groom: Just as they were being led to the wedding canopy, they were murdered by Bogdan Khmelnitsky.* In more than fifteen or sixteen

---

*Bogdan Khmelnitsky, the Cossack general, led a revolt against the Poles in 1648 to drive them out from the central Ukraine. His troops killed the majority of the Jewish population.

shtetls I was shown a small headstone near the synagogue and always told the same story about the bridal couple. This is practically the only widespread tale that has come down to us from Khmelnitsky's massacres. Jews saw themselves symbolized by the bride and groom killed just before their union, and so unable to continue their family and their tradition. The couple was like a tree chopped down just as it began to blossom.

Unlike Khmelnitsky's attacks, our current war did not threaten the Jewish nation's survival, but it would prove to be one of its greatest tragedies. Jews on both sides fought each other, brother against brother. From the start, the Jews were gripped by this horror, and represented it in a legend of two soldiers meeting in battle. One soldier bayoneted the other and then heard him shout as he lay dying, "Hear, O Israel, the Lord our God, the Lord is one."

I'm not exaggerating when I say that I heard all versions of this story in nine or ten different places, from St. Petersburg, to Moscow, Minsk, Kiev, and Warsaw—in short, wherever I ran into Jewish soldiers and refugees. Of course, each variant was presented not as a rumor but as a true event involving such and such a person.

In St. Petersburg I was told about a Jewish patient in a military hospital. During an attack, he had bayoneted an Austrian soldier, and the victim had cried out, "Hear, oh Israel . . . !" The patient had instantly lost his mind.

In Kiev, I heard the tale about a Jewish soldier who, when he heard his victim cry, "Hear, oh Israel," flung himself down and begged forgiveness. The dying man produced a pouch filled with money, gave it to the soldier, and asked him to send it to his wife. But before he managed to convey the address, he died.

At the military hospital in Moscow, I was telling this story to a physician when Katz, a soldier listening to us, exclaimed, "I had an experience just like that. Once I was about to bayonet a soldier when he shouted at me 'A Jew killing a Jew?' My first thought was, 'He's an enemy, what does it matter?' Still, I pulled away the bayonet, grabbed the soldier by his shirt, and took him back as a POW."

A few weeks later, I ran into the same soldier. He didn't recognize me. I brought up the story again because I wanted to see how he would respond.

"The very thing happened to me," he said. "We were sent out. I ran with other troops. I couldn't see or hear anything around me. They came pouring out of their trenches and a free-for-all began. One soldier pounced on me, I rammed my bayonet into his heart, killed him on the spot. When we had captured the trenches, I saw a pouch sticking out of the soldier's pocket. In it I found a pair of phylacteries and I realized I had killed a Jew."

The story was not a conscious lie. As with any myth, the narrator had lost his ability to distinguish between fact and fiction; his subconscious mind contained a different truth—a symbolic and historical one.

7

From the start of the war and even earlier, the German and Austrian governments had relied heavily on Russia's reactionary spirit. The Germans exploited the czarist court's strong ties to their country and made good use of the help provided by high-ranking Russians. But at the same time Germany railed against Russian despotism, attacking France and England for allying themselves with a backward tyrant. Germany presented itself as an enlightened warrior fighting a savage Russia that posed a danger to European civilization.

The czarist government did nothing to rebut these charges; on the contrary, everything it did only served to reinforce them. The Russian army committed the most shameful atrocities in East Prussia and Galicia, often with the approval, tacit or otherwise, of the czar's court, thereby outraging the entire world, including its allies. Great indignation was sparked by the czarist government's antisemitism and its lies about the Jewish people. Hundreds of thousands of Jews were driven from entire regions; innocent people were summarily hanged or shot; Jewish property was looted and destroyed. In the neutral countries, especially America, the fiendish quality of the antisemitic bacchanalia stirred a profound hatred of Russia—even in those circles that sympathized with France and England. French and British diplomats tried in all sorts of ways to get Czar Nicholas to soften his attitude—at least for the sake of the war. They were not successful. Supposedly, Alexander Protopopov, one of the czar's ministers, tried to explain that Russia's antisemitic policies were damaging the Allies' interests. But when Protopopov raised the issue, Nicholas started sulking and impatiently drumming his fingers on the table, a habit of his. The minister faltered and held his tongue.

When the war erupted, a rumor spread throughout Europe that Nicholas had issued a manifesto granting equal rights to Jews. The German press even published the text of this apocryphal manifesto, which began "To my dear Jews." The Germans and the Austrians also printed leaflets in Yiddish and Hebrew to this effect, dropping them over Lodz, Warsaw, and other cities.

Still, throughout the war, both during the czar's reign and after the revolution, the Germans and Austrians exploited the Jewish persecution in Russia for their own political ends. Their newspapers were filled with stories about the Russian army's cruelties. Entering a town after the retreating Russians, the Germans would photograph the corpses and the injured, the ruined stores and homes, and circulate the images around the world. In 1917, the pogroms in Tarnopol and Kalushts enabled them to compromise the Russian Revolution.

Of course, the protests against Russian barbarism were driven by political motives. There was no real sympathy or commiseration with the persecuted. While railing against Russian cruelty in German-occupied territory, the Germans themselves displayed no small amount of brutality. They didn't perpetrate massacres or pogroms, but their harshness and scorn were nonetheless hard to endure. German forced labor was no easier than a Russian prison, and their appropriation of property was no different from outright theft.

On the whole, the Austrians (except for the Magyars) treated the Jews in occupied territory far better and more humanely. Thus Polish and Ukrainian Jews tended to idealize the Austrians, creating great myths about the Austrian military. They talked about a general whose first act was to spend an entire evening with the town's rabbi; they had stories about the severe penalties imposed on Christians who took part in pogroms. But these claims were quite inflated; the Jews were mistreated by the Austrians as well. Still, nothing compared with what they suffered from our own Russian military. Itzik Rosenberg, a resident of Yuzefov, a shtetl in Lublin Province, lived through it all. His story is called "The Destruction of Yuzefov."

8

At around ten A.M., we heard the loud boom of a cannon on the other side of the Vistula. An hour later we saw blazing shells falling on the village across the river, Tshishitse. The village was in flames.

After a short while, a few Cossacks appeared on the opposite bank. They yelled at us to let them have our scows; otherwise they would bombard the town. The scows were all loaded with planks and low in the water, which was so shallow it was impossible to push the scows out immediately. The people who owned the planks begged us not to destroy their property, but the minutes were ticking away.

Finally, the whole town came and started to work. People also started collecting bread to send on a skiff to the soldiers across the water. Suddenly, in the middle of our work, there was a terrible panic and people began running into town, wondering what had happened. We saw an Austrian cavalry squadron charging through the village, on the way to Anopol.

When the Cossacks across the water saw the Austrians, they began firing at the town. We ran to the houses, and luckily no one was hurt. The shooting went on for about twenty minutes until the Austrians were gone.

It was already evening, and the parents were collecting their children, about to head home, when a blast of artillery resounded from Ribit and Netshebo, the neighboring villages. The whistling bullets exploded over our heads, and the noise was deafening. We shrieked, running every which way, not knowing where to go.

We heard the Russian artillery respond five times. . . . You can imagine how we spent the night. Twenty or thirty people sat in one dark room, scared of lighting the lamp. No one had the courage to stick his head outside. We huddled there, trembling at every sound from the street.

At eleven that night, we heard the rumbling of wheels, the galloping of horses. We couldn't tell whether the troops were Russian or Austrian. But soon we heard them knocking on all the doors. The door to our room opened, and we were face-to-face with Austrian soldiers. They screamed at us to light a fire. Carrying lamps, they were scouring attics and basements, hunting for Russian soldiers, and they missed only one house. Upon leaving, they said good night and told us not to worry, we could go to bed.

The next day . . . squadrons of Austrians passed through from dawn to dusk, marching from Anopol to Opolye. They didn't touch a single Jew or Christian. The following morning, the government rabbi, Yekhiel Litman, received a visit from an Austrian officer, who ordered him to send for the scribe and the administrative head. He told him that three hundred Jews and one hundred Christians were to report at noon to a place on the Vistula, and they were to bring saws, spades, and axes to build a bridge across the river. The officer said that anyone who refused to work would be hanged or shot within twenty-four hours.

Of course, the town was terrified, and anyone who could lend a hand grabbed a tool and hurried down to the Vistula. Hundreds of soldiers from the Austrian engineer corps supervised the project, urging the men to work faster. In the evening, they dismissed the workers, telling them to report back the next morning at ten.

But by seven, the soldiers were already driving the men out to work. It was harsh drudgery, and the men weren't allowed a free moment to catch their breath. A line of ten people had to shoulder forty- or fifty-foot logs. The sun was boiling, everyone was sweating, and the soldiers were bellowing: "Move it! Move it!"

We imagined our ancestors toiling in Egypt, and we were comforted. "How are we any better than they?" we said. Since time immemorial, we Jews in exile have been building pyramids for other nations.

The Austrians allowed us to rest on the Sabbath. All that day, more and more battalions kept crossing the bridge. They came from various towns in Radom Province, and the torrent continued through Sunday, Monday, and Tuesday night.

After so many soldiers had passed through, we had no food left and were in a state of famine. There was no bread—a sentry had been posted in every bakery to prevent people from buying even a single loaf—and sugar was selling at sixty kopeks a pound. We suffered dreadfully. There was no question of making even a ruble. Craftsmen, shopkeepers, and teachers were out of work. The women set up tables and sold glasses of tea and coffee, earning a few rubles a day, and that was the only source of income. There was no way to bring food in from somewhere else because we weren't allowed to leave town. No one could come, and no one could go.

Meanwhile, with nothing to buy, the soldiers began requisitioning whatever food was left in people's homes. The hunger grew unbearable. Occasionally, someone was permitted to go to another town, but the little food he brought back was of almost no help.

Life got worse with each day. An epidemic of fires broke out in all the surrounding villages. We could tell that there were dark days ahead.

Then one morning, we saw lots of battalions with a large amount of artillery retreating toward Anopol along all the roads. Suddenly, a cannon could be heard booming. The army's withdrawal lasted two days. On the second day, we saw shells flying in the mountains. Toward evening, rifles began firing along the banks of the Vistula. The next day, the Austrians blew up the bridge and took down the telephone wires.

No one could doubt that trouble was coming. When the bombardment began, the women and children fled into the brick houses—there were one or two hundred people in each house. After midnight, the Russians began shooting at us. The windowpanes fell out. The women and children were weeping; men were reciting prayers and calling out, "Hear, O Israel, the Lord is God, the Lord is One."

At the first glimmer of dawn, many of the men grabbed their wives and children and ran off to other villages with lots of Jewish residents. There was no chance of finding refuge with any of the Christians. They wouldn't even allow us into other Jews' homes; they threatened to burn down houses that took in Jews. From all sides, all we heard was Yid and Beilis. As a result, many people ended up coming back to town.

We spent all day in the cellar with nothing to eat or drink. Although the shooting stopped in the evening, no one dared go out. We stayed there through the night, while the children slept. They had asked for food, but we had none to give them. Still, this agony was nothing compared with the next day. The Russians launched a terrible bombardment. Shells and shrapnel came raining down on us. The houses were burning. We realized we couldn't stay inside. The strongest buildings couldn't hold up against the cannonballs. To avoid being killed, we had to get out as fast as possible.

Hundreds of people were dashing every which way under a shower of bullets, and the Russians intensified their fire at people moving in groups. Some people turned back to the cellars, where many had been killed. But most ran over the dead and wounded, who covered the entire path. People dropped like flies. A man, Itzik Halberstam, held one son in his arms and another by the hand. The boy he was carrying caught a bullet in his mouth, and the blood poured over his father.

At every step, we heard the wounded moaning, begging to be taken along. That evening, when the shooting stopped, people began looking for their families. Besides the dead and the wounded, the air resounded with the screams of people dying in the basements—because of the fires we couldn't bring out the dying. All night long, we hovered near the cellars, but there was nothing we could do to save the victims.

The next day, we might have been able to do something, but the Russians arrived and started beating or killing any Jew they could lay their hands on. We risked our lives getting a few people out of the basements. The rest were dead. All day, we struggled to help the injured, moving them from out in the open to the only synagogue still standing.

We found Harenfeld lying in a puddle of blood. His money was gone; his head had been smashed; his brains were on the ground. By Friday, we had buried forty-one bodies.

And so we had had a week of curses. The next day was the Sabbath, and we read the passages of God's curses and inflictions in the synagogue while gazing at the bloodied faces and the burned remains of our town.

That was followed by Bloody Sunday, for at the crack of dawn bands of peasants—men and women, young and old—started arriving in town. Clutching baskets, they formed lines and jeered at the scorched, mourning, half-naked Jews poking through the rubble, trying to find a charred pot, a plate—anything. The peasants called out "Kike" and "Beilis." Obviously, they were waiting for a chance to loot the cellars and run off with the valuables the Jews had buried. Although we knew what was going on, we didn't respond. Meanwhile, people who had fled their burning homes began returning from the countryside. The soldiers didn't harass them in any way. Then we suddenly saw a few peasants talking to two officers and some soldiers with a number 7 on their epaulettes. The group broke up, and the soldiers yelled, "Stop!" With their whips and sticks, the soldiers and the peasants came charging at the Jews, waving their knouts and rifles. Whoever was caught bore the scars. Seventy-year-old Itshe Fuks was attacked by a band of peasants, who smashed his head. What did he plan to be in the Austrian army—a lieutenant, a colonel? They laughed at him. The Russian officers dashed around in a frenzy, hitting us and ordering us to hand over the Austrian rifles we'd supposedly concealed.

Frightened men, women, and children converged on a house where Rabbi Epstein was sitting with his two motherless children. The crowd assumed they'd be safe there, but the mob followed them. The soldiers were ordered to drag out each Jew out and beat him—"but not to death"—until we gave up our caches of Austrian rifles. They hit us ruthlessly and kicked the people who collapsed under the first blow. Nor did they spare the rabbi, who was holding his two little boys in his arms. The soldiers pulled him out by his earlocks and gave him a dreadful thrashing. One man, Leyzer-Yekhiel Englender, who was in fact an engineer in the army, took out his military papers and showed the officer he had been furloughed for three months. He thought it would help, but he received death blows in return. They didn't want papers, the officer barked, they wanted rifles. Heaven and earth and rifles!

Next they took several Jews, including the rabbi, down to the Vistula. I don't know what happened to them because I managed to escape into the synagogue, which was packed with wounded people. Taking advantage of the turmoil, the peasants rioted through our town, doing anything they wanted. They showed the soldiers a basement in which cloth and other goods were hidden. The soldiers removed all the contents and sold them to the peasants dirt cheap. For a thirty-five-yard roll of "Polish linen," the soldiers got fifteen kopeks. In another cellar they unearthed four hundred pairs of boots, which they gave away to the peasants for a total of three rubles. Mobs of peasants headed home with brimming baskets, and no Jew dared say a word. Once all the basements were emptied, the soldiers began looking for "revolvers" in every Jewish pocket and even in the breasts of the women. The Russians thereby took the last few rubles and the meager bits of jewelry that the women had tucked away. The Jews only begged the soldiers to stop harassing and clubbing them. Then, at nightfall, a platoon commander started galloping around, chasing away the soldiers and the peasants from the long-depleted cellars and preventing them from beating the Jews.

In the dead of night, we lay in the synagogue, battered and hungry. Two soldiers came in. They didn't hit anyone. They said they had strung up three Jews: Lippe Shenker, for having an Austrian pass allowing him to travel and obtain merchandise; and Leybesh Cohen and his son Mayer, who had been found lying in a trench during the shooting.

The refugees started flocking into the synagogue. Some had no boots, some no overcoats. We spent the whole night there, shivering and starving, until daybreak. That morning, the first of September, the rabbi and I, together with nearly the entire Jewish population, tearfully left our desolate, gutted town.

Jews were victimized by Gentiles and fellow Jews, by soldiers and their own neighbors. They were trapped between two infernos, two pitiless forces. There was nothing to expect from either but threats, looting, lies, rumors, and terror.

9

During the battles of Lodz, fifty or sixty trainloads of wounded men were evacuated daily, and there was nowhere to send them. The tracks were backed up for a distance of four or five miles. Thousands of railroad cars were stuck in the countryside for days, and the wounded men were without food or medical attention. Luckily, a medical division of the Zemstvo Alliance had been set up some three miles outside Warsaw and was able to stop by on its way to the Carpathian Mountains. The division volunteered to bring food and aid to the wounded, but as it had to move on very quickly, the alliance decided to establish a permanent center. A staff of some twenty-five people would include a physician, five nurses, ten orderlies, and a few administrators.

As with all Zemstvo projects, everything cost three or four times more than normal, but money was no object The Poles were willing to pay exorbitant prices. They spent money like water, never giving it a second thought, recklessly agreeing to pay tens of thousands of rubles, only to discover that the merchandise was useless and the money wasted. The same was true at the new center. Fixtures, inventory, ovens, kettles, tableware, food—it all came to some ten thousand rubles, not to mention the salaries, of course, which totaled more than two thousand rubles a month. And then when the place was ready, the center proved to be superfluous. We waited a whole week but never set eyes on a single wounded soldier. Winter was already moving in, the battles were slowing down, and the occasional trains carrying the injured never stopped at our center. Furthermore, the medical division that was supposed to head for the Carpathians lingered for a while, so we had two centers with more than one hundred people on staff who had absolutely nothing to do. Our one useful activity was feeding a few railroad workers as well as fifty or sixty peasants and their children from the nearby villages.

Virubov's solution was to close the center. Then he said, "We'll transfer it to Blonye," a small town seventeen miles from Warsaw. "They've got epidemics raging—cholera, typhus, black pox, scarlet fever. Go there right away, find an empty house, and set up the center there to serve the population." He quickly changed his mind. "No—that won't do. You're Jewish, and so is your woman doctor. The way things are, with everyone suspicious of the Jews, there is no point in your going to a place where there's cholera. God only knows what could happen. They could pull out that old chestnut about Jews poisoning the wells."

That same day, I ran into Fyodorov, one of the best war correspondents. "My advice," he said, "is that you shouldn't go to a place where there might be some kind of disturbance. You have no idea how intensely the army hates Jews. All it needs is just one little spark to set off the rumors and trigger a savage pogrom."

Without debating it, the alliance members unanimously voted to move the center to Blonye.

"As for your going there," Virubov exclaimed, "my fears were groundless. You're free to go. It turns out the entire population is Jewish."

"Well, not the *entire* population," said Ladizhensky, a writer and delegate. "But probably at least fifty percent."

"In that case," I replied, "I'll have to organize the center in a slightly different way. I'm sure you know that Jews have their dietary laws, so there will have to be a special cauldron supervised by a Jew."

Virubov grimaced. "No, you can't do that!" he snapped. "We can't give in to superstition!"

"We can't possibly cater to every taste," said Oliw, a Pole.

"This isn't a taste issue," I retorted, "these are religious convictions. And even if they're superstitions, it's not the job of the Zemstvo Alliance to fight them. There are other institutions for that. The alliance is supposed to feed the hungry, and that's what it should be doing. After all, the Jews of Blonye didn't come to you for help. You're going to them, so you ought to make sure they'll eat the food you serve them."

"If people are really starving," Virubov replied, "they're not so picky about how the food is prepared; they eat whatever they get."

"Our job," said Ladizhensky, seconding him, "is to serve the food. And if they don't eat, that's their business."

"That's a bureaucratic response," I exclaimed. "No true welfare organization would ever follow that tack. When the Free Economic Society sets up food centers in areas with a Jewish population, they always have two kitchens."

This made an impact on Virubov and his friends. "You know what?" Virubov said. "We'll also put up a tea center to distribute bread. That shouldn't be a problem. The tea center can cook buckwheat too. I know that Jews eat buckwheat if there's no meat in it. . . . So, leave for Blonye tomorrow with your doctor, get all the details in place, and we'll decide how to proceed."

Upon returning to the center, I found a note from Peretz asking me to see him immediately. I rode back to Warsaw and went to his home, where he told me that Feygenboim had arrived—an acquaintance of his with large contracts in Galicia. Peretz had told him about me, and he had agreed to take me along to Galicia as an employee.

Feygenboim suggested I leave for Brody with him in a few hours, but I couldn't until someone replaced me at the center. So we agreed that I would head for Rovno a week later, and he would meet me there and take me to Brody.

IO

Before the war Bloyne was a rich and elegant Jewish town: wide streets, a large municipal park, several monuments, many tall buildings, large stores. But when the war came through, the town was passed from hand to hand; occupied by the Germans, then by the Russians, Bloyne was totally destroyed. At its center, the town hall, with its roof torn off and its walls riddled and shattered, looked like an ancient ruin. It symbolized the annihilation of Bloyne. Most of the houses and buildings had burned down. The rest were empty and desolate, their doors and windows ripped out; whole houses, especially Polish ones, had survived only in the side streets. Not a single large store endured; they were all deserted and their doors were gone. A few shops had been taken over by new proprietors, who sold bread, ham, cigarettes, paper, tea, and sugar. There was no other merchandise in town.

The large synagogue was unscathed. But all its contents were looted or smashed; the Torah scrolls were tattered and sullied. Now the building was used as a military hospital for cholera patients since the local city council had informed the army authorities that this would be the most appropriate site.

Ravaged as the town was, the streets were bustling and filled with nervous military movement. Baggage convoys and heavily loaded wagons rumbled incessantly; the artillery kept up its iron clatter; infantry and cavalry units slogged by one after another. They were all streaming toward Suchostow. The few terrified civilians hurrying along stood out against the gray military mass. They looked like useless, alien creatures entangled underfoot.

I traveled to Blonye with Dr. Berlin, our center's female physician. Upon arriving, we went straight to the city council, where we found one of its members, a Polish doctor. He told us that only four or five hundred townspeople, one tenth of the population, were left—many of them refugees from the countryside. As for Jews, no more than ten or fifteen families had stayed put. The rest had scattered to wherever they could flee—mainly Warsaw. The city council, he went on, had organized a soup kitchen, which dispensed 150 to 200 lunches a day. The Zemstvo Alliance also had a free teahouse, which, however, didn't have enough manpower to take care of everyone. A second teahouse was needed. Tens of thousands of tired, thirsty soldiers were passing through town, and if they couldn't get tea they would drink plain water—sometimes even from the muddy street puddles, which caused epidemics.

"Who is your soup kitchen set up for?" I asked the Polish doctor.

"We don't discriminate," he answered. "Anyone who comes gets fed."

"I'm sure you know what I mean—Jews won't eat food that hasn't been specially prepared."

"Yes. . . . I know."

"And have you established a Jewish soup kitchen?"

"No. . . . There's little call for one. The few remaining Jews don't need free food. They're involved in business, and they're doing quite well."

"Why was the synagogue converted into a cholera hospital? Couldn't they find any other building?"

"That's none of our concern. It's a military matter," he responded dryly, apparently sensing my contentious tone.

"How did the Germans behave here?" Dr. Berlin asked.

"Some were very decent, courteous, and didn't touch anyone. They paid for everything. Others set houses on fire and committed the worst sort of atrocities. In a farm granary a mile from here, there were 192 wounded soldiers and patients with epidemic diseases. The Germans put straw around it and torched it. All the men were burned alive. The Germans did it to prevent the epidemic from spreading to the German army."

. . .

Dr. Berlin headed over to the Zemstvo Alliance's teahouse, while I walked through the town to find out what was happening to the Jews. I stepped into an old shop where an elderly woman was selling rolls, herring, and other cheap food. She confirmed that most of the Jews had fled.

"How many Jewish inhabitants were there?" I asked.

"Who counted them? Half the town was Jewish—like everywhere else."

"Why did they run away?"

"Not because they were doing so well here. There was something to run away from. Oh."

Her son came in, a young man with a bandaged head. He started to talk. "Before the Germans marched in, they shelled the town to bits. One girl was killed and about ten people came to the funeral. On the way back from the cemetery, they encountered a Russian patrol. The soldiers began firing and they killed two men. . . . But that wasn't the worst of it. The Jews ran away from lootings, beatings, from the lies. The Russians always assume that a Jew is a spy, and they arrest him."

The proprietor then said: "On an estate not far from here there was this tenant farmer. He was washing the dishes. . . . He was awfully dim-witted; he never understood anything; he didn't know his top from his bottom. And they suspected him of espionage. How could anyone mistake him for a spy? A spy has to have at least a little bit of gray matter. But try reasoning with them."

"How is the military treating the Jews now?"

"Now that there's nobody to beat up and nothing to plunder, everything's quiet, thank goodness," the woman replied with bitter irony.

"Well, to tell the truth," the young man explained, "ordinary troops don't do anything. They seldom bother anyone. The real problem is the Cossacks. The moment they ride in, they start looting and beating."

"Do you need a Jewish soup kitchen here?" I asked.

"No," the young man said. "The few Jews still here have stayed because they're earning a living. The poor ones have all gone to Warsaw."

Wandering through the town, I entered what had once been a dry-goods store. Now three men sat there, each at his own table, one sold bread, one ham, and the third, a Jewish youth, sold cigarettes. I introduced myself.

"I'm from Suchostow," he told me. "I had my own store there, and I had a nice income. When the Germans were approaching, the town was thrown into a panic. Then General Rennenkampf arrived, and he took his revenge. His men beat us and arrested us, and forced the best men to clean toilets—and of course they looted our property. Then they began expelling the Jews. Many had already scattered. I took off for Warsaw, but then I thought it over. How can I leave all my property? I rented a wagon for sixty rubles and drove back to Suchostow. Where was my store, what had happened to it? They had torn it to pieces. My merchandise was worth fifteen hundred rubles, and the stuff that was left, which my neighbors salvaged, was worth maybe one hundred rubles. So I brought it here and set up shop. In Suchostow they forced out the last Jews who came here. They were starving, exhausted, battered. A lot of them came barefoot; their shoes had been stolen on the way. One of the refugees was a young woman who gave birth as soon as she reached Blonye. She's lying in an empty store for now; we don't know where to put her."

I got hold of Dr. Berlin, and we went to find the new mother. On a pile of straw on the muddy floor of a small, empty shop lay a young woman covered with tattered clothes. Her feverish face was calm, but she was breathing heavily. Next to her, wrapped in dirty rags, lay the newborn infant. Two little boys, one four years old, one two, wandered aimlessly around the tiny room. Their oversized coats, hems dragging behind them, were covered with wet mud up to the collars. The children were scared, disoriented, and their bloodshot little eyes gaped at us. The instant I or the doctor moved toward the mother, the boys began wailing dreadfully.

The woman's elderly mother, careworn and embittered, stood off to the side. When I addressed her, she murmured with the deathly indifference of supreme despair.

> We'd already gone through enough misery and horror. When the Germans came back to our town and began shooting at us, we hid in the cellars for five days without food or water. Somehow or other we managed to get by, but the thirst was unbearable. A father and mother went down to the river to get water and they never came back. Later on, we found their corpses. The day before yesterday, when the shooting fell off slightly, we ventured

out of the cellars. The general ordered all Jews, including children, to assemble in the marketplace. There were sixty-eight of us. Thirty men were pulled out, arrested, and put in the trenches. We don't know what's going to happen to them. The rest of us were banished. We left on foot. Walking was terrible. It was raining. The road was covered with thick mud, and my daughter was pregnant, ready to give birth any moment—and we also had the two little boys. We dragged ourselves along for twenty-four hours.

At one point, my daughter asked me: "Mama, look! What's hanging from those trees?"

I looked. There were three Jews. I was afraid to take a closer look—I might know them. A few miles on, my daughter collapsed in exhaustion, and the children couldn't walk any farther. So we settled in the mud on the side of the road. A soldier riding by in a wagon—a Christian, mind you—felt sorry for us and offered us a lift. The moment my daughter climbed in, she went into labor, and she kept screaming in agony all the way. When we arrived in town, she gave birth right away. We didn't even have time to carry her to a home.

Dr. Berlin took the new mother and the entire family under her wing. She found them a place to stay and managed to obtain milk, eggs, barley, wine, tea, and sugar. We got all this from the only food center in Blonye.

When we decided to open another teahouse here, we went looking for a suitable place. Checking out over twenty deserted locations, we noticed that every burned house and every devastated apartment had the trace of a mezuzah on the doorjamb. Perhaps the looters and arsonists had deliberately chosen Jewish homes. The mezuzahs themselves had been ripped out. A few were lying in the mud.

There is something eerie and horrifying about ravaged, empty homes; you can still feel the tragedy, they have been struck deaf and dumb. . . . We desperately try to detect some trace of the residents. We want to know who they were, how they lived, and what they went through before they left.

We took over a deserted house. It had been repeatedly occupied by soldiers, who had left straw, dirt, and empty tin cans. With some scrutiny I was able to find a clue to who had lived there before. On a wall in one room there were two small, round plaster images. Rachel's grave was painted on one, and, on the other, a portrait of Max Nordau.*

Where are you now, my brothers, who have gone into your dark second Diaspora, leaving behind a spark of your yearning for the ancient, eternal homeland?

II

Upon returning to Warsaw, I went to the Zemstvo Alliance and gave my report on Blonye. I expressed my opinion and Dr. Berlin's that a second teahouse was necessary there, not a Jewish kitchen, since almost no Jews were left. However, I let Virubov know how I felt about Jewish soup kitchens.

Virubov was slightly embarrassed, but said, "This is not just a local issue. In Gora-Kalvaria, the city council opened a kitchen for Jews and Poles. But the local tsadik decreed that it was better for the Jews to starve to death than eat with Christians.

"I know only one thing," he went on. "Cholera is raging in the town, the Jewish population is starving, a food center is crucial—and it can't open because of the tsadik." He added, "Go there, find out what's happening, and let the tsadik know that at a time like this, he needs to reconsider."

I left the alliance and went to see Peretz. First he explained that "the tsadik" was the rebbe of Gora, the greatest of Poland's Hasidic leaders, and that he exerted a tremendous influence on just about all the Orthodox Jews in Poland. Peretz, who had actually met him a few times, felt that this was a special case.

Peretz then phoned Vegmayster, a wealthy resident of Warsaw and one of the rebbe's most devoted followers, and told him the whole business. Vegmayster was shocked. He regarded the story as a deliberate

---

*An Austrian writer and Zionist leader.

attempt to smear the rebbe's name. In these times the stupidest lies could have very bitter consequences.

At seventy-five, Vegmayster was still strong and lively, and he talked about how much he was doing for the Jewish community. There was no Jewish institution he didn't chair, and no famous person he didn't know. But he was especially close to the rebbe of Gora. Sitting with us was Vegmayster's son, about sixty years old, who listened to his father's chatter in reverent silence.

The rebbe had left Gora three months ago and was now in Warsaw; and even if he was still in Gora, he wouldn't have interfered with such mundane business as a soup kitchen. He was very far removed from worldly matters.

It turned out that Vegmayster had informed the rebbe about the "smear," thereby frightening him. I visited Vegmayster at his home and while we were talking there were several phone calls from the rebbe's home, and Vegmayster transmitted every word I said to him. Not satisfied with that, the rebbe's sister called and apologetically asked me to come by, if only for a few minutes. I couldn't refuse, and so I went over with Vegmayster's son. The rebbe's elderly sister, an intelligent, self-possessed, refined woman, was waiting for me impatiently. The instant I walked in, she began assuring me that her brother was free of any sin in regard to both the city council and the Zemstvo Alliance, and that he would never presume to issue any kind of contradictory orders. Her arguments persuaded me. I finally managed to assure her that she needn't try to convince me of the rebbe's innocence. I attempted to put her at ease, reassuring her that not the slightest libel would result.

She calmed down a little and began telling me about Gora. "Our town has suffered every possible calamity. For days the Germans showered us with shrapnel and cannonballs. Who knows how many Jews were killed? Countless numbers! When the shooting started, we ran to the synagogue; about two thousand people gathered there. Suddenly a cannonball hit the synagogue. It plunged through the roof, smashed the table, and sank into the ground. But not a single person was hurt! A divine miracle! The crowd should've stayed in the synagogue. But people panicked and dashed out into the street, and then another cannonball struck, killing twenty-three people on the spot. In the whole town a total of perhaps several hundred died—who can say? And then the horror began—the looting, the pogroms, first the Russian soldiers, then the Germans, and then the Russians again.

"So many innocent people were killed, and about three-quarters of the town ran away. But now that it's quiet again, the armies are gone, the Jews are starting to trickle back."

"What about a Jewish soup kitchen?" I asked her. "Do they need one?"

"Hard to say," she answered vaguely. "It depends on what kind of kitchen and for whom."

"Naturally I mean a strictly kosher place under the supervision of the rabbi or some observant Jew."

"The city council established a kitchen, but no Jews showed up."

"Why not?"

"You have to know our town. We have many destitute people, but they aren't simple paupers; they used to be part of the rebbe's court, and they spent their time studying the holy texts. A Jew like that won't go to a free kitchen organized by the city council—no matter how kosher. There are also quite a number of upstanding men who've come down in the world. But, you see, no matter how poor they might be, they'd sooner starve to death than eat in a soup kitchen together with beggars and lowlifes. Anyone down on his luck hopes to obtain a loan, receive some kind of help from a relative, and get back on his feet. But if he lowers himself to go to a soup kitchen, it's over—he's considered a beggar."

"But aren't there ordinary paupers who are starving?"

"Certainly. But they'll eat wherever and whenever. Why, we've even got Jews who joined the pogroms and looted Jewish property."

In her words I sensed an attitude permeating the Hasidic aristocracy—the brutal indifference to the simple poor.

Vegmayster's son kept silent all the while. After we left the rebbe's sister, and said good-bye to him, he broke in: "When you return from Gora, you have to visit the rebbe! You have to see him! I tell you, you'll see a wonder. He's so far above the ordinary run of men!" And with sparkling eyes he murmured: "You know what he is? He is *the wisdom of the world.* All I need to tell you is that whether he's awake or asleep he has never, for even a second, forgotten *who he is!* . . . He says little, almost nothing; he is silent. But the most important thing isn't his words—it's his expressions. . . . He has a different expression on his face every moment, and each expression contains whole worlds of wisdom."

12

Gora can be reached by a narrow-gauge trunk line, which was built almost exclusively for the tens of thousands traveling to see the rebbe. Otherwise this line would have no reason to exist. In the half-destroyed shtetl of Pyasetshne, from which the Jews were driven out as the Germans were approaching, we saw the first signs of the war: trenches, barbed wire, bomb craters, houses burned down or stripped to their foundations.

Gora, a large town, had suffered terribly from the fighting. Yet this shtetl was not as destroyed as Blonye. The marketplace was functioning, lots of stores were open, and Jewish tradesmen sat in them. This seemed at least a normal picture of small-town Jewish life. No army was stationed here. The war seemed to have receded for a while, as if it had forgotten all about this town.

An old man I met in the street took me to the rebbe's court, a veritable palace with dozens of rooms. Now it was locked up; the shutters were closed. Only the yeshiva was open. A few scrawny, gloomy students in long caftans and with long earlocks were wandering about in the courtyard.

The old man led me into the synagogue—a large, bright, but desolate building, which hadn't been cleaned in ages. The shrapnel had entered the synagogue when several thousand had taken refuge here. The gaping hole in the ceiling had been patched up. Otherwise, neither walls nor floor showed signs of damage. When I asked the man what had become of that shrapnel, he replied in a secretive and enigmatic voice: "Shhh! That's the problem. No one can tell what's become of it."

A wartime miracle. Who knows what legends have sprung up around the shrapnel?

Vegmayster had told me to look up two intimates of the rebbe's, Hokhberg and Varm. I found Hokhberg at his leather shop. He was an elderly man, in a belted Hasidic caftan, with almost shoulder-length earlocks, a furrowed brow, and sad, intelligent eyes. When I told him why I had come, he promptly sent for Varm. The latter, a more secular Jew, started off by telling me what had been happening here throughout the war.

There are ten brick factories around Gora, and nine are owned by Jews. Together they have some ten thousand employees. When the war broke out, it was rumored that the workers were about to plunder Jewish property, and the rumor kept spreading and spreading.

One day, a Polish worker came to me, took me aside, and whispered into my ear: "I've been breaking bread with Jews for years, and I want to save them from a terrible disaster. An organization has been formed at all the factories—its goal is to beat up Jews."

"How do you know?" I asked him.

"It's very simple," he answered. "I'm a member myself; I'm even a delegate from our factory. If you like, I'll bring you some written evidence."

But in the marketplace, people were already saying quite openly that a pogrom was being planned.

I consulted the rebbe, and he told me to meet with two men from the brick factories—Lukrec and Witlicki—and ask them what to do. I went to them, and they advised me to see the district leader. Several days later, when he arrived in town, I went to his office; after sending out the mayor and the guards, he asked me: "Speak frankly. What's going on with you people, how are you getting along with the Poles?"

"Very well," I responded.

"I've been hearing rumors that the Poles are about to plunder Jewish property."

"Yes," I said. "We know. Even the children are talking about it."

"Then why do you say you're getting along with the Poles?"

"Why do you ask when you know what they're planning?"

"Well," he said, "don't worry. I'll come on the Holy Days, and I absolutely won't allow a pogrom."

Meanwhile the Russian military reached our town, and the Poles immediately started an anti-Jewish agitation among them. They claimed that Jews were spies, that Jews were using cloths to signal the Germans, and all kinds of similar fairy tales. Two Polish engineers, who supervised the digging of trenches around the town, turned out to be fierce antisemites. They concocted all sorts of lies about Jews, forced them to work on the Sabbath, beat them. Late at night, when I was in the militia, I ran into one engineer, and he tried to shoot me. . . . In short, disaster was closing in on us from all sides.

I went back to see the rebbe and repeated everything to him. I also told him that the town commandant, Colonel Yefremov, was a friend of mine from long ago.

The rebbe heard me out and then said: "Throw a large banquet fit for a king. Invite the commandant with all his officers. And also invite the two Polish engineers. And in the midst of the feast, kneel before the commander, as Esther knelt before the king, and describe all the injustices and persecutions, point to the two Poles, tell him that they are brutalizing Jews terribly— and God will help you."

I followed the rebbe's advice. I prepared a banquet fit for a king—you couldn't imagine a more sumptuous one: the finest food, the costliest wine, with all the trimmings. I invited the commandant with his entire staff and all his officers; I also asked the two Poles, but they declined. The commandant and his officers came, and they ate and drank, constantly praising the feast, especially the liquor. "When the heart of the king was merry with wine" [Esther, 1:10]—that is, when the guests were all in high spirits—I told them about how the Poles were planning to kill us, agitating against us in the military, preparing a pogrom, about how the two engineers were going to get even with Jews. In short, I poured out my heart to the guests.

They all listened carefully. Yefremov had tears in his eyes, and the others were also moved. But no one knew how to help me. Then the commandant's aide exclaimed that he would take care of everything.

"During your High Holy Days the town will be declared off limits for our soldiers. And we'll issue very strict orders that no one is to touch a Jew!"

The commandant agreed. He kept his promise, and the holidays went by calmly, thank God; they couldn't have been better.

Soon after the Days of Awe, Yefremov left our town. A new commandant arrived, and everything began all over again—the libels, the denunciations, the persecutions, the foul efforts of the Poles. Now Jewish shops were looted; initially a few, then any and all. The Poles showed where, and the Russian soldiers plundered. They began with the large stores and ended with the small ones. They missed almost none. The first was Hokhberg's leather business. They pillaged it all night, snatching merchandise worth tens of thousands of rubles. What you see here are the meager leftovers. . . . When they were done with the stores, they started in on the Jewish homes. The Poles showed the Russians the cellars where the Jews had buried their few belongings. During the looting, a general happened to pass by. Brandishing his knout, he drove the troops away. One soldier grabbed him and threw him into a ditch. I've heard that the soldier was court-martialed and shot.

Several days later, the Jerries arrived. They managed nicely too. First they seized only food, then anything they could lay their hands on. They took my bike and two overcoats—and not a word about payment.

After the Germans marched in, a Russian colonel was still here—I think his name was Komarnikov. He hadn't succeeded in getting out with his army. We hid him. We put him in a Jewish kaftan, stuck a yarmulke on his head, fed him, and kept him locked up. Only four people knew about him. When the Germans left, he got out and went to meet the Russian military. He told them how he'd been treated, and in front of everyone he hugged and kissed the Jews who had concealed him.

The Jews whose house he'd been in all that time asked him loudly, "Do you still believe Jews are pro-German?"

"No! I swear they're not!" he replied.

The colonel was surrounded by officers, who asked him how much he'd paid the Jews for hiding him.

"Not a single kopek!"

The officers were surprised, and they praised the Jews. There was an atmosphere of joy and good humor, so that for a while earlier troubles were forgotten.

But several days later the army marched off together with the colonel whom we'd hidden. A new military arrived, and the old plunderings resumed. This time they stripped us bare—leaving us nothing.

Hokhberg's elderly wife was with us in the store. When Varm was telling us about the lootings, she grew very agitated and began talking and gesticulating hysterically, describing everything that had happened: "They burst in, yelling, 'Give us money!' I said, 'We don't have any!' And they began hunting like wild beasts, knocking over everything in the store. They ran to the table where you're sitting now, and they started yanking at the drawer. It was locked. So, as you can see, they broke off the edge of the table. Inside the drawer there were pawned items, gold and silver articles, which they grabbed. One soldier gave me a gold chain; then another one ran up to me and shouted, 'Give it to me,' and he was ready to stab me!"

And now, equally agitated, but with a childish naïveté, she cried, "Well, tell me? Isn't that total brutality?"

We then discussed my reason for coming to Gora: the Jewish soup kitchen.

Varm told me: "The instant the war broke out, a civic commission was formed here in unison with the five closest communities. There were thirty-six people, two of them Jews—Lukrec and myself. Out of the thirty-six, nine men were elected as the actual councilmen.

"By the time the Germans marched off, over two-thirds of the one thousand Jewish families had fled, leaving less than three hundred. Bilczynski, the engineer who was chairman of the city council, was Polish, but he was decent. He suggested establishing not only a Christian soup kitchen but also a kosher one. He asked that it be supported by the Jewish community. But we refused."

"How come?"

Varm cited the same reasons as the rebbe's sister. He then added:

Simple people don't need a soup kitchen. They have jobs in town. Besides, fifty Jews are employed digging trenches, with the men each earning a ruble and a half a day and the women one ruble. Granted, they have to pay the guard twenty-five or thirty kopeks a day so he'll keep the Poles from beating up the Jews. But there's enough money left for food.

When the commission offered to establish a kosher soup kitchen, I pointed out that we really wanted a store where the poor wouldn't have to pay for merchandise—the same food they would receive cooked at the soup kitchen. Three members of the council voted in favor of that idea, but Bilcyznski and the other five dug in their heels: a soup kitchen or nothing! When I expressed my opinion, they asked if I was speaking for myself or on behalf of the Jewish community. I answered, "I'm speaking on behalf of all the Jews in Gora and also on behalf of our holy rebbe."

I hadn't even discussed it with the rebbe, but I knew perfectly well he'd be opposed to a soup kitchen. That was why I took that position. And apparently that's what triggered the lie that the rebbe decreed it was better to starve to death than use the soup kitchen.

In the midst of our conversation, someone came and announced that it was now illegal to hire Jews for the trenches. We were also told that ninety Germans were being sent here today—three of them bakers. That was why they had made the Jewish bakers agree to bake bread all week long, including the Sabbath.

13

After my conversation with Varm, I went to Bilczynski, head of the civic commission, whom Varm had described as pro-Jewish. I introduced myself to him as a representative of the Zemstvo Alliance. He welcomed me very amiably, but his very first words showed that he didn't realize I was Jewish. I had to choose: either tell him right off and thereby caution him to be careful when talking about Jews; or else keep mum and find out how a decent Pole, who was regarded as pro-Jewish by the local

Jews, actually felt about Jews. I must confess that I gave in to temptation, I didn't inform him. And although this "friend of the Jews" said things he wouldn't have said to someone he knew was Jewish, I felt very dejected and insulted after my visit—as if I'd robbed someone. Next time I'll ward off such temptations.

Bilczynski, an intelligent and educated man of about forty, acquainted me with the activities of the civic commission. So far, the Warsaw chapter had sent it 3,600 rubles, which was being used here to establish a low-price store as well as a home for sixty to eighty poor children. At the same time, the local convent, the Sisters of Charity, had set up a soup kitchen that could feed 150 people.

"The kitchen is only for Christians—Jews aren't allowed to eat there because of their religious laws," he added. "The civic commission wanted to establish a special kitchen for Jews, but they refused."

"How come?"

Smirking, he said with venomous irony: "Listen, Jews are too fine and too aristocratic to eat in a free kitchen. What can you do? Such a noble race! And they also claim it can hurt their image." He paused for a while. "I must tell you," he went on. "I'm an ardent antisemite. But before being an antisemite, I'm a human being. I'd never go so far as to buy anything from a Jew, but when I see a poor Jew in distress, I try to help him. Besides, I feel that this is not the right moment for a national war against the Jews. Because of my conduct, the local Jews want my advice, and the instant something happens they come running to me. They usually do what I tell them, but in regard to the soup kitchen they ignored me. I assume that the tsadik interfered. . . .

"Do you know what a tsadik is?" he suddenly asked.

"I do."

"The local tsadik is the supreme head of all the Polish tsadiks. Jews idolize him."

"So far as I know, he doesn't get involved in secular matters," I said. "Besides, he's been in Warsaw for several months. How could he have interfered in the soup-kitchen issue?"

"Maybe he didn't," Bilczynski agreed. Then he added: "I've met with the tsadik several times. He doesn't understand Polish or Russian. We spoke through an interpreter."

"What kind of an impression did he make on you?"

"He seemed like a deep, earnest, reserved man. By their lights, he's probably even very moral. But they have their own peculiar ethics, which is absolutely incomprehensible for us Christians."

I brought him back to the issue at hand: "How did things remain in regard to food for poor Jews?"

"This is how matters stand: Jews rejected the idea of a soup kitchen and requested that the Jewish poor should get their share in the form of groceries. But we didn't go along with that."

"Isn't it all the same whether you give a hungry man cooked or uncooked food? Raw food is also more efficient. It cuts down on kitchen overhead, and it saves time for the poor man since he doesn't have to show up every day; you can hand out groceries weekly or semiweekly. Each recipient can use the food any way he likes. Furthermore, the same system can be utilized by peasants and other people who live a long way from town and can't get to the soup kitchen."

"The peasants," he replied, "don't need our help. They've hardly suffered, and they're doing quite well now. About three thousand of them are getting high pay for working in the trenches. A peasant and his family can earn as much as thirty rubles a week. As for Jews, there's a different reason why I oppose giving them groceries. You just don't know what sort of people they are! A Jew is content with eating very little. If you hand him a pound of barley, he'll sell three-quarters of it just to pocket the money."

"I think you're mistaken. But even if that were true, who cares?"

"Well, we don't want our assistance to be turned into profiteering."

And no matter how much I argued with him, the "friend of the Jews" stuck to his guns, refusing to provide help in the form of raw food.

When I returned to Warsaw and went to the Zemstvo Alliance, Kzewicki, the Polish secretary, welcomed me with a friendly smile and said: "Well, we now know that the denunciation of the tsadik of Gora-Kalvaria was wrong. He left his town three months ago and has been living in Warsaw."

At the alliance committee I gave a report on Gora, making it clear that the town needed help, which should be extended to Jews in the form of groceries. But the members were indifferent. Since the civic commission didn't like the idea, they said, it was probably worthless. If Jews refused to patronize a soup kitchen, they probably weren't starving. The committee decided to open just a teahouse in Gora.

At ten P.M., upon reaching my hotel, I found Varm. He had taken an earlier train in order to tell the rebbe about my trip to Gora. He had a message from the rebbe, who was asking to see me. Varm was upset. He was afraid I would decline, and in a pitiful voice he begged, apologized, and explained that the rebbe never went out and couldn't come to me himself. So together with Varm, I went to see the rebbe.

14

We entered a spacious wooden house. Varm escorted me through several large rooms containing beds heaped with featherbeds and pillows without pillowcases. Youngsters and adolescents sporting long caftans and curly earlocks were passing back and forth. One of them hurried off to announce our arrival.

Varm led me to a room where there was yet another unmade bed with a symphony of pillows and featherbeds. At the center of the room stood a circular table with a couple of chairs.

A few minutes later the rebbe walked in. He was a middle-aged man of medium height, with broad shoulders, a round face, and a round black beard. His clear, bluish eyes were either weary or lost in thought, and he had a naive, childlike expression with a touch of pity—for himself or for others?

All in all, he was soft, rotund, and compassionate. He shuffled unsteadily like a person unaccustomed to walking. His dressing gown was old, threadbare, and light-colored. Coming to the table, he modestly shook my hand, wishing me peace; his hand was soft, with stubby fingers. He sat down at the table and remained silent, as if not knowing where to begin. He looked at me, helpless and compassionate as if I had the power of life and death over him. Finally, as if unsure of himself, he murmured: "You were in Gora? Someone denounced me?"

I described my trip and put his mind at ease, assuring him that people were now convinced of his innocence.

He listened, gazing at me with dreamy, childlike, compassionate eyes, nodding in silence. I scrutinized his face for the changes of expression that Vegmayster had raved about. But I noticed nothing.

After telling the rebbe about Gora, I brought up other Jewish woes. I wanted to see what impact that would have on him. He listened for several minutes, then stopped me: "The rabbi of Nowomiasto is here. Should I call him in? He ought to hear what you have to say. He'll describe what happened in his town."

We were soon joined by the rabbi of Nowomiasto, a tall, bony man with twisting, shoulder-length earlocks and large, slightly bulging eyes. He came striding in as if gearing up for something. His words were loud, quick, ardent, his movements energetic, fervent. He contrasted sharply with the mystically aloof tsadik.

The rabbi listened impatiently to my story about Suchostow, and before I could finish, he began telling me about Nowomiasto. His account was smooth, almost literary, with some Russian words mixed in with the Yiddish. It turned out that he also functioned as the government-appointed rabbi, even though he was a fiery zealot.

> In our town the Poles began agitating against us on the very first day of the war. They spread lies, incited the military, and wouldn't let the Jews into the militia. The Russians were the first to march in. It was a Sabbath. Soon the militia chief came dashing over to me: "The army's arrived. The shops have to be opened."
>
> I replied that I wouldn't allow the shops to open on the Sabbath. A few hours later he came back and snapped, "The town commandant, General Morozov, orders you to tell the Jews to open their shops without further delay."
>
> I repeated: "Tell the commandant that I'm not his flunky; I don't take orders from him. I will not allow the stores to open on the Sabbath no matter what!"
>
> Another hour passed, and two soldiers with rifles came and led me to the commandant. The general was furious, and he hollered, "You the rabbi?"
>
> "I am."
>
> "Did you say you weren't my flunky?"

"I said that I was God's flunky and no one else's."

"How dare you ignore my orders to open the shops?"

"Your excellency!" I answered. "I assume that in wartime the same God is in Heaven as in peacetime, and if our laws do not allow us to do business on the Sabbath in peacetime, then it is likewise forbidden in war. I also believe that we have to be even more pious now, so that God will send us a victory!"

"Do you want my men to go hungry because of your piety?"

"God forbid!" I said. "They mustn't go hungry. I've told the shopkeepers that when a soldier comes and asks for food, they should give it to him but take no money, because that's prohibited."

Apparently my answer pleased the general, who gaped at me and said: "I like you. Go and observe your religion."

A week passed, and then the commandant ordered the streets to be cleaned on the Sabbath. I ordered the opposite. So he summoned me again: "You told the Jews not to clean the streets on the Sabbath?"

"It's not I who told them. Our religion won't allow it."

"In a war people have to forget about religious laws."

"If that's so, why did you send for me instead of having the Catholic priest order Jews to work? If the Jewish religious laws have been annulled, then, logically, so has the rabbi. Do you expect Jews to ignore our commandments and yet obey the rabbi? If there are no religious laws, then there is no rabbi."

He saw that I was right, and, waving his hand, he said so in Russian: "Ravvin Prav" [the rabbi's right].

A few weeks later, the Germans marched in. We suffered the most horrible ordeals. They threatened to shoot us for the slightest offense. They forced Jews to clear away the mud and clean the roads even on the Sabbath. My pleas fell on deaf ears—I could barely convince them to have the soldiers leave the synagogue. They billeted soldiers in the homes. I protested against their placing them in my home; I said that I was exempt because as a licensed rabbi, I was a government official. I had sworn an oath to my emperor and couldn't break it. They exempted me.

When they retreated, they hauled off the grain, the horses—anything they could. As they were leaving, we put out Russian flags, and when they saw this they started shooting up the town.

During the German occupation, the Poles had kept quiet, even acting friendly toward Jews. But when the Russians returned, the Poles went to meet them and didn't allow us to get near the military. I told the baker to bake a white roll, I took a pouch of salt, a Torah scroll, and forced my way through to the military. I approached Supreme Commander Pleve, wished him good luck, handed him the scroll, the salt, and the roll, blessed him, and burst into tears as I said: "The Poles are maligning us to you. We ask you not to believe their libels. We are loyal to God and the czar." And I described what we had endured under the Germans.

The supreme commander was accompanied by a grand prince, whom he addressed as "Your Highness." After hearing me out, Pleve said: "I won't listen to any libels or denunciations about you. I haven't received such a cordial welcome anywhere else."

We felt relieved.

Eight weeks passed, and then policemen arrested eight of our congregants, the finest and most pious, who were anything but political. One of them was our ritual slaughterer, who I'm sure didn't know there was a war going on or who was fighting whom. The military freighted them off to Warsaw. They fasted for the entire trip. In Warsaw they dropped to the ground and stuffed snow into their mouths in order to revive themselves. Now they're in prison. . . . And what do you think they're accused of? When the Germans pulled out, they were pursued by Russian troops. On the edge of town, at the barrier, two or three Russian soldiers were shot and killed by the Germans. So now the Russians decided to charge Jews with deliberately closing the barrier in order to get the Russian soldiers killed. And they arrested the Jews who live near the barrier. The whole story's a fabrication. Hundreds of people can testify that the barrier was open; the priest is willing to swear that the Jews are innocent. But none of this helps.

I've heard that they're looking to arrest me too. I'm not scared—let them arrest me, hang me. . . . Martyrdom isn't such a bad thing. But meanwhile we have to try and save the prisoners. That's why I've come here, but I have no access anywhere. If I had a letter of recommendation to Tumanov, I could accomplish something.

"Have you approached the community administrators?" I asked.

"I've seen them, but they haven't visited our town; they haven't been in our hell. So they're calm. 'Write a petition,' they tell me. 'We'll look into it.' I tell them we have to act now and not lose another minute. And they reply that this is an individual case and they deal only with community affairs. They don't understand that the community is made up of individuals. Just try talking to them—they're cold fish! . . . So now I'm appealing to you. Since you're well connected with the highest-ranking people, you absolutely have to get me a recommendation to Tumanov!"

I started explaining to the rabbi that I had no connections whatsoever with the "most important people," but he wouldn't listen.

It occurred to me that Baron Alexander Gintsburg and Oscar Gruzenberg, the defense attorney at the Beilis trial, had been here four or five days ago and had gone to the front lines with a boxcar full of presents from St. Petersburg Jews. They were due to return today. I told the rabbi I would ask either man to receive him and help him as much as possible.

The rabbi, excited by my idea, pulled me aside to whisper: "Get Gruzenberg and Gintsburg to see the rebbe. It'll absolutely have a big effect. Don't forget that the rebbe is the head of the Polish Jews."

I suggested to the rebbe that he meet with the baron and Gruzenberg. He gave me a pitying look and helplessly pulled his hands apart. "What . . . can . . . I . . . do?"

And he refused.

15

When I got back to the Hotel Bristol around midnight, I met Baron Gintsburg. Just a few hours earlier, he and Gruzenberg had come back from the front lines after delivering gifts to the troops there. I acquainted the baron with the events in Nowomiasto and asked him to receive the rabbi. He agreed to see him tomorrow morning. (I transmitted the message to the rabbi, and he showed up on schedule. But I don't know the upshot of their meeting because I left Warsaw the next day.)

I also asked the baron about his impressions of his trip to the front.

Had he managed to meet with the army's commander in chief about the Russians' behavior toward Jews. He said he had had no chance to talk about the Jewish question but was generally satisfied with his visit—though not enthusiastic. He saw no major political significance in his journey.

However, it was assessed quite differently by Gruzenberg, the other delegate, with whom I spoke the following morning. "We viewed the front lines and met face-to-face with the Russian military and its commanders. These events are history-making. We've finally found the right way to battle the nightmare haunting the Jews."

He described the distribution of the gifts. The delegates were taken all the way out to the frontline trenches. The troops were summoned company by company and ordered to line up. The general explained that Jews had sent these presents for the holidays. The soldiers yelled, "Hurray!" and "Thank you!" The general personally thanked the delegates and asked them to convey his gratitude to the St. Petersburg Jews. Then the officers invited them to a dinner, at which speeches were given. Lastly, the delegates were escorted with great honor to the train.

"Imagine!" Gruzenberg concluded. "What a welcome! You said that the military carries out pogroms and hangs and shoots Jews. But the troops we met cried 'Hurray!' and practically carried us on their shoulders. The Russian soul is like a pendulum. First it swings down into the darkest abyss, and then it zooms up to unequaled heights. I was so deeply moved that I couldn't speak—I was choking back my tears. . . . But that's not all. Just listen to this! When the general thanked us, he asked me to say a word to the soldiers. Do you hear? He allowed a civilian to address the frontline fighters! It was virtually a rally. I was amazed, and I told the general: 'Your Supreme Excellency, I know the meaning of discipline, and I won't venture to address the soldiers directly. But please tell them that we bow in deep appreciation for their great suffering and self-sacrifice and that we look with great delight upon their courageous and heroic struggle.'

"The commander in chief, Sheydeman, also received us and thanked us, but his reception was a lot colder. . . . He didn't even ask us to sit down."

"And did you talk to any of the commanders about the behavior toward Jews, about the libels and persecutions?" I asked.

"We had no chance to broach the topic."

"Are the front lines you visited out in the countryside or near a populated area?"

"Near a shtetl. We were there for twenty-four hours."

"Did you meet with the local Jews? Did you question them?"

"We didn't meet or even see a single Jew there, but we did stay in a Jewish home. And imagine: I walk in, and what do I see? My picture of the Beilis trial hanging on the wall."

"Well, did your hosts tell you anything about the Jewish situation?"

"No. Our host had just returned home. He had been arrested and very nearly hanged."

"How did he manage to get released?"

"This is strictly between us: he bought his freedom for one thousand rubles."

Several days before I left for Gora, I received a telegram from Feygenboim, the businessman who had offered to take me to Galicia: he would be staying in Brody for only a few days, and if I wanted to take advantage of his offer, I would have to start out immediately. I wired back that I would be leaving for Rovno on December 29, and I asked him to dispatch my travel permit there or bring it to Brody.

I put my departure off for several days in order to complete my work at the Zemstvo Alliance. I also nurtured a glimmer of hope that the alliance would send me to Galicia. Virubov, claiming he couldn't help in this regard, added each time that I ought to approach Prince Lvov, who was due to visit Warsaw any day now. He arrived on December 27. I met with him, and he instantly recalled our conversation in Moscow, when I had asked him to help me enter Galicia.

"It's very difficult now for a civilian to go there," he replied. "Two weeks ago they published an order that absolutely no travel permit to Galicia was to be issued to any individual. Just imagine: Virubov, the supreme plenipotentiary of the Warsaw division of the Zemstvo Alliance, had to struggle for two whole weeks before wrangling a permit."

"I'm not asking you for a permit," I responded. "Just give me a document stating that you've ordered me to go to Galicia. I'll manage to obtain a permit myself."

"We're not allowed to send any missions there. Shlikevitsh, our plenipotentiary in Galicia, does everything he has to."

"You know my purpose in going there," I replied. "I need your mission document only until I reach Lwow. Once I'm there, I'll fend for myself. Maklakov and Demidov have promised to put me into one of their divisions."

Igor Platonovitsh Demidov, a member of the Duma and a prominent Constitutional Democrat, was in charge of one of the army divisions. He was stationed in the Galician town of Tarnow.

"Demidov is in Moscow now; he's forming a new detachment. Why not try him? It would be easy for Demidov to take you along. But we can't give you any authorization from here."

It was clear that he wouldn't give me a document because I was Jewish and especially because I planned to investigate the Jewish situation in Galicia.

As I passed through the next room on my way out, Kzewicki, Prince Lvov's secretary, smirked and said: "Well, so was I right? I told you Lvov wouldn't give you a document for Galicia. I knew it."

Virubov then caught up with me and said apologetically: "Come by tomorrow. Try to talk to Lvov again. I'll discuss it with him."

I appealed to Lvov again, but it was pointless. I left him without shaking hands or saying good day.

To reach Rovno, I had to start out immediately. I just had time to hurry over to Peretz and say farewell. But he wasn't at home. I didn't realize that we would never meet again, that three months from now he would depart from us forever. I left Warsaw without seeing the man who had become dearer to me than a brother.

En route I telegraphed I. Nayditsh, a well-known Zionist and community leader in Moscow, who had given me a letter of recommendation to Demidov. I explained that I had failed to accomplish anything in Warsaw, and I beseeched him to ask Demidov to take me into his new division, and asked him to please wire me back in Rovno.

On my train, there were officers in my compartment, and I had the pleasure of hearing their stories about Jews. One officer told us:

"Imagine: a friend of mine, a second lieutenant, was on furlough, and when he got back he didn't find his company where he had left it. He asked around, but no one knew, and those who knew wouldn't say. Orders had been issued that the destinations of these army divisions were strictly classified. He was in agony for three days. So what do you think he did? He summoned a broker, promised him a couple of rubles, and told him to find out whatever my friend needed to know. One hour later the broker brought him the most precise data: when his company had marched off, where to, and even the route they had taken! God only knows how they found out. We were in the town, we knew nothing, but we could tell from the Jewish faces that we were about to withdraw. And the orders actually came the next day: 'Retreat!' It's obvious the Jews have a huge espionage network with a lot of agents, who give one another all the information."

A short while later, another officer spoke up: "All the misinformation is spread by the Jews. They deliberately circulated a rumor that the Germans had taken Kielce. And their insolence! They openly call out, 'Soon our forces will be here!' They mean the Germans. And they talk German to one another. They should all be strangled! Those traitors know our victory will spell their doom. The Poles'll kill them all! That's why the Jews are looking forward to a German victory."

In Rovno, I did not find the expected telegram from Feygenboim. But I did receive an unexpected wire from I. Nayditsh: "Come to Moscow. Demidov's division is pulling out. It has a place reserved for you."

I immediately left for Moscow.

Demidov, in search of medicine, had come to Moscow several weeks earlier. Nayditsh, upon receiving my cable, had talked to him about me, and Demidov had promptly agreed to take me along to Galicia. But he had had to leave before I could reach Moscow. So he had told his brother, Lev Platonovitsh, his Moscow representative, to authorize me to escort two freight cars of medicine to Galicia.

I went to see the brother, who handed me my authorization and explained my assignment: I was to make certain the medicine was packed in the freight cars according to the list, accompany them to Tarnow, and turn them over to the division. A member of the Artyél, a labor batallion, would be coming along as well. Another authorized person (a Moscow lawyer named B. Y. Ratner, who wanted to go to Galicia out of sheer curiosity) and I only had to make sure the shipment wasn't held up along the way. In Brody we would have to transfer it to an Austrian train because the lines outside of Russia have a narrower gauge, and we would then accompany the consignment to Tarnow. I didn't need a travel permit; official authorization was enough.

VOLUME TWO

I

Galicia is one of the poorest regions of central Europe, if not *the* poorest. It has few natural resources, few mineral deposits. The soil is not particularly fertile; the farming methods are primitive and the harvests meager. Industry, manufacture, and commerce are also underdeveloped. The deeply rooted Galicians, especially the Ruthenians in the eastern part, are barely educated and live roughly; they are more backward than even the Russian *muzhik*. All this has of course affected the economic condition of Galician Jews, who numbered between nine hundred thousand and one million before the war. Even though Jews in the Austrian Empire enjoy equal rights, with equal access to all the professions and government jobs, those in Galicia are very poor and unsophisticated. This is confirmed by two sets of statistics: Galicia has the highest death rate among Jews and the highest rate of immigration to America.

Galician Jews clearly lag behind other communities in cultural terms as well. True, they've gone through the same ideological upheavals as Jews elsewhere. They too have lived through the false Messiah crisis,* the spread of Hasidism, the onset of the Enlightenment, and the assimilationist, revolutionary, Zionist, and nationalist movements. Galicia has certainly contributed great leaders and other personalities to these developments. But it has never played a central role. Galicia's sole distinguishing feature is that the ideological battles have always been fought more passionately there. Galicia's Hasidism degenerated into blind faith in wonder rabbis, while Orthodoxy waged an especially savage and

---

*Refers to the phenomenon of Shabbtai Zvi, who in 1665 proclaimed himself the Messiah.

relentless war against the Enlightenment, and assimilation here has been a poor joke, a pale imitation of other Jewish centers.

Although Jews in Austria-Hungary have enjoyed civil equality, their political situation has been complicated. In the fierce national struggles of various ethnic groups, Jews formed no single national entity with a political agenda; instead they navigated their way among all the other brawling forces. As each nationality in Galicia—be it the politically dominant German speakers, the Poles, or the Ruthenians—considers itself the worthiest and most legitimate, the Jews are always seen as subjects, required to demonstrate their loyalty and devotion. Having no single political platform of their own, the Jews have mostly gone along with the de facto ruler, whoever has had the upper hand: first the Austrians, then the Poles. More recently, the Jews have tended to follow the Ruthenians. Because of these shifts, the various ethnic groups resented the Jews all the more and viewed their behavior as treacherous.

At the same time, the generally favorable political situation gave Galician Jews a feeling of self-worth and security, a conscious sense of being full-fledged citizens. Their Austrian patriotism was strong, and their dedication to the old kaiser, Franz Joseph, was cultlike. They loved him deeply and respected him as their protector and helper. At the start of the war, Austria's Poles were in an ambiguous position, while the Ruthenians stood apart from everyone. The Galician Jews, however, stuck to their pro-Austrian orientation, flaunting it in the most delicate of circumstances, with no concern for horrible consequences. Their self-sacrificing allegiance was extraordinary. I saw Jews shedding bitter tears when they heard about the fall of Przemysl to the Russians. Jews could not hide their delight at Russian defeat, and, when overrun, they heroically told the invading army that as Austrian citizens they were devoted heart and soul to their government. In some places, the Jews reacted with hostility even to me and Dr. Lander as representatives of the enemy.

Although the Galician Jews, whether Orthodox or enlightened, drew spiritual support from their Russian brothers and shared many bonds with them, a large gap existed between the fraternal tribes before the war. They were alien to each other, even inimical, and always cool. The Galician Jews looked down on the Russians as disenfranchised Jews and were unable to grasp how anyone could live and breathe under arbitrary rule, deadly pogroms, and random persecution. The Orthodox among them saw Russian Jews as licentious and heretical. For their part, the Russians despised the Galicians as backward, fossilized—an ignorant mass without culture or aspirations.

For more than a century they had lived side by side in estrangement and misunderstanding. It took a terrible catastrophe, an ocean of blood and tears, to bring Russian Jews closer to their Galician brothers. At the very least, the war will lead to a rapprochement between these two parts of the population.

2

Radziwillow and Brody, two small border towns, had faced each other, armed to the teeth, for more than one hundred years. They were separated by customshouses, tollgates, and barbed wire. Still, the people of both towns maintained a close rapport and were interdependent. Their separation actually brought them together and provided their livelihood, since commerce between Russia and Austria passed through Radziwillow and Brody. Then the first shots of the war shattered the barrier, bringing down the tollgate and the customshouse. Both towns died instantly. With trade—the chief source of income—gone, they lost their raison d'être.

The towns lie some four miles apart, and my train to Brody covered the short distance in barely fifteen minutes. But that quarter of an hour felt very sinister. In Kiev and, earlier, in Moscow, I had encountered the harsh military regulations that prohibited any Jew from entering Galicia. I had been told, in Kiev, about Dovid Faynberg, a famous St. Petersburg social worker, who was friends with Count Bobrinski, East Galicia's governor-general. Bobrinski had turned down Faynberg's request for permission to go to Lwow. (Eventually, though, I heard that he had managed to enter Galicia anyway.)

Would I be allowed in? My authorization, from the committee of the members of the state Duma, enabled me to escort two boxcars of medicine to Tarnow; but my documents hadn't been stamped by any military institution and didn't even bear my photograph. My name and my father's name were obviously Jewish. I had little doubt that when my papers were checked, I would be stopped; in any case, the process was certain to be troublesome.

But I was wrong. The officer, accompanied by two policemen, went through the train, checking documents, and didn't even look at my authorization. He quickly penciled something on my papers and handed them back.

Later on, I crossed the border several times, free and undisturbed, even though Galicia was strictly off-limits. And during the months when I visited dozens of Galician towns and even the front lines, no one ever asked to see my papers. It was very difficult for civilians to reach the front lines. They had to pass through dozens of checkpoints, where documents were scrutinized. In Russia, these hurdles were eliminated in a highly original way. The army decreed that delegates or employees of the Red Cross or other welfare organizations had to wear uniforms with special epaulets, and they had to carry swords, even though most of these people were civilians. In their uniforms they had roughly the same privileges as army officers, and they were protected against suspicions of espionage. Nothing was easier than joining an organization, donning the military garb, and freely gaining admission anywhere. There were probably many German spies among the tens of thousands of welfare workers, moving along the front lines and among the officers, seeing and hearing whatever they needed to see or hear. When it transpired that the enemy knew all Russia's military secrets, Russia comforted itself by accusing the Jews of treason.

At the start of the war Brody's train station had gone up in flames. Now, a ramshackle buffet had been set up in one room of the ruins. When I entered, the place was packed with officers, who were standing at the buffet or around small tables, consuming borsht. I noticed that the soup bowls bore a Hebrew inscription that read "mazel tov," congratulations. The china had evidently been stolen from a Jewish hotel.

Next, I went into the town with my travel companion, Mr. Ratner. The town was about a mile or so from the station. The day was just breaking. The road to Brody was flanked by burned and desolate cottages. In the distance we saw a broad field covered with charred ruins. Soon the devastated town emerged from the gray mist of an early winter morning. There were blackened chimneys and burned walls as far as we could see, visible beneath a dusting of downy snow. The town looked like the ancient, mossy remnants of Pompeii. I noticed the scorched wall of a synagogue. Above the door, some Hebrew words had survived: "How awesome is this place" [Gen. 28:17]. The verse was fitting for the ruins of the house of worship and for the entire spread of the shattered neighborhood.

Nestled among the wreckage I saw a small cottage almost embedded in the earth. It looked as if it had crouched down during the conflagration, hidden in the ground, and therefore had survived. An old Jewish man was standing nearby, as poor and hunched as the cottage itself.

When he saw me and my friend in our uniforms, he whipped off his cap and bowed deeply. I went over and asked in Yiddish, "How come your cottage escaped the fire?"

The old man gaped at me, then shrugged and sighed. "Perhaps a miracle. . . . Heaven granted us a place to starve to death."

I gave him a ruble. He was so amazed he forgot to thank me. He stood motionless, gawking.

We walked on among the burned ruins. I noticed something that I would see again and again: at every street corner, shiny metal signs in Russian had been nailed to the walls. The occupiers had given every street a fancy, new name: Pushkin Street, Gogol Street, Lermontov Street, and even Turgenev Street, if I remember correctly. The irony of naming these horribly deformed streets after the luminaries of Russian culture had escaped the victors; they didn't realize how offensive it was to the memory of our great Russian authors.

3

The burning of Brody had devoured almost half the town—several hundred exclusively Jewish houses. It had happened during the early days of the war, when the Russians crossed the border into Austria. The first Cossack division had met little resistance taking Brody; it had started the fire and blocked all attempts to put it out. Later in the war, this crime was repeated in dozens, indeed hundreds, of Galician towns and villlages, becoming normal, not worthy of notice. The burning of Brody, however, was the first such atrocity committed by the czar's army and so the soldiers felt the need to devise an excuse, to rationalize the savagery. They came up with the lie that would be adopted as the standard pretext for all the pogroms and violence against Jews: a girl standing at her window had fired at the Russian army.

Before I'd arrived in Brody, I had already heard this story in military circles: When the first Cossack division galloped into town, a Jewish girl, the daughter of a hotelier, had shot at the commander. The troops killed the girl, then shelled Brody, burning down the district where the attack had taken place.

Dr. Kalak had lived through the Brody disaster. He told us this story:

> As the Cossacks headed down the main boulevard, we heard a shot. One of the Cossacks was wounded or killed. This happened outside a Jewish hotel. When the owner's daughter heard the shot, she got scared and came rushing out. The Cossacks took her for the culprit, and they hacked her to pieces. Then they raced out of the town and started bombarding it, sending two or three heavy shells. One of the shells hit the bank, totally destroying it and claiming several lives. A day or two later, the Cossacks returned and went from house to house in that neighborhood, kicking out the Jews and torching their houses. They wouldn't allow the residents to carry out anything from their homes or to douse the flames. The entire neighborhood went up in smoke—hundreds of houses. The damage is estimated at several tens of

millions of crowns. Six people perished: five Jews and a Christian woman, a teacher. Curiously enough, before the arrival of the Russians, the father of the accused girl had been jailed on suspicion of sympathizing with the Russians. He was released by the czarist military.

A Jewish drayman, who drove me to Radziwillow for several hours and then back to Brody, gave me his impressions of the events:

> On August 14, around six A.M., we suddenly heard a nearby cannonade. We didn't know what that meant because we hadn't expected the Russians to enter Brody so fast and so easily. Our army scooted out of town. A couple of hours later, at eight-thirty, a horseman came riding up, a Cossack. He charged through town, stopping only long enough to ask where the post office was. Then he dashed back. Next, a whole division of Cossacks arrived, and soon we heard some heavy firing, which went on for forty-five minutes. My family and I hid in a cellar. Others concealed themselves wherever they could. No one dared look into the street. When the noise died down, we crept out of our hiding places. There was no trace of the Cossacks. The streets were filled with a deathly hush. No matter who we asked, nobody knew what had happened. Around ten-thirty, we heard a cannon boom. Then it boomed again. The cannonball hit the Prague Bank and wrecked it—but no one died. There was turmoil in the streets again, and so we started looking for a new hiding place. My family and I ran over to the Jewish cemetery. All at once, several Cossacks turned up. We were terrified; we thought they'd slaughter us on the spot. But they didn't touch us; they only asked for drinking water. When we gave them some, they wanted one of us to taste it and make sure it wasn't poisoned. After drinking, they rode off. The town fell silent, and we didn't set eyes on another Russian or Cossack soldier for a whole week.
>
> But then a Cossack division came galloping in. They halted at the end of town, dismounted, and, not saying a nasty word, used their spears to toss something through the windows of the houses. The houses then burst into flames. They allowed the residents to leave only with the clothes on their backs and without carrying anything out. And while some Cossacks set fire after fire, others looted the houses. They broke into the shops, stormed into

the homes, and grabbed everything they could lay their hands on. They didn't relax until the entire neighborhood was burned down and the town grew silent.

About a month later, a Russian soldier walked into a garden and started picking apples. The maid yelled and hurled a log at him. He ran off, but then after a while he returned with a few more troops, and they torched the house.

In Brody, I heard yet another version of the story about the shooting and the Cossacks: When the Cossacks rode in, they encountered a young Christian woman, a Ruthenian, accompanied by a Pole. One Cossack got pushy with her, and so she hurried away. He chased after her, so the Pole shot him dead. That triggered the turmoil.

Generally, there's reason to believe that the whole story about the killing of the Cossack officer or simple soldier was a fabrication that the invaders spread to justify the pogrom and the burning of the town. Dr. Helman, whom I met several weeks later in Tarnow, told me that he was the physician attached to the first Cossack regiment that entered Brody. If an officer or soldier had been killed or even wounded, Helman would certainly have known about it—but he had heard nothing of the sort.

4

With its old marketplace, the unsinged area looked impoverished and dejected. Many stores, especially the bigger and richer ones, were locked or boarded up. They had been ransacked during the pogrom, their owners perhaps butchered—or else the owners had fled the Russians in time. Despite the early hour, the shops still open were enjoying a brisk business. The customers were generally Russian troops jamming the entire square and buying mainly food and the most basic necessities. The instant my companion and I entered the market, we were surrounded by a whole army of poor, ragged, famished kids, who were begging for a kopek. Most of them were Christian, but three or four were Jewish. I gave each child a few kopeks, no matter what his religion. But the instant I handed a coin to a Jew, all the Christian children began shouting at me: "Don't give him anything! Don't give him anything! He's a Jew!"

The children were joined by a Jewish beggar, a strange woman of about sixty. She wore a red dress, her gray hair was powdered, and her movements were nervous. She stood before me, grinning, her nasty, hungry eyes glaring at me, and she sort of danced a little. Then, in a hoarse voice, mangling the language, she began warbling a sentimental Russian song, "Ptitshka Kanareyka," dearest little canary, about a young man who sends out a canary with a greeting for his beloved. The old beggar woman's screechy voice and outlandish appearance made a terrible impression on me. I gave her some coins and tried to hurry off. But she blocked my way, staring into my eyes and squawking her horrible song. She plainly expected me to be surprised that she could sing in Russian. I was haunted for the rest of the day by the nightmare of the beggar's appearance and performance.

In town we discovered a hotel, where we rented a large room. When I stepped into the adjoining café, I found a large group of young men playing pool. I was astonished to see Russian officers playing with young Jews, acting as friendly to them as to their own people.

In Radziwillow I was sent to Dr. Kalak, who, I was told, could fill me in on the Jewish situation. His reception wasn't very cordial. When I introduced myself and told him why I was in Galicia, he acted very leery. Because of my epaulets, he thought I was an officer, and, knowing that a Jew could never achieve that rank in Russia, he gave me the third degree. He absolutely refused to believe that a Jew could be the authorized agent for a welfare organization. Ultimately, I managed to put his mind at ease and convince him that I hadn't converted to Christianity.

He and his wife told me about the overall situation created by the arrival of the Russians. They had dissolved the town council and announced that they would allow the election of a new council—made up of people who were not suspect in the eyes of the military. They found an alcoholic butcher, who claimed to be a Russophile and took it upon himself to organize the election. Instead of making public announcements, he called his friends and acquaintances together, and without any voting he designated them members of the new town council. When they started running things, these people were unbearable.

The military authorities kept a sharp eye on the council. There were no more "overt" pogroms as there had been at first. But there was a non-stop silent pogrom. A nine P.M. curfew was imposed, after which the whole town, with all its shops, remained under the supervision of the military patrols till morning. And almost every night, the patrols broke into one or more of the best shops, particularly the ones that had been closed down because their owners had fled. The soldiers pillaged the merchandise and sold it to special dealers. In this way, they cleaned out dozens of businesses, stealing goods worth millions of rubles.

The Jews were suffering the worst persecutions at the hands of the military. The Russians had immediately dismissed all the Jews from any official positions: in the law court, the railroad, the post office, and so forth. Every single day they commandeered private homes and public institutions for military purposes, throwing the people into the street. A few days ago they had taken over the Jewish old-age home and simply booted out some forty elderly residents. Near Brody there was a huge farm with many well-appointed lodgings that would work very nicely as military facilities. The farm belonged to a rich German blacksmith, who, with all his employees, had fled into Austria at the outbreak of the war. The farm was totally deserted, but the Russians didn't move in. One group tried to occupy the place, but they soon received strict orders to evacuate. It turned out that the blacksmith was very well connected—with friends in very high places.

Having arrived in Brody on Friday, I stayed on through the Sabbath. I visited the old synagogue, which had played a major role in earlier Jewish cultural life. It had once housed the leaders of the Jewish intelligentsia: Yekheskl Landa, Meyer Margolis, and others. And it was a center of anti-Hasidism. Gershen Kitever [secretary to the Baal-Shem-Tov, the founder of Hasidism] had come here to defend his employer when they were preparing to anathematize him. A whole era of Jewish life was bound up with Brody and its synagogue. The old building had a very splendid interior. The beadles showed me many ancient silver rarities: menorahs, crowns for Torah scrolls, candelabras from the sixteenth and seventeenth centuries, as well as lavish curtains for the Holy Ark.

When I pointed out that this was a dangerous time for keeping these precious articles in the synagogue, the beadles smiled at me. One of them said: "Don't worry! We hide them in a place where no one could ever find them."

Did they manage to hide these ancient treasures during the many pogroms that took place in Brody after my visit? I don't know.

Upon leaving the synagogue, I witnessed the following scene. An old, small, emaciated horse was struggling to pull a huge wagon piled high with all sorts of poor household items: dishes, bedding, old, broken furniture. An old Jewish couple was pushing the wagon along with all their strength. They had probably been given twenty-four hours to clear out of their home. The Jews leaving the synagogue were deeply grieved by the unusual sight of Jews moving out on the Sabbath. There wasn't the slightest hint of a rebuke—no one was reproaching the old Jews for publicly breaking the Sabbath.

I spent several days in Brody because I had to transfer my load of medicine to non-Russian freight cars on the Austrian tracks. During the six months since the arrival of the first czarist soldiers in Galicia, the Austrian railroad gauge had been widened to Russian specifications only within five or ten miles from the border. For that reason, the countless shipments of goods or troops heading in either direction had to switch trains near Brody. You can imagine how disruptive that was for normal transportation.

While dealing with the boxcars at the depot, I made the acquaintance of two Jewish doctors attached to the large army medical barracks nearby. They told me that hundreds of thousands of wounded men had passed through here. Now, thousands of soldiers a day were arriving from the Carpathian front—with more frostbite than wounds.

Like most frontline Jewish doctors, these two were uninterested in the plight of the local Jews, and so they were unable to give me any concrete data about the persecutions. To make up for it, they described the hardships suffered by the local peasants under the Russian priests. The instant the Russians occupied a section of Galicia, they were followed by whole armies of priests under the leadership of Yevlogi, a famous archimandrite of the Black Hundreds. The Ruthenian peasants belong to the Uniate Church, and the black army instantly began working on them, trying to bring them back to the Orthodox faith. And the proselytizers used deeds as well as words: they threatened to confiscate the land belonging to the obstinate Ruthenians and to forcibly take away their children and induct them into the Orthodox creed. They didn't go through with such actions, but the peasants were terrorized, and many converted against their will. One doctor told me that the Ruthenian woman in whose home he was billeted had locked herself in during the past few days and refused to admit anyone because of a rumor that the children of the Uniates were to be taken away. She had decided it was better to starve to death behind locked doors than give up her children to the Orthodox faith.

5

From Brody to Lwow I took a special military train, which, commuting daily between the two destinations, provided all the comforts of home. During the ninety-minute ride, I saw no traces of the war. I shared my compartment with some officers, who, while gazing out at the mountains near Lwow, were astonished that the Austrians had abandoned the town without offering any resistance.

I found Lwow to be an elegant, cultivated European city. In some ways it reminded me of Kiev. At every step you see old, historic buildings from the days of Polish rule. Indeed, the entire city is imbued with Polish culture. The largest and most glorious structure was the train terminal, one of the most beautiful in all Europe. Later on, while pulling out, the Russians blew it up, totally destroying it.

Here, too, there were no signs of war, no burned or shattered houses. The city was bustling, the streets were filled with cars, wagons, and pedestrians, but most of the people belonged to the czarist military. In the center of town, all the shops were open, and I noticed that many of them were selling luxury items—gold and diamonds. As I heard later, the Lwow storekeepers did a thriving business with the Russians.

I had been told to look up two people in Lwow: Dr. Yankev Diamant, a lawyer, and Dr. Hoyzner, a rabbi, who were both involved in organizing relief for the local Jews. I went to call on the attorney. My arrival caused quite a bit of turmoil in his home. Dr. Diamant had been arrested three times; the last time together with thirty other Jewish and Christian hostages. The Christians had been released the next day. The Jews, however, had been incarcerated for several weeks and had been set free only days ago. No wonder that Dr. Diamant, upon hearing that a Russian officer wanted to speak to him, assumed he was being taken in yet again.

Dr. Diamant proved to be an inveterate assimilationist and an ardent Austrian patriot. From the very first moment, I felt his coldness, almost hostility. He saw me as a Russian, even though he knew perfectly well that I was anything but a chauvinist and was interested only in the Jewish situation. Still, being well bred, he was very polite and said he would be willing to help me with anything I needed.

He told me that Dr. Lander from St. Petersburg had been here several times and had suggested forming a relief committee for the needy Jews in Lwow and, insofar as possible, in other areas of Galicia. For now, Dr. Lander had left a certain sum of money for welfare purposes. Dovid Faynberg, the famous community leader in St. Petersburg, had been here several weeks earlier, when Count Bobrinski, the governor-general of East Galicia, had given him an audience. Faynberg had obtained the count's permission to organize a Jewish committee.

"I consider the whole attempt to form a relief committee absolutely unnecessary and even harmful," Dr. Diamant said to me. "This action can easily be implemented by the community administration, which has organized help for the population in the past. You have to understand that installing a Russian committee with the official approval of the Russian authorities is impossible for us. We were and we remain Austrian citizens. We are loyal to our fatherland and to our gracious monarch, to whom we Jews especially have a lot to be thankful for. If we went along with the proposal to establish a Russian-Jewish committee, we'd be entering into an official relationship with the Russian authorities, and that would constitute profound ingratitude toward our government, if not treason."

I pointed out that, to my mind, this would not in any way constitute a lack of gratitude toward Austria. The relief committee had absolutely

nothing to do with politics. Its only goal was to help the devastated Jewish population, which would suffer terribly if it received no such aid. The
community administration couldn't possibly replace this committee.
Given the Russian government's suspicions toward Jews and given the
lies being spread about Jews, the St. Petersburg committee couldn't privately hand over any funds, much less hefty amounts, to a Jewish community board made up of subjects of the enemy country. They were
bound to arouse suspicions that Jews were donating large sums to the
enemy. Indeed, Jews had been accused of doing just that. It had been
hard enough to convince the czarist authorities that there was nothing
treasonable about setting up a relief committee for the Jews in the
Russian-occupied sector.

"I heard all that from Mr. Faynberg," Dr. Diamant replied. "Rabbi
Hoyzner agrees with him one hundred percent, and they've gained support from other local Jewish community leaders. Ultimately, I have no
objections to such a committee, but Faynberg and the local leaders actually want me to be chairman and to go and introduce myself to Bobrinski. But I absolutely refuse. As an Austrian patriot, I simply can't do that."

I then went to see Rabbi Dr. Hoyzner at the community administration. The Lwow community has its own large building. In the hall, where
I met with Hoyzner, a life-size portrait of Emperor Franz Joseph was still
hanging. The Russian authorities had not demanded its removal even
though his picture had been taken down in other official institutions.

Unlike Dr. Diamant, Hoyzner was a Zionist and fervent nationalist.
Needless to say, he had a very different approach to the relief issue:

> We knew early on about the Russian army's atrocities toward
> Jews in our country, and anyone who could flee did so, abandon-
> ing all his property. People also urgently pressed me to leave. I
> may have owed it to my wife and children to escape. But after a
> lot of soul-searching I told myself that it was my duty to remain
> for the sake of the poor and helpless population. So I've re-
> mained. During these past few months I've had plenty of adver-
> sity. And I'm bound to have more. I'm convinced I'll be taken
> hostage, and I could easily be shot or hanged. But I don't regret
> staying on. There's so much to do here for the Jewish population.
> I'm definitely an Austrian patriot, and I was frank about it with

Count Bobrinski. But Mr. Diamant's position is foreign to me. Our brethren in Russia are thinking about us and are trying to help us. We have to accept their help with the greatest thanks and enthusiasm and not indulge in any exaggerated sense of loyalty. To tell you the truth, even if anybody saw this as ingratitude toward our government, I still wouldn't oppose it—given the dreadful Jewish plight. With the help of Russian Jews we can prevent thousands of people from dying in a famine. But I'm not afraid that the Austrian government may regard the committee as illegal. Our government is smart enough and civilized enough to see that we're not committing any sin.

The rabbi also told me about his visit with Count Bobrinski. The governor-general had received him cordially, expressed his satisfaction with the Jewish populace's loyalty to the Russian military, and promised to allow the establishment of a Jewish relief committee. On the whole, Bobrinski had made the finest impression on Dr. Hoyzner, who described him as a civilized European trying to live in peace with the people in the occupied region.

I heard the same opinion from others who had met the count. He was indeed highly educated and good-natured, striving to avoid violence, even toward Jews, whom he perhaps didn't much care for in his heart of hearts. Unfortunately, his power was very limited. He had to reckon with all kinds of forceful influences, with the moods of other men in power. On the one hand, there were the local military authorities, the commanders and generals, who totally ignored his orders and decrees and often flouted his policies. On the other hand, he was dependent on the czarist government, its cabinet, and especially the St. Petersburg bureaucracy, which pursued its own agenda in Galicia. Furthermore, Bobrinski had to execute the fiats of General Headquarters, which was filled with the worst Jew-baiters, such as Nikolay Nikolayevitsh and Yanushkevitsh. And finally, within Lwow and other parts of Galicia, the count had to deal with local Russophiles who had formed a Black Hundreds group led by a man named Dudikjevic. Its members terrorized not only the local populace, especially the Jews, but also the Russian authorities— even the governor-general.

Bobrinski had to navigate through all these currents as best he could.

A few times he was on the verge of resigning. He did remain in his post until the end. But he never managed to carry out his own independent policies—if only because nearly all the officials on his staff, whether in Lwow or elsewhere in Galicia, were the lowest elements of the Russian bureaucracy: thieves and bribe takers, many of whom had been tried for serious crimes in Russia. The government had developed a kind of system for sending the worst scum to the occupied areas—men who had even been kicked off the Russian police force or constabulary.

Rabbi Hoyzner told me about the Lwow pogrom:

> The Russians marched in with no anti-Jewish violence—a very rare occurrence. They spared only the large towns such as Lwow and, later, Czernowitz. But soon after their arrival, some shooting broke out on the eve of Yom Kippur. A rumor spread that a Jewish girl had shot at the Russian military from a window and wounded or killed somebody. An echo of the Brody legend. A bloody pogrom erupted. Eighteen Jews were massacred and dozens of stores were pillaged. The Jews were too frightened to attend synagogue for the Yom Kippur Kol Nidre prayers. The hundreds of Jewish soldiers in the czarist army here went to the synagogue, but, finding it closed, they assumed that the Russian authorities had prohibited worship, and so they sent a delegation to the then governor-general (before Bobrinski). The governor-general instantly summoned the rabbi and yelled at him for closing the synagogues in protest against the pogrom. The rabbi replied that no one was protesting—Jews were simply afraid to go outdoors. The governor-general then set up military patrols at all synagogues and yeshivas and assured the Jews that there would be no second pogrom.

Ethnic relations in Lwow, indeed throughout Galicia, are immeasurably better than in Russian Poland. There have never been any anti-Jewish boycotts. The Gentiles paid little heed to antisemitic lies, and Poles and Jews have coexisted quite peacefully, especially now, during the Russian occupation. Indeed, they stuck together when negotiating with the Russian authorities and did nothing without consulting one another.

6

Rabbi Hoyzner told me a dreadful story. It was hard for him to talk, but impossible for him to hold back.

He had been summoned to a Russian military hospital to attend a mortally wounded Jewish soldier, who wanted to confess. When the rabbi arrived, the man was already dying.

"Rabbi! I can't die. . . . I'm burdened with a great sin, and I beg you to grant me forgiveness."

"What is your sin?" asked the rabbi.

"Our regiment occupied a Jewish shtetl," the dying patient began. "As usual, there was a pogrom. The troops broke into a wine cellar and started drinking. I shared the liquor with them, got drunk, and set out to rob Jews. I stormed into a house and found an old man with a *shtreymel* and long sidelocks. Later on I learned he was the town rabbi. I grabbed the front of his shirt and screamed: 'Jew! Give me money!' He said he had none."

The dying man fell silent.

"What happened next?" Rabbi Hoyzner asked.

The soldier clammed up for a while, then murmured, "I ran my bayonet through him."

He moaned and pleaded. "Rabbi, grant me forgiveness so I can die in peace."

Rabbi Hoyzner was shaken, at a loss for words. He promised the dying man that he would think about it and give him an answer. But within a few hours he was told that the soldier had died.

This story was extraordinary but not unique. When savage instincts are unleashed by war, nightmares are bound to occur when even the weaker, backward Jewish soldiers yielded to the ferocious intoxication and joined their Russian comrades in perpetrating the most shameful atrocities, even against Jews.

In this connection I heard another story from Dr. Lander. When his regiment had entered a certain shtetl, a pogrom began. Lander went to the colonel and demanded that he find a way of stopping it. The colonel sent an officer and a few troops to accompany Lander into town. Upon hearing yells from a house, they ran in and encountered two soldiers who were dashing out with plunder. The looters were promptly arrested. Lander was shocked to see that they were both Jews.

Still, these things were very rare. From everything I heard and saw in Galicia, I can confirm that the Russian-Jewish soldiers normally treated the local Jews like brothers, often endangering their own lives. They were the only czarist troops who could defend the Jews against the Russian army. Though they didn't have equal rights, the Jewish soldiers frequently managed to save a shtetl or people from violence. In that climate, the Jewish troops provided moral and often material support. Despite the strict ban on fraternizing, the soldiers secretly visited the local Jews, gave them advice on how to cope, and helped them in any way they could. In many places, a Jewish soldier virtually became part of a family, and I know of soldiers who courted real danger for their Galician brothers. When Cossacks raped women in the street, the few dozen Jewish troops who happened to be there fired at the Cossacks, killing many of them.

During the pogrom in Sokal, Jewish soldiers either joined the Cossacks in taking merchandise from stores or asked them for a portion of the loot, which they then returned to the owners. In areas afflicted by a famine, Jewish troops shared their crusts with the locals. In Suchostow, I heard a great deal about a soldier named Srulik Vaisbord, who kept practically the entire town alive for six months, supporting it with food and money. Legends were created about him. Some people said that his father had come to him in a dream and ordered him to spend everything he had to maintain the shtetl. Others claimed that the soldier was actually the prophet Elijah.

I was good friends with one soldier, Abba Lev, who devoted himself to the interests of Galician Jews. During my prewar ethnographic expedition, I had encountered him several times in the shtetls of Volhynia, where he had helped me gather material. This educated young man was something of a writer; he had published a few articles in Jewish newspapers. He had, of course, endured a great deal in the war, but he had managed to gain the regimental commander's trust, and so the officer sent him on numerous missions to Kiev, Moscow, and St. Petersburg to buy food. I crossed paths with Lev in five or six Galician shtetls and was always amazed at his efforts on behalf of the Jewish population. He developed close ties to local people everywhere, was familiar with all their needs, brought this information back to Kiev, and demanded help. Once I ran into him just as he was returning from Kiev. Before reporting to his commander, Lev, exhausted from his trip, vulnerable to arrest, headed toward a shtetl some three or four miles from his camp. It was midnight; he had a sack weighing over one hundred pounds slung over his shoulder, containing food, medicine, mezuzhas, daily prayer books, and the ritual fringed garment worn by Orthodox Jews. He had collected these things in Kiev and was donating them to the town. After the outbreak of the Russian Revolution, he was in Romania, providing the same kind of help; he went to St. Petersburg to report on the hardships facing the Romanian Jews.

To my regret, I can't say the same about the Jewish surgeons, of whom there were several thousand in the czar's army. They had more privileges than the rank and file, and since many were colonels and even generals, they constantly fraternized with other officers and had access to the commanders. They were in a position to help the persecuted. But as I discovered, they showed a fearful indifference to their Galician brothers. I don't wish to accuse all the Jewish physicians—there were certainly exceptions: Dr. Lander, who spent four self-sacrificing years working for the Galician Jews; Dr. Helman, Dr. Shabad, and several others. But the other Jewish doctors I encountered during those years were totally uninterested. Some even hid their Jewish backgrounds and swallowed all the anti-Jewish lies and insults they heard.

I once met a surgeon named Shabshayev from Orenburg. He told me he avoided meeting local Jews in the occupied region. "I was also more severe with Jews than with Christians so nobody would suspect me of favoring Jews," he said. He was unaware of any "terrible things," and yet he told me that all the Jews had been removed from government bureaus, military hospitals, baggage transports, and other institutions and sent to the trenches. A survey about Jewish soldiers was taken, and naturally few officers had the courage to say a good word about them. They were asked whether Jewish troops had close relationships with local Jewish civilians, and how many of the killed, wounded, or captured soldiers were Jews. In Shabshayev's regiment 10 Jews had been killed, 40 wounded, and 190 taken prisoner. The percentage of Jewish captives was no greater than that of the Gentiles. But no survey had been taken among the latter, and everyone was surprised by the figure of 190 Jews.

At one point ten men sent out on reconnaissance had all been captured. A normal occurrence. But one of the ten was Jewish—and he was blamed for the entire disaster. The company commander was to be severely punished for including a Jew in a reconnoitering mission.

At the close of our conversation, Dr. Shabshayev entreated me: "Don't repeat anything I've told you. Don't even let on that we've met, much less talked about Jews. It could be dangerous for me."

Other physicians did not hide the fact that they were Jews. But since they were not particularly concerned about the local Jewish situation, I was unable to elicit any information from them. Many had even spent months on end in Jewish shtetls where their military hospitals were located, but they remained uninterested in the Jews around them. With a great deal of effort I managed to talk some physicians into passing me copies of the official orders for expulsions of Jews. They knew how crucial it was to convey these facts to the community leaders in St. Petersburg, but they were terrified of being found out. Some doctors I met were stationed at hospitals in out-of-the-way villages with very needy Jewish populations that I was unable to visit. I asked these doctors to take back a few hundred rubles and distribute the money to the poor or hand it over to the local committee or the rabbi. Most physicians refused. Others consented very reluctantly, as if making the greatest sacrifice.

7

I was very eager to see Dr. Lander, who was now in Zolkiew but, I was told, had left for several days. I traveled from Lwow to Tarnow via Yaroslav and Rzeshov. On the train there were some officers, who talked about Slavic troops in the Austrian army and their attitude toward the war.

"We captured a few dozen Slavic soldiers," an officer stated. "One of them said his entire company was ready to surrender. He told me that if I let him return to their trenches, he'd bring them to us. Naturally I didn't release him. So he offered to write a letter that one of our men would take via a secret route and leave in a specific place at the Austrian trenches. This time I agreed. In his letter he coaxed his comrades to switch sides. He said this was a paradise for POWs. One of our men volunteered to deliver the message, and the prisoner told him how to get there. Our soldier carried out his mission and returned safe and sound.

"And what do you think?" he said. "Two days later two Slavic companies joined us, together with their officers and all their ammunition."

Another officer on the train accused the generals and commanders of treason. He spoke bluntly, and none of the other soldiers protested. On the contrary, most of them agreed with him.

"Russia is fighting three enemies: the Germans, lice, and our generals—the most dangerous."

I had heard many nasty comments about the czar's generals and commanders. They had been accused of selling out to Germany. These charges had a certain basis in fact. The generals' lack of talent, their indifference, their squabbles over honor and medals had produced crushing defeat, more than any real treason might have caused. The suspicion that the generals were traitors, even the greatest and most popular, was long-standing and widespread. Every war has its rumors of treason. Under Catherine the Great, the people accused Prince Gregory Potyomkin of selling out the Russian army to the enemy after losing a drunken card game. In 1812, during Napoleon's attack, the same allegations were made about Mikhail Illarionovich Kutuzov. And during the Russo-Turkish War, suspicion fell upon a whole series of generals.

In this war, the story about Baron Korf, the governor of Warsaw, who had been captured by the Germans, provided material for a huge mass of rumors: supposedly he had given the enemy all the military plans and millions of rubles. A soldier told me that General Rennenkampf's brother was a German general and the brothers met secretly every night so that Rennenkampf could pass on everything he knew. Until he was discovered and hanged.

The writer and revolutionary Rusanov told me that while living in a village in Yaroslav Province he had heard peasants accusing the generals of treason. When he tried to defend some of the generals, one peasant shouted, "Have you ever been to Yaroslav?"

"No."

"Well, go there, and you'll see that the generals are traitors."

"What will I see?"

"A pole in the marketplace, and eight generals chained to it—they've been condemned for treason. And each one's got a sign on his chest that says, 'Spit in his face—spit but don't hit!'"

The train inched alongside barefoot, skeletal peasants, children and adults. They held up their hands to our windows, yelling, "Bread! A kopek!"

We only went as far as Zheshov. We had to spend the night there and wait for the next train, which would carry us and our freight to Tarnow. Zheshov, a beautiful town with a large Jewish population, had suffered little from the war. I had no time to meet with any of the community leaders, but I wanted to see the town's ancient brick synagogue. The interior was mournful and deserted. It was time for afternoon prayers, but no one was there aside from the beadle, an old man in his eighties, still strong and with all his wits about him. He instantly sensed that I was Jewish, and he talked to me like an old friend.

"You see the synagogue? People used to sit here day and night, poring over the holy books. It was mobbed; you could barely squeeze in. Men had to prop their copies of the Talmud on the next man's back. And now the synagogue is empty, like a ruin."

"How did the Russian troops behave?" I asked. "Did they harm the Jews?"

After a long pause, the old man murmured, "There are bad people in your army, and there are bad people in ours." Following another silence, he pensively added, "A man can harm only himself, and not others."

Our boxcars of medical supplies were hooked to a train carrying high-explosive shells, and off we chugged. In my heated freight car I found a young officer with an intelligent face, and we got to talking. There was something a bit odd about his rigid, dreamy stare and his habit of slowly weighing each word before he spoke. I wondered whether he was quite all right.

"You know," he said as we got better acquainted, "you know, when I was young I led a shameful life. I drank, I debauched, I beat the young soldiers, and I did other wicked things. Then I came across Leo Tolstoy's *What Do I Believe In.* I read it and I was reborn. I became a completely different person. I even stopped eating meat."

"And yet you go to war, and you kill people," I said.

He sat awhile with a downcast head. At last he murmured with deep conviction: "War is a different matter. This war will renew the world; it will cleanse mankind of its dirt. For such a goal one can make the supreme sacrifice."

Our train stopped three or four miles short of Tarnow because the approach to the station was being shelled. The station itself and the surrounding buildings had long since burned down. I had to reach town on foot. My belongings and the medical supplies would be driven in by automobile.

8

Tarnow, a large European town with an old town hall and historic buildings, was relatively unscathed and quite bustling. The front lines were only three or four miles away, along the Bzura River. The czarist army had advanced a lot farther, taking Bachny and reaching Cracow. But some three months ago, the Austrians had pushed the Russians back to Tarnow, and now the two enemies were on opposite banks of the Bzura. They engaged in skirmishes but no pitched battles, and it looked as if neither side planned to launch a serious attack.

The inhabitants, hardened by now to the sporadic cannonades, barely noticed them. Life was virtually normal. Two cafés were open, and they were constantly packed, especially with officers. There was also a movie house, and the building walls were covered with posters announcing a symphonic concert under the baton of a man named Smirnov.

The instant the front lines had been established, the Austrians had started shooting 42-centimeter mortars at the Tarnow railroad station, wreaking absolute havoc. I was told that the cannon had remained there accidentally because the military had been unable to move it. They had been firing at the depot to prevent ammunition from reaching the front. When the townsfolk had seen that the enemy was aiming only at the station and the tracks, they had calmed down. But then a couple of weeks before my arrival, the enemy had begun targeting the town—with that same Big Bertha. Two houses had been destroyed, but nobody had been killed. Once the enemy had stopped shelling Tarnow, the inhabitants had calmed down.

The medical corps I was joining had been established with funds provided by some members of the state Duma. Demidov had been put in charge. A thin, nervous man in his forties, he had a thick beard and large, dreamy, mystical eyes. Though he looked for all the world like an aristocrat, his face and his gestures had a strange, almost peasantlike simplicity, such as you find among sectarians.

As I grew more familiar with this corps, I noticed that it reflected Demidov's personality. Most of the members were aristocratic volunteers, dedicated patriots intent on serving the Russian soldier and helping the war effort. Along with Demidov there was the head nurse, Countess Bobrinskaya, an elderly but energetic woman, accompanied by her two young nephews. And there was also a prince. All these titled men and women behaved very simply, acting as bureaucrats and merchants, eating the same food as the rank and file with the same wooden spoons.

The corps had a forty-bed hospital with two physicians, and there were also two mobile units with hospitals. One hospital, run by Demidov's wife, was stationed in the small town of Tuchow, while the second hospital was somewhere in the Carpathians. The corps also had its wagon for transporting wounded men from the front.

The work was endless and hard. Relations among the volunteers were friendly, without petty friction. This was unusual among the medical corps, which were always bristling with intrigue.

Though Tarnow was very close to the front, a large number of hospitals and medical units were concentrated here. Aside from Demidov's hospital, there were: the Red Cross hospital; two or three army hospitals; and, under the leadership of Prince P. T. Dolgorukov, the corps and the hospital of the Association of Towns.

When I arrived in Tarnow, Demidov was away. The corpsmen gave me and my companion, Mr. Ratner, a warm and friendly welcome. They were delighted with the medicine we had brought. We were inundated with questions about the events in Russia and especially the mood there. When I said that people in Moscow were very pessimistic, the old countess became agitated and exclaimed: "What right do they have to feel that way about the war? We're under fire here, yet we believe in victory, while they moan and sigh. It's disgraceful!"

From the very start I sensed no antisemitism in the corps. Deep down the countess and her colleagues may not have felt very kindly toward Jews, but they didn't exhibit any prejudice here. The climate was liberal, in the spirit of the Constitutional Democrats, and there were several Jewish nurses and orderlies.

Demidov showed up the next day. I found him in the committee room, but he was very busy, and he said he would stop by my hotel that evening: "I've got a lot of important things I want to discuss with you."

When he came over, he began talking nervously but with deep conviction. "First I must tell you: Not only am I a friend of the Jews, but I worship them as a nation that trusts in God. I'm a mystic and a theosopher, and I'm deeply interested in everything that Jews have created on the foundation of mysticism and religious thought. But I must tell you: coming here, to Galicia, I've changed my mind."

"Why?"

"Please don't think my impression is based on the stories of treason. I know how worthless all those rumors are. In every town some Jewish girl shoots at the Russians, and she just happens to be in a building with wealthy stores and apartments. . . . But the Galicians aren't like our Russian Jews. They are very unappealing."

"How?"

"They're hostile toward us, and it makes people suspicious. They're not loyal to our military."

"But they're Austrian subjects, and if they stay loyal to their fatherland under such difficult conditions, they deserve the greatest respect."

"Yes, yes, yes!" Demidov agreed, avoiding my gaze. "But you won't be able to convince our people. And one must admit that the Jews—not all of them, to be sure—fleece our troops and rack up huge profits, which causes great resentment. This is a minor complaint, no doubt, especially considering how much the Jews have been robbed and ruined." He quickly added: "Well, enough about that. We'll have plenty of time to talk about this. Why don't you tell me about your trip and what you intend to do here. What are your plans?"

My first goal, I said, had been to enter Galicia, and I thanked him for enabling me to do so. "Now I have to get permission to travel around and investigate the Jewish situation to organize assistance. You're my only hope for a pass."

"Definitely! Definitely!" he exclaimed. "We'll have to figure out how to do that. I think Prince Dolgorukov can help. He's a good man, and he has a friendly attitude toward Jews. I'll introduce you, and you can discuss it with him yourself. I'll talk to him too, but only in a few days. Right now I'm very busy."

We talked about the war. Demidov spoke in a mystical tone and was convinced that the fighting would renew mankind. He repeated almost word for word what the Tolstoyan officer had said to me on the train.

"Igor Platonovitsh," I exclaimed, "I've been in the thick of the war for three months now, and I've seen a lot of soldiers. I've seen men who have looked death in the face, soldiers who have killed and been wounded. But I haven't seen anyone who has been renewed. The liar is still a liar; the thief is still a thief, perhaps an even greater one. There are the same intrigues, and a medal is still the highest goal a soldier can strive for. No, Igor Platonovitsh, bloodshed won't bring any renewal of mankind."

Demidov sat gazing silently at me. Finally, he said, as if to himself, "How can you prove that bloodshed is a sin and not a supreme act of heroism?"

The war's ability to "cleanse mankind" and "renew the human soul" was evident in the pogroms and atrocities that occurred. When I met people from the army and the welfare organizations, I could see how even they had grown more savage with each passing day and were losing their moral foundations.

At the outbreak of war, the Russian intelligentsia had protested the German cruelties, which they contrasted with our own soldiers' humanitarian attitude toward the enemy. But very soon other opinions were heard.

"I don't understand our sympathy for the enemy," said an old lawyer in my sleeping car. He was an agent for a relief organization. "If they fire at us, we have the right to fire at them. If they kill Russian POWs and raze our towns, we have the right to do the same. We have to learn from the Germans and outdo them."

"Frankly, I don't much care for your theory," said his neighbor, an elderly military physician. "And not for moral reasons. No matter how angry I feel toward the Germans, I can't forget that I owe my cultural development to Germans and Jews. Nearly all my instructors and professors were Germans, and my best friends were Jews. The books that influenced me were by Germans or Jews. So I simply can't accept just killing the Germans, and I can't listen to this antisemitic incitement."

Many months later, I found something rather interesting, which reminded me of my conversation with Demidov. I noticed that officers who had fought in battles and had met the enemy face-to-face looked and behaved with a mystical serenity. They spoke softly, slowly, never grew excited. They seemed to have grasped a great truth that made them calm. I wondered if this was the renewal Demidov had talked about. Later, I reached a different conclusion. Perhaps the lust for bloodshed has stayed with man since his animal beginnings. Perhaps blood keeps him calm, while the lack of it makes him nervous, so he unconsciously tries to appease his passion for it. Perhaps people who have shed blood are so tranquil because they have sated their need. I was shocked by the idea, but the more officers I met who had actually fought, the more I was convinced it had merit.

9

I had been advised to look up Dr. Ader; he would apprise me of the local Jewish situation. I visited him the day after my arrival in Tarnow. He told me that the Russians, upon entering the town, had killed several Jews. The wealthier Jews had fled early on, while the remaining ones were totally ruined. There was no way to earn a living, and they were trapped in a famine. There were a lot of well-stocked stores, but the owners were in Austria. The Russians had taken over the stores and staffed them with Christian saleswomen, paying them high salaries, which they charged to the owner's account as overhead. The income was transferred to the owners, but it was all done without supervision. You can imagine the brisk business that went on in these shops.

The Russians disbanded the Jewish community organization (which had gone underground) and dismissed Jews from social and governmental institutions. Those who stayed were taken hostage. Dozens of Jews were forced into labor. In short, life was unbearable.

According to Dr. Ader, there was one teacher, an informer, who was blackmailing the prosperous Jews, threatening to turn them in to the commandant.

Since I had a tiny sum from Kiev, I gave Dr. Ader three hundred rubles to distribute among the neediest.

In Tarnow I also met Dr. Helman, who was attached to the first regiment that had entered Galicia. He described bloodcurdling atrocities inflicted by the Cossacks. They had beaten, tortured, massacred, shot, and hanged people with no semblance of a trial or even an excuse. And women had been raped in almost every town.

"The worst violence was in Yaroslav," Dr. Helman said. "A pogrom went on during the day, and then at night, when the streets were deserted and the houses dark, I heard terrible, heartrending shrieks of women from various houses. Suddenly, their shrieks were cut off, as if they had been gagged. What could I do? How could we rescue someone if we couldn't pinpoint the exact location? And the shrieking went on all night! I'm amazed I didn't lose my mind!"

In Galicia there were a great number of Jewish landowners and lease-holders. The Russian army treated them worse than other Jews. They ruined them, down to the last penny, seized their horses and cattle, grain, and machines. And they killed a lot of them or deported them to Russia. Galicia has an old tradition of peasants kissing the hands of landown-ers—including the Jews, something which infuriated the Russians. A Christian kissing the hand of a Jew? In some places they forced the Jews, with their wives and children, to kiss the peasants' backsides.

"In the town of Brzostek," Dr. Helman went on, "a dreadful thing happened. The Cossacks arrested two Jews, a father and a son. They sus-pected them of spying and, with no investigation, no trial, dragged them off to be hanged. On the way, the Cossacks told the son they would let him go if he strung up his father himself. The son refused, but the father pleaded with him to do it and save his own life. So the son hanged his father. The Cossacks laughed their heads off and then strung up the son."

I visited a few synagogues in Tarnow. The new synagogue was a huge brick building. Dr. Ader told me that its construction had begun fifty years ago, and a Christian general had been given the honor of laying the first stone. This greatly upset the Orthodox Jews, who had placed a pro-hibition on the building. A terrible feud erupted, and for half a century the synagogue had remained shut. It had finally opened just several weeks before the war broke out, and now the Orthodox were convinced that this had caused the war.

Ever since my arrival in Tarnow, the cannons had been boom-boom-booming day and night. The blast was so systematic that I soon got used to it. The first evening, I went out around nine and heard a rat-a-tat-tat sound like peas clattering into a tin. Machine guns were active, and I could hear the distinct and regular firing of rifles. The noise came from the front lines. It was the first time I heard a battle, and I could picture the bloodbath: men hurling themselves on their enemies, digging into each other's throats, a whole blood-soaked field strewn with bodies.

The next day, I was told that no battle had taken place in the evening. The troops liked to shoot just to intimidate the other side. . . .

While sitting in the hotel on my third day in Tarnow, I heard an explosion that was slightly louder than the usual cannon. An hour later, I heard a noisier blast. I learned that the town was being shelled by a 42-centimeter cannon. I headed toward the Duma corps. The second projectile had struck its courtyard. The two-story brick structure, a former high school now occupied by the corps, was intact, except that all its hundreds of windows had burst. Inside, everything was topsy-turvy.

The shell had scooped out a huge pit some twenty-five feet deep and fifty-two feet around. In its flight, it had knocked off and dragged along a log from an unfinished house. A horse standing close by had been slashed in two; one half had zoomed over the roof and landed one hundred yards away. Next to the pit they found a bloodstained vest with a military ID in its pocket; a bit farther on, human innards were dangling from a tree. Apparently, a soldier had been torn to smithereens, and all that remained of him were those bowels and that shred of clothing with his pass. Acquaintances told me they had seen an unidentified projectile. Coming from a Big Bertha, it was almost nine feet high and weighed over one ton.

The hospital was in turmoil. The old Countess Bobrinskaya was despondent because every window had shattered. There was no glazier in town. And even if a glazier were unearthed, it would take a long time and a lot of money to replace all the panes. How would these people endure open windows, especially in a hospital? The nurses were with the patients, calming them. Some of the corpsmen were in high spirits, and they gleefully reported that Dolgorukov's unit, which was lodged in the next house, had no food for supper. The explosion had ripped through the kitchen wall, dropping bricks and clay into the cauldron where supper was cooking. No one had displayed any fear, but the older surgeon had taken refuge under the table. This made him a laughingstock. Very embarrassed, he gazed foolishly at the others, trying to rationalize his action: "I swear I don't know how it happened. I wasn't scared, and I absolutely don't remember crawling under the table."

That evening, I met with Demidov. "Do you know why the shell landed right in our yard?" he asked me. "Last night some ordnance reached us: shells and cannon. If the enemy shells had landed ten yards over and hit our artillery, it would have blown up half the town. It's obvious someone told the enemy about our ordnance."

"I think it's a lot simpler," I said. "Enemy planes flew over town this morning. They could have spotted the artillery and notified their ground forces."

It seemed obvious to me. But the rumor going around was that someone had signaled the enemy. The Jews, of course . . .

IO

I had achieved my first goal: to enter Galicia to find out what was happening to the Jews. Now I had to tour the occupied towns and villages and conduct a thorough investigation. I focused on this plan, suggesting to Prince Dolgorukov and Demidov that they order me to travel in search of fur and leather for the corps. As a matter of fact, they were badly in need of leather. It was impossible to get shoes from Russia or in Galicia. The people who had leather or boots were terrified that if they showed their supplies, they might be commandeered by the military. But since I was a representative of a welfare organization and a Jew, they wouldn't be afraid to sell me their wares.

Though I had stopped only in a few towns, I had a general idea of the Jewish situation. Just fact-finding made no sense. It would be awful to come across Jews starving and not be able to help them. So I set myself another task: to secure some cash and bring at least a bit of aid to the places I would visit. With that in mind, I decided first to go back to St. Petersburg, Moscow, and Kiev, describe the hardships in Galicia, and drum up tens of thousands of rubles from relief committees and individuals. When I got back to Tarnow, I found another reason why I had to leave for St. Petersburg immediately.

Ader came and told me that the military authorities had plastered the town with Polish and German notices inciting the army and the Christians against the Jews. It was virtually a call for a pogrom and could have the most terrible consequences. I went and read the notice. It was staggering.

· NOTICE ·

Our experience in the present war has revealed the open hostility toward us on the part of the Jewish populations in Poland, Galicia, and Bukovina.

Whenever we leave a place and our enemy marches in, he inflicts all sorts of punishments upon our pro-Russian friends mainly because of denunciations by Jews, who stir up the Austrian and German authorities against the population.

To free the population from persecution and protect the military from espionage, which Jews are committing along the entire front, the commander in chief has made it illegal for Jews to stay in the same area as the army or to enter the region west of the city of Yaroslav. And to shield the peaceful population against false denunciations, and also because Jewish spies have been exposed, the commander in chief has issued the following order: Take hostages. For every peaceful inhabitant who has been denounced to the enemy and for every secret Jewish spy, two hostages will be held responsible and will be sentenced to death by hanging.

This decree is issued in the interest of the peaceful pro-Russian population to protect it against the punishments that might be inflicted on it by our enemy. This decree is based on six months of experience, which has led the military authorities to the firm conviction that Jews have behaved and are behaving disloyally and cruelly toward the local population.

There was no signature.

I ran into Dr. Shapiro, who was also upset by the notice. That morning, she had made a copy and brought it to Prince Dolgorukov. Furious, he had written a letter to the newspaper *Ruskiye Vyedomosti,* but he thought the censor would likely block its publication. He was certain the notice had been issued by headquarters, which meant nothing could be done about it. Subsequently, I learned that Dolgorukov, unable to act against the notice, had protested the blatant Jew-baiting by hanging a

Yiddish sign in his outpatient clinic: "Dispensary for all sick people regardless of nationality."

I had to let the St. Petersburg Jewish community know about the notice. To do so, I needed a copy. But how to get one? The only way was to tear it off the wall, which I had to do very carefully; if I was caught, I could be handed over to a court-martial. That night Dr. Ader and I went through town, hunting for a poster that we could remove without being seen. The notices were displayed in all the streets, and, luckily, they were pasted only at the corners, so it was easy to tear them off. We wandered for over an hour until we found an alley with no passersby. I swiftly tore down a poster, and we went home.

That evening, I met with Prince Dolgorukov and presented my plan to travel about in search of leather. He liked the idea, and he gave me an official pass to tour the whole of Galicia and seek leather for the medical corps. I wanted to obtain a similar authorization from Demidov, who was due back tomorrow.

That was on February 12, 1915. I decided to leave on the fourteenth.

II

The next morning I went to Dr. Ader to say good-bye. He lived alone in a three-story house, very close to the corps. In a small neighboring street there was a one-story cottage belonging to a Jewish tailor. Since I needed to have some mending done, I went in, spending an hour there until the tailor was finished.

Because of what would happen a short time later, everything I saw at the tailor's home was etched in my memory. He stood at his table, cutting cloth. A young man sat in a chair, cross-legged, in typical tailor fashion, mending my overcoat. A young woman, the tailor's sister-in-law, stood at the stove. Her husband was in America, and she and their two sons, five and six years old, were staying with the tailor. The two boys were in the opposite corner, transferring potatoes from a sack to a crate. The tailor described recent events, the poverty and deprivation. He himself had nothing to complain about. If only the same could be said about all the Jews. He explained he was earning a lot more from the Russian officers than from the Austrian.

At noon I went to see Demidov. We sat at the table, discussing my plan for buying leather goods. Suddenly, we heard a thunderous crash, as if a house had caved in. The windowpanes broke, the glass shattered, and we were both hurled from our chairs.

"They're bombarding the town!" I yelled.

We dashed outdoors. I saw a dense cloud of yellow dust enveloping Dr. Ader's house, rising swiftly. We heard desperate shrieking. I ran over and saw that the roof had been torn off and the facade of the second and third stories was shattered. The wall of the tailor's cottage had a gaping hole. After smashing through Dr. Ader's roof, the shell had flown across the street and hit the tailor's home.

In Ader's house, the staircase was intact. I hurried upstairs but found no one there. The place was a shambles. All the furniture was in pieces, including the piano. The floor was thickly covered with shards of clay and brick. Everything was coated with lime dust and clay. On the back wall a large, unblemished picture was hanging, and some glassware was still lying on a small table. Things were worse on the top landing, where the floor had a big hole. I couldn't walk up because the stairs had been destroyed. In a back room, four or five Russian soldiers were playing cards. They hadn't been touched, and for the first minute they hadn't even grasped that the house had been hit by a shell.

I was worried about Dr. Ader, whom I had left in his office a couple of hours earlier. It was impossible to get in there because the door had been blocked by furniture and stones. I was certain he was behind the door, injured or dead. But when I headed downstairs, he was coming in from the street. Half an hour earlier he had been summoned to a patient, and this had saved his life. But he wasn't thinking about this miracle; he was stunned by his misfortune: his house had been wiped out, and he was ruined.

I went to the tailor's courtyard. The first thing I saw was a stable. The front wall had been torn off. There were two horses inside. A black horse, covered with blood, stood trembling, but it wasn't injured. A white horse lay next to it, in its final convulsions. Its guts had been ripped out. Orderlies were carrying out the injured on stretchers. The first was the young man who had mended my overcoat an hour earlier. He was pale as chalk, and his frightened eyes were staring. Blood was dripping from beneath the stretcher. Next came the young mother. The blast had torn off both her legs. Shreds of flesh and tatters of cloth were dangling from the stumps, mixed with bloody clay. Then came the younger of her two children. He had been killed by a piece of shrapnel stuck in his chest.

The cottage was devastated. Everything was wrecked and mixed with clay and blood. In the next room, where the wall had been badly hit, an old woman was lying in bed, surrounded by several orderlies. She was unharmed, and the orderlies were suggesting she get up and leave because the wall could tumble at any moment. But she didn't understand them and wouldn't move. When they started lifting her from her bed, she screamed. A neighbor came in and explained that the woman was lame and couldn't walk. Finally, they put her on a stretcher and took her to a neighbor's home. As I left the cottage, I found the tailor walking back and forth. Although unhurt, he seemed to have lost his mind. He grabbed my arm and yelled: "Did you see? Did you see? Everything was gone in a second! My luck! What am I going to tell my brother in America? His wife and children—all killed!"

Ader's street was unrecognizable. A stretch of fifty or sixty yards was filled with bricks, chips, glass fragments, and snarled telegraph lines.

All told, one of the tailor's boys had died, as well as a young woman in the next street, where a piece of the shell had landed. The tailor's sister-in-law and his helper had been injured. I went to check on them at the military hospital. I found the assistant naked on a table, with two physicians tending him. When he saw me, he began talking rapidly, but the doctors signaled for me to leave. One doctor followed me out.

"His spine has snapped. He's only got a few hours left."

"What about the woman?"

"She's lost both legs. Let's hope she makes it till the morning."

I went back to the hotel. Prince Dolgorukov's clinic was on the ground floor. Looking in, I saw the tailor's second nephew sitting on a high chair. His hands were bandaged, with clumps of gauze in lieu of fingers. He was alone and forgotten. I asked him how he had gotten there, and his answer was tranquil and direct. He was still reeling from shock. I picked him up, carried him to my room, put him to bed, and gave him tea and food. He took it all in, calm, indifferent, as if it were part of the daily routine. I asked him whether he remembered what had happened.

He replied softly: "I remember everything. . . . There was a loud boom, like thunder. I fell down. Something scalded me and bricks dropped all over me. I woke up, and I saw my brother lying next to me. He had a hole in his heart, and he was covered with blood, and Mama was lying on the floor; her legs were torn off and the blood was pouring out. So I began screaming. Then some people came and took everyone away and me too. . . ."

While he was talking, an explosion thundered nearby, rattling the windowpanes. The boy hadn't heard the blast—he hadn't even shivered.

I went over to the window. Three streets away, the three-story building containing the officers' club was shrouded in a billow of yellow dust. When the dust cleared, I saw that half the building was gone. Luckily, no one had been there. Within minutes dozens of people from the surrounding streets came scooting over to the damaged building to gather chips and wood.

12

The next morning, February 14, when I was preparing to leave, I was visited by Colonel Markevitsh, the town commandant. I was surprised because I had met him only once, at Prince Dolgorukov's.

"I need a big favor from you," he explained. "I was told you're going to Kiev today, and so I'd like to ask you to take a letter to my wife, as well as a small package, and give her my best wishes. I'm worried that when my wife hears that the town's been shelled, she'll be very anxious."

I promised I would do as he requested.

"I was ready to talk to you as to a journalist," he went on. "The local population keeps complaining about the military authorities, and maybe they're complaining about me too. But my attitude toward them is very humanitarian. A few months ago, when I was appointed commandant here in Tarnow, I summoned the town representatives and gave a speech. I told them I understood that since they're subjects of an enemy government, I can't expect them to feel any devotion to the Russian authorities. The only thing I demand is that they remain neutral and decent. . . . I'd really like you to read my speech, which I wrote down. You might find it interesting enough to publish in a Kiev newspaper."

"Well, give it to me in any event, and I'll see."

"It's at my office. Why don't we drive over in my car—I'd be very grateful."

I agreed to ride with him.

Colonel Markevitsh, having viewed the sites of yesterday's hits, talked about them in a very agitated manner. I noticed right away that he was in a very nervous state.

"It's a heinous action—bombarding an unfortified town without a military but with a dozen hospitals. I've decided to take measures against it!"

I was surprised. "What kind of measures can you take?"

"I'm going to find a way to inform enemy headquarters that there's no army in the town and that it's an atrocity to shell peaceful inhabitants. I'll make sure the information is conveyed by the mayor and the bishop. I'm simply going to order them to write the appropriate report."

After a pause, he added: "I'm sure that all the shooting is aimed at me. They're targeting my billet. . . . But I've found a good way to deal with that."

The plan to communicate with enemy headquarters struck me as outlandish. But I held my tongue.

As we got out at the commandant's office, a carriage drawn by two good horses came rolling along. The commandant halted it, and out stepped an elegant man in his forties; he greeted Colonel Markevitsh in a cold, dignified manner. I was introduced to "His Honor the Mayor of Tarnow."

The colonel began talking to him in an agitated Polish. The mayor's replies were icy and resolute. Not knowing the language, I barely listened. But from the few words I did glean I realized they were talking about notifying enemy headquarters.

When the mayor took his leave, got in his carriage, and sped away, the commandant told me with a grimace:

> I proposed my plan to the mayor, and he replied, "You can string me up, of course, but I simply refuse to go along with that."
>
> I asked him, "Why?"
>
> "It's quite simple," he answered. "If I send a letter like that to Austrian headquarters, the Russians will respond by shelling my city hall."
>
> "And if you don't write it, they won't bombard city hall?" I asked him.
>
> "I'm sure they won't."
>
> "If that's the case, then I'll move into your city hall today and ask you to move into my office, because I'm convinced they're aiming at me."
>
> And that ended our conversation.

We went to the commandant's office. On the table in the first room, I saw a huge bundle of the anti-Jewish posters in Polish and German.

"What sort of notice is this?" I asked.

"They were sent to me from the commander in chief's headquarters. I'm supposed to paste them up."

"How come it's not signed?"

"I don't know. I don't like it, and I didn't put any up. But then I had to comply with the order."

"Could you possibly give me a copy or two?"

"Take as many as you like."

I took several dozen, and the colonel didn't even ask why I needed them. He handed me the letter and the package for his wife and the text of his speech, and we said our good-byes.

Since there were no trains leaving Tarnow, the medical corps lent me an automobile as far as Dembits. I took along an injured nurse from Dolgorukov's division; she was being sent home to Russia. She asked me to stop off for a few hours in the small town of Filzne, so she could see her brother, who was serving in the investigation unit at the headquarters of the Russian Third Army. Since the train for Lwow wouldn't be leaving Dembits till late at night, we woud have to wait anyhow. So I gladly went along with her request, partly because I wanted to have a look at Filzne.

After dropping the nurse off at headquarters, I wandered about. On the outside, this tiny townlet had sustained little damage in the war. All the Jewish shops were open; however, the faces of the storekeepers hinted that they didn't feel very relaxed or comfortable. I stepped into a shop and chatted with the owner. She told me that a bloody pogrom had taken place, ruining most of the Jews economically. Filzne was much more tranquil now that army headquarters had settled here. But the poverty was dreadful. I gave her a few rubles to distribute among the poor. Astonished at this unexpected charity, she burst into tears, repeating again and again: "God Almighty, Jews are so wonderful! Jews are so wonderful!"

I went over to the synagogue, an old wooden building in a small muddy alleyway. The women's section was occupied by soldiers, who sat there, cleaning their boots and singing. The men's section was free, but it showed fresh signs of the pogrom: everything was ripped and smashed. Only the Holy Ark was unscathed. I ran into an old man, who told me about the many calamities the Jews had suffered. The looters had also carried off the precious silver articles. The old man offered to take me to the rabbi, who had set up a small synagogue in his home. Today was Purim, and soon they would be reading the Book of Esther. But I had to drive on, and so I put off my visit to the rabbi until my return.

I went to army headquarters to pick up the nurse, who introduced me to her brother and offered me some tea. Her brother gave me a few details about his work in the investigation unit. His main job was to interrogate captured spies. I asked him which nationalities had the most spies, and I was sure he would point to the Jews. But he replied that the important thing wasn't the number of arrestees, nine-tenths of whom proved to be completely innocent. What counted was the type of espionage. Dangerous spies, experienced and dogged, were found chiefly among the Poles.

He showed me a few proclamations dropped from Austrian aircraft along the front. Most of these leaflets were attributed to fictitious

Russian revolutionary organizations. Written in a corrupt Russian, they advised the soldiers to stop obeying their commanders and go home. In one particularly interesting text, the czar supposedly addressed the army, stating that he was against the war, but that his uncle, Nikolay Niko-layevitsh, had started it and was continuing against the czar's wishes. He therefore asked the soldiers to side with him, to end the war and go home. The signature read, "Your unhappy Emperor Nicholas."

I asked the officer to give me several leaflets for a museum in St. Petersburg.

"With the greatest pleasure!" he exclaimed. "I just want to check with the administrator."

He left, soon returning with a colonel. I recognized Aleksandr Zvya-gintsev, a member of the fourth Duma.

"You'd like some of the Austrian proclamations for a museum." He spoke to me in a friendly tone, indifferent as to who I was and what I was doing at the front. "I'd be delighted to give you copies, and also another interesting item. Our soldiers shot down a plane coming from a belea-guered Przemysl. It was carrying thousands of letters, some of which are very interesting. So I'll give you a couple."

I was truly astonished at the reckless trust that the head of the inves-tigation unit was showing toward an unknown person.

On the train from Dembits, I met a railroad engineer, who, while serving at the Tarnow depot, had endured his first shelling from a Big Bertha.

It was on New Year's Day. We'd ushered in the new year in high spirits by partying until five A.M. I'd been asleep for something like an hour when all at once I was thrown out of my bed and I heard a terrible crash that sounded like thunder. I ran outdoors, and there I saw that the pump house had shattered and caved in. I was certain that a shell had been dropped from an airplane. But since there was no plane in the sky, I calmed down and went back to bed. About twenty minutes later, there was another huge blast, but again no plane in the sky. I now realized the station was being bombarded by a long-range cannon. Several trains full of shells and explosives were standing here. If a shell were to strike, it would cause the most horrible catastrophe. There were also medical trains with wounded men. All these trains had to be quickly evacuated from the target area—but there were no locomotives.

I had to spend another five or six hours at the depot until everything was moved out. After the third or fourth shell, I realized that the shooting occurred regularly—every twenty minutes. Whenever twenty minutes were almost up, everyone at the station grew very nervous. Some hid under the railroad cars as if that could protect them against an explosion. As for me, whenever I heard the terrible whistling of the flying shell, I'd automatically yank up my overcoat collar and pull in my head. I knew very well that the best thing to do was fall to the ground, but the mud was so deep I couldn't get myself to do it. During the hours I was there, around twenty shells landed, destroying the depot and long stretches of the tracks. When I was done and leaving that awful place, already out of danger, I began shaking so hard my teeth chattered. And just imagine: after I arrived at the next station and prepared to lie down and rest, I received a phone call ordering me to come back with a train car—it was a makeshift office. I felt as if someone were holding me back, not letting me go. I had to exert all my strength to force myself to return.

All the passengers in our train car were military personnel, who never stopped talking about their combat experiences. One officer said that he and a sixty-man unit had sneaked over to the Austrian trenches and stormed them. The Austrian officer was so surprised that he waved a white cloth and yelled, "We surrender!" But when they were about to hand over their guns, the Austrian officer noticed that there were only a small number of Russians against four hundred Austrians. So he changed his mind, drew his sword, and shouted something at his troops. The Russian officer promptly shot him and ordered his men to attack. The carnage was appalling—most of the Austrians were slaughtered.

A young man claiming to be a doctor ranted and raved about Jewish treason: Jews were installing telephones in their synagogues and dispatching secret reports in bottles across the Vistula to the Germans.

"I treated the Yids like dogs!" he boasted. "Whenever we got to a new town, the stores were all closed or else the prices were astronomical. So I'd pull out my whip, give the Yid storekeepers a few good strokes—and I'd get anything I wanted, and at half the price."

There was also a young Russian physician there. He started questioning the whip hero about where he had gotten his medical degree and what professors had taught there. It turned out that the pseudodoctor had never attended a university. Eventually, he had to admit that he was only a medical assistant. When the train arrived in Lwow, and the passengers were saying good-bye to one another, the medical assistant tried to shake hands with the physician, who, however, refused, saying, "I won't shake hands with a good-for-nothing like you."

And I said the same thing when the assistant held out his hand to me.

I spent only a few hours in Lwow. But I did manage to see Rabbi Hoyzner and show him the Tarnow poster. He was devastated.

"This is catastrophic!" he cried. "It can cost hundreds and thousands of Jewish lives. The last few intellectuals in the towns and villages will be taken hostage! You have to go to St. Petersburg immediately and make sure they do their utmost to get the decree annulled! This takes priority over anything else—even the problem of economic aid!"

Lwow still didn't have a relief committee. Diamant hadn't gone to Governor-General Bobrinski. It was rumored that Bobrinski was leaving his position and would be replaced by Fyodor Fedorovich Trepov, a well-known member of the Black Hundreds.

During my twenty-four hours in Kiev, I filed a report about the situation in Galicia, indicating that I couldn't go back there without a significant amount of cash, particularly with Passover coming. The Kiev office promised to give me a certain sum when I returned from St. Petersburg. The Tarnow poster likewise made a dreadful impact on the community leaders in Kiev.

In St. Petersburg I handed the poster over to the Political Bureau, which called a special meeting about it. The members passed a resolution to appeal to Prime Minister Goremikin, and they also prepared a new formal report to the supreme commander in chief, Nikolay Nikolayevitsh. They even discussed sending a deputation to the czar.

I showed the poster to Milyukov, who asked me to leave a copy—the one I had torn down from the wall so people could see that the notice had already been pasted up around Tarnow. He promised to speak to Foreign Minister Sazonov and to Buchanan, the British envoy.

Since I spent only a few days in St. Petersburg, I couldn't see the results of these various measures. Later on, I learned that the head of the cabinet had warmly received a Jewish delegation, which showed him several documents, including the Tarnow poster. The minister had condemned the persecutions of Jews but added that the government was powerless in this matter because army headquarters strongly resented any interference from the civilian authorities. In short, the delegates left empty-handed.

The formal report to Nikolay Nikolayevitsh took a long time to write. There were difficulties involved in submitting it, and to this day I still don't know if it was ever delivered.

Nor can I say whether Milyukov ever spoke to Sazonov or Buchanan about the poster. All we know is that the British envoy did try to talk Nicholas into at least softening the persecutions of Jews. But he got nowhere.

Some hope was pinned on Dovid Margolin, a millionaire and community leader in Kiev. He was personally acquainted, indeed supposedly friendly, with Commander in Chief Ivanov, and perhaps he would seek him out at headquarters. But nothing came of this either. Margolin didn't go to Ivanov's headquarters, apparently because he failed to obtain permission.

As for the Jewish leaders' campaign against the fiat, none of their lobbying bore fruit. Not in high places, nor at army headquarters, nor among the local authorities, especially in Galicia. Our leaders operated on the assumption that all the edicts, restrictions, and persecutions were meant as punishments for crimes. And so they set themselves the goal of correcting the authorities, convincing them that the Jews were innocent of any wrongdoing. This approach was wrong. Granted, the government and the army cited all kinds of causes to justify their actions. But they were just a cover for the real motives. In fact, the authorities didn't even believe the clumsy lies about Jewish espionage, and they said as much. It wasn't only Count Bobrinski and Goremikin who didn't believe all that nonsense. Nikolay Nikolayevitsh and Yanushkevitsh also said they didn't regard Jews as spies. Even Nicholas II stated, "I'll allow that a Jew will charge a soldier three kopeks more for a roll, but I don't believe that all Jews are spies."

Still, the persecution didn't stop—because the Russians wanted to annex Galicia and create a political system there without the complications of the Jewish question. They wanted to reduce the Galician Jews to the level of Russian Jews as far as rights were concerned.

13

On the way back to Galicia, I spent a day in Kiev, where the relief committee gave me eight thousand rubles for Passover assistance. I received another two thousand from private sources.

While in Kiev I was visited by a young lawyer, Goldenvayzer, the son of the famous leader. He had a plan to go to Lwow to set up protective institutions for young girls. His idea greatly appealed to me. The famine and the savage instincts of the army had led to wide-scale prostitution in Galicia—above all in Lwow. I later ran into Goldenvayzer in Lwow, where, with the help of some local women, he had organized several such institutions, and they functioned smoothly until the Russian withdrawal.

While in Lwow, I found Rabbi Hoyzner and others in very low spirits. During the past few weeks, a whole series of decrees had immobilized the Jewish population. Jews were not allowed to travel from one district to the next, which had brought commerce—already severely disrupted—to a halt. The military authorities had also been told to break off all business with Jews and not to order anything from them in the future. Hoyzner, together with the assistant to Mayor Rutkowski (a Pole), had gone to see Bobrinski about this and had explained how unjust and damaging these regulations were. The governor-general agreed but said he couldn't help because the regulations had come from on high.

When I heard that Dr. Lander was in Zolkiew, I went there. I arrived in the middle of a blinding snowstorm that knocked me off my feet. But I was still able to see that this was a highly unusual town. It looked like a museum of antiquities. Ruins of old palaces, walls of a bygone fortress, massive gates, historic buildings and monuments. An ancient Polish church that, as I later found out, was interwoven with legends about the battles with the Russians in the days of Peter the Great. The church contained some original paintings by Rubens. At the center of town there was a monument to—if I was not mistaken—Jan Sobieski.* I noticed that the inscription had been torn off. I heard that this had been done by Zolkiew's Russian commander, who had been ordered to destroy all Polish signs and inscriptions.

Indirectly, this fight against Polish unexpectedly led to official recognition of Yiddish. The Jewish administrative center had remained, but the commander prohibited the use of Polish in its bookkeeping and correspondence. The community was in a predicament.

"We don't know any Russian," people explained, "and if we can't use Polish, how are we supposed to do our bookkeeping and correspondence?"

"Well, but you're Jews," the commander replied. "You can do it in Yiddish."

I arranged to meet Dr. Lander at the home of a druggist who headed the local Jewish relief committee. He made an excellent impression on me. Though he had his hands full as a physician, he was devoted to the needs of the Jewish population. Aside from visiting Lwow several times a week to organize the relief committee there, he toured other Jewish places. He had devised a system of aid for the Galician Jews while maintaining a correspondence with the relief committees in Kiev and St. Petersburg. In all his efforts, he displayed a remarkable commitment and self-sacrifice.

As Lander explained, he still had conflicts with Diamant about establishing an official relief committee: "The two of us must stick to the principle of creating a committee under the jurisdiction of Kiev and St. Petersburg. Then we can develop a broad range of activities and obtain major funding. We have to work on Diamant till he agrees to be chairman. It's absolutely crucial."

---

*King John III of Poland, 1629–96.

As Lander was talking, we heard strange music from the street, something truly Asiatic—melancholy and monotonous.

"Those are soldiers of the Wild Division," said Dr. Lander. "Yesterday a lot of them arrived for a few days of rest. They're making the town very jittery."

Outside, fifty or sixty soldiers with typically Asian faces and tranquil, frozen expressions came charging by on small black ponies. They were wearing Caucasian quilted jackets with red hoods on their backs. The first rider was playing a zurn, and behind him two men were dancing to his melody. They were calm and earnest as if the dancing were a military ceremony. Jewish tradesmen were peering out with fear on their faces. Some hurriedly locked their doors.

The Wild Division was important in the war. It consisted of Georgians, Chechens, and other Caucasians. Their commander in chief was the czar's brother, Mikhail Alexandrovitsh. These troops accepted no form of discipline. They were devoted to their commander in chief and excelled in savage heroism. But they also excelled in barbaric cruelty toward the enemy and toward civilians, especially Jews. I heard many stories about their conduct in the war. Initially, they couldn't understand why civilians should be allowed to live.

One officer told me he had gone on reconnaissance with twenty Georgians from the Wild Division. After sneaking over to enemy lines, they discovered two or three companies stationed there. The officer quietly ordered the soldiers to return, but they insisted on attacking.

"Twenty men against two companies?" The officer had to force them to head back.

They were furious at his timidity and demanded that he be replaced.

Another officer told me that in his company there was a Chechen father with two sons. One day one son's corpse was brought back. The next day the second son said good-bye to his father and went off to avenge his brother's death. Several days later they brought back his corpse too; he had been hacked to pieces. The father didn't shed a single tear or utter a word. He knelt on his rug all day, praying. The next morning he put his dagger between his teeth and grabbed a revolver in each hand. Climbing out of the trench, he walked across the open field toward the enemy lines. The Russians were flabbergasted. And so, apparently, were the Austrians. They started shooting but the man dodged the bullets, walking calmly as he reached the enemy, and leaped into the trenches. It's hard to say what he did there and whether he got his revenge. But late that night, the Austrians placed his mangled body in the field, with his dagger at his side, expressing their admiration for the warrior's heroism.

In its conduct the Wild Division followed a savage knightly code. Once a detachment tore into enemy trenches. The Austrians threw up their hands in surrender, but the wild troops wouldn't accept this. "Why do you put your hands up? It's shameful!" they yelled. They handed the Austrians their rifles and forced the soldiers to fight. The wild troops won, but they lost a few of their men in the process. When the wild soldiers take a town, they consider everything their property. They loot down to the last thread.

14

My next stop was in Stri, a big town with a large Jewish population, over half of which had fled with the Austrians. The town had suffered greatly, passing from Austrian to Russian hands a number of times. And every arrival of the Russians was accompanied by atrocities and violence.

I stepped into a Jewish-owned shop and asked for the rabbi's address.

"The rabbi's been arrested," the merchant said. "He's been taken hostage together with fifteen Jewish civilians."

The detainees included people I had wanted to contact. I had no idea where to turn, but the shopkeeper came to my rescue.

"Why do you need to contact them?" he asked.

I had come from the Lwow relief committee, I said, and we were trying to organize Passover aid for the needy.

"For such an important matter," he replied, "you can arrange to see the rabbi."

"How is that possible?"

"They aren't in prison; they are in a room at the commander's office. For a few rubles, we can sneak some of them out for a couple of hours."

The shopkeeper called over to one of his sons and sent him out on an errand. Then he told another boy from a neighboring store to escort me.

"The boy will walk ahead, and you follow him unobserved," the shopkeeper instructed me. "He's going to enter the home of one of the hostages; it's right across from the commander's office. Go in and wait there for the rabbi."

I followed the boy to the house. After thirty minutes four of the detainees showed up. The rabbi was feeling ill and couldn't join them. I spent a few hours with these men, carefully mulling over the local Jewish situation. They indicated the number of paupers and listed a few surrounding shtetls, where assistance could be organized. Stri already had a relief committee, which had been operating for several weeks with money collected here in town. The members consisted of the rabbi and a few local men, including these four. I gave them twelve hundred rubles for Stri and eight hundred for the surrounding shtetls.

A couple of months later, I met the Stri hostages in Kiev, where they were being detained. Their final destination was Siberia. One of the hostages gave an account of their expenditures and the receipts. I was very touched that he had remembered to take along these documents at such a moment, when he had been deported from his town.

VOLUME THREE

I

On May 6, 1915, I left Kiev for Lwow. But this time, instead of going via Brody, where the entire railroad line was crowded with military trains, I traveled through Volotshisk and Tarnopol. At the outbreak of hostilities, the Russians had occupied this [Austro-Hungarian] region almost without firing a shot, and so there were barely any noticeable signs of war along the entire route: no burned villages, no ruined farms, no abandoned trenches or barbed wire. In the distance you could see entire hamlets and churches. There were tall haystacks in the fields and herds of cattle grazing in the pastures. The few scattered wounds in the earth—a tiny number of trenches and holes left by shells—were becoming more and more overgrown, covered by the fecund energy of nature, which had only just awoken in the light of the spring sun. And in these vast fields, human beings, farmers, were participating in nature's fruitful labor: plowing the soil, building houses, taking their products to town. The entire area was so peaceful and secure—you could scarcely imagine that some seventy or eighty miles away the armies were waging the fiercest and bloodiest battle and that the storm of combat was approaching these quiet meadows and villages.

But despite the springtime mood, despite the security and fertile energy of nature, a feeling of nervousness and vehement agitation accompanied the narrow and unending track running through fields and forests toward the gory tempest. Packed military trains dashed by every few minutes. All the stations were mobbed by military personnel. Our train, an express, scheduled to reach Lwow at one in the afternoon, didn't arrive until nine that evening. We spent hours at almost every depot, letting trains go past—trains bursting with troops, with projectiles, with cannon. At the same time, other trains were coming toward us—trains filled with wounded soldiers, POWs, refugees. Now a medical train flew by. In every window you could see bandaged heads, hands, and other parts of the body. Pale, earnest, tearful faces were peering out—gloomy, curious gazes—and they were all drawn to the springtime sun.

Next—a freight train stuffed with prisoners. They looked as if they were sitting atop one another's heads. The ones who hadn't found any space inside the cars were perched on the roofs. No one was watching them. Either the guards were sure they wouldn't escape, or else they didn't care. Most of the POWs were barefoot, ragged, and unshaven. But their expressions were brisk and calm, and their postures and movements full of self-confidence. Their animated conversations were punctuated with booms of laughter. These men were nothing like the bowed, gloomy, despondent, intimidated captives that I had encountered a few months before. Perhaps they had felt like that because of the winter, when the temperature was several degrees below freezing. But now, every creature was warmed and delighted by the lovely spring sun. Earlier, the Russians had been seizing town after town; but now the POWs knew that their side was winning, that the Russians were pulling back, getting crushed, and were sliding toward a total defeat, so that peace would be concluded. The captives sneered scornfully and arrogantly at their captors and felt like the real victors. But the main reason for their sanguine demeanor was that they weren't Slavs; they were Magyars. Many stories were told about their ferocity and savagery, though they didn't look brutal—these were strong, healthy peasants with open faces and proud eyes.

I walked over to one of the cars and tried speaking German, Russian, and French. They shook their heads; they didn't understand me.

"Magyars?" I asked.

They nodded buoyantly, gesticulated proudly, and quickly replied: "Magyars! Magyars!"

Long, long trains, one after another, kept lumbering by, carrying Ruthenian refugees, mostly women and children. The passengers were crammed together like chickens in a cage. Some cars were packed with schoolboys, others with intellectuals. No baggage, no belongings were to be seen. Either they were stored somewhere else, or the fugitives had had no time to take anything along. But we heard no sighs; we saw no despair.

"Where are you from?" I asked someone.

"From Toorki."

"Why'd you leave?"

"They forced us out!"

"We were scared of the Magyars!" a second person explained. "Wherever they arrive, they take along the healthy young men and slaughter everyone else!"

"What are you going to do in Russia?"

"What do you mean? We'll be farming!"

These homeless people, by tens and hundreds of thousands, will come into the interior and spread across the endless fields of Greater Russia, Ukraine, and Siberia. Along with them, hundreds of thousands of POWs will come from Ruthenia and from other frontline areas and scatter throughout the same fields: Slavs and Magyars, Germans and Turks. And they'll meet the Russian peasants. And all those former antagonists and deadly enemies will come together on those endless fields and work solemnly by the sweat of their brows. They'll till the same soil, eat from the same bowl, drink from the same pitcher, express their deep gloom and yearning with the same universal sigh. And perhaps by then they'll sober up; they'll be unable to grasp how they could have ever have pounced on each other like bloodthirsty beasts.

And as they grow even closer and discuss things openly, they'll find so many universal interests, universal joys and sorrows. And when they remember their neighbor, the Jew, who fought none of them, who killed none of their people, they will nevertheless unanimously agree that the Jew is the one responsible for everybody's misfortune.

2

Military circles, from the highest to the lowest, were cruel and cold-blooded when talking about the most horrible violence perpetrated on Jews. This attitude was, of course, rooted in the bestial antisemitism permeating the entire army. And a large part was also played by the savaging and systematic deadening of the most elementary human feelings—a process I witnessed day after day.

In the beginning of the war, the Russian military wouldn't stop carrying on about the German atrocities—practically the main topic of every conversation. The Germans, it was said, were flouting all divine and human laws. They were disregarding the traditional rules of war, bombarding unfortified towns, destroying historic buildings, inflicting all sorts of calamities on the peaceful population, and brutalizing POWs. At the same time, the Russians underscored their own kindness, softheartedness, and especially lawfulness. They were, needless to say, incapable of such crimes; they would never dream of using explosive bullets or torturing captives.

But within a few months, the tenor changed. Intelligent and liberal officers were arguing that the Russians had to respond to the German cruelties with even greater ones—like shooting explosive bullets and taking no prisoners. And soon these convictions evolved into an overall theory: war is war, and if you want to win, you have to be merciless, stop at nothing, and, wherever possible, exterminate the enemy.

"It's no use our being humane!" said one educated volunteer. "It's time we started wiping out everything in our path. We've really grown smarter and stopped showing the enemy any consideration!"

If such was the prevailing temper among the most intelligent members of the social institutions, then we can picture the mood in the army. This frame of mind can best be characterized in a statement made to me by a wounded aviator. He told me about watching Russian soldiers hang a man—neither a Jew nor a Pole—who had been perched on a tree branch. They had ignored all his explanations. And then afterward he turned out to be innocent. He had been returning to his nearby home, but first he wanted to climb a tree to check if his house was still in one piece. There was no way he could have signaled anyone from up there.

"Naturally, such a case is sad," the pilot concluded. "But what can you do? It's better to string up ten innocent men than let a guilty one go free."

That was the moral standard to which the war had reduced its participants.

The four military men sharing my compartment and describing the most dreadful anti-Jewish atrocities also told about the orderlies gathering the wounded.

"There was this officer lying on a stretcher," said the colonel, "and he felt someone filching his money, his watch, and other items from his pockets. He pretended to be unconscious so he wouldn't be killed. There've been so many instances of medics killing the wounded and robbing them. Another officer got shrapnel in his belly, and he died on the spot. It took several minutes for the orderlies to arrive—and by then all his pockets were inside out."

"If the medics don't get any money, they simply refuse to carry anyone from the battlefield," added the second lieutenant. "Our company adopted a rule. Before going into battle, every officer has to leave twenty-five rubles for the medics in case he's wounded."

Several days later, a Cossack officer I was traveling with was ranting and raving about the Jews, and he also provided a graphic depiction of the bestial outrages committed by his fellow Cossacks. "We captured six hussars," he recounted cheerfully. "And our men stabbed five of them to bits. But I liked the sixth one, so I said to him, 'If you want to be my servant, I'll spare your life.' Well, naturally he agreed. So I took him in and then sent him to my home in Tsarskoye Tselo. I called him Ivan. An excellent servant!

"Another time," he continued,

we were attacking, and when we got within fifteen feet of the trenches, those damn Austrians were still shooting at us. And when we were just a few feet away, they held up their hands. Surrendered. But we were furious. If you're going to give up, why the short-range firing? Our sergeant major jumped into their trenches and smashed into their officer's face with all his strength. "That's for shooting at such close range!"

The officer started arguing, "What is this? I'm a POW!"

"A POW? Hack them all to bits, guys!" our sergeant major yelled.

But we came up with something different. We told them, "Choose: either we cut you all to ribbons, or you join us in our shooting."

They picked the second option. We put them in the trenches, gave them rifles. And for two days we forced them to fire at the Austrians. We made sure they were aiming at them. It was only then that we sent them to prison camps.

"And in the last few battles," he added, "we stopped taking prisoners. We had no time to deal with them, so we got rid of them on the spot. . . . They say the Germans killed our wounded men—they sprayed them with machine guns."

There was a widespread conviction in the Russian army that the Germans took no Cossack or Circassian prisoners, that they tortured them horribly and just murdered them. I don't know how accurate this claim was.

With regard to the Wild Division, everyone agreed that it took no prisoners. They simply didn't understand how you could let the enemy live. And that was why they never surrendered and usually demonstrated the knightly heroism of savage Asian warriors.

By contrast, I feel duty-bound to state that men captured in the rear positions, beyond the fiery circle of a battle, generally received humane, often merciful treatment. Both the Russian soldiers and the civilian population showed compassion toward these unfortunates. It was nothing like the atrocities that the Germans inflicted on Russian POWs.

In regard to prisoners of war, I would like to quote a Russian document proving that the higher military ranks stopped at nothing to hurl charges against the Jews and compromise them in the eyes of the army.

I herewith publish this copy of military orders nos. 272, 278 paragraph 3, and 282 paragraph 3, issued by the Third Army of the southwestern front of the current year, in order to make them known and have them carried out.

No. 272. During the attack of the 240th Infantry south of Ustranki Gorniye, the captured Austrians included the soldier of the Twelfth Vyeliko-Lutsky Infantry Company Aleksey Grigoryev Kharitonov, who was a prisoner March 8–23.

On March 8 he was sent to Ustranki Gorniye, and from there, together with other prisoners, chiefly Jews—a total of thirteen men—he was sent on foot to the Berezino station.

There, together with other groups of Russian prisoners of war, he was employed in repairing the dam under difficult conditions, dragging heavy rocks from the river and from the mountain, drudging no less than twelve hours a day. The overseers were Magyar cavalrists and other soldiers—Jews.

Captured Jews are not made to work. They serve as interpreters and overseers, and they brutalize the prisoners.

The prisoners are fed very poorly. They get tea in the morning and a mug of soup plus two and a half pounds of biscuits in the evening. Prior to their imprisonment, they had been given bread twice a day and half a pound of lard once a day. On the farm where the prisoners had spent the night of March 20, the soldier Aleksey Grigoryev Kharitonov decided to escape. He got as far as the Austrian lines, where he was detained and carried the officers' belongings. On March 23 he was liberated by the detachment of the Sixtieth Infantry Division.

The above-issued order is to be read aloud to all the troops. . . .

Note: the telegrams from the chief of staff of the commander in chief of the armies of the southwestern theater of war of March 27 of the current year under no. 4511. The original text was signed by the commander of the Third Army, Infantry General Radko-Dimitryev, and the staff administrator, Lieutenant General Dobrovolski.

3

In Lwow I found a very tense mood, which worsened from hour to hour. The Austrian army was still very far away. It first had to pass through Przemysl and dozens of other towns. But the charge was so fierce and tempestuous that it shocked everyone; it felt as if the enemy had already reached the gates of Lwow. Neither the civilians nor most of the military people knew any details of the battles or their sites; but it was clear to everyone that a tremendous catastrophe had taken place. People were saying out loud that Russia's Third Army had been completely shattered and was retreating chaotically, and that two corps had been totally anni- hilated. The figure announced for the Russian casualties was colossal: a quarter million. Three hundred thousand men [*sic*] were killed on the first day of the onslaught while the enemy poured out fire and steel, vir- tually inundating a sixty-mile area occupied by the Russian army. The commander in chief and the commander of the Third Army were openly accused of criminal negligence for failing to fortify the rear points during the past eight months. And it was true. While traveling twice from Brody to Tarnow and Jasla, I had seen no fortifications anywhere along the way—no trenches, no barbed-wire fences, aside from the old ruined ones left by the retreating Austrians. It was only now, with the erupting catastrophe, that the Russians were hastily fortifying the approach to Lwow. Jaroslaw had fallen on August 28, and the Russians had decided to dig trenches around the town only two days before the Austrians took it back.

Needless to say, the generals and the commanders pointed fingers at one another. The headquarters of the commander in chief of the south- western front accused Radko-Dimitryev. And he, for his part, placed the entire blame on the administrator of the commander in chief's head- quarters, Abram Mikhailovich Dragomirov, who had been carrying on intrigues all that time, trying to wipe out Radko-Dimitryev, ignoring his queries, refusing to send him any help. For instance: at the last moment, Radko-Dimitryev had urgently asked for two divisions, but Dragomirov had dispatched only a single company—and so on. In the end, both men were driven out.

Characteristically, with all the often exaggerated information on the defeats of the Russians, nearly every day brought rumors about a mammoth victory. It was said that the Russians had beaten off the enemy and captured seventy thousand men. The next day, it was claimed as a bona fide fact that the Austrians had lost forty thousand men in a single battle, that the Russians had deliberately withdrawn in order to fool the enemy and trounce him thoroughly. At the same time, people kept whispering that two divisions were about to arrive or that two Japanese corps with a powerful artillery were nearly here, and that they had already been spotted at a particular station—and so forth.

All this encouraging news had little effect on the overall mood. Everyone knew that the Russian army was about to give up Lwow, that all the officers' wives had been sent away several days earlier, that all the supplies had been brought to the railroad and were ready to be shipped off, and that the various institutions would start evacuating any day now.

Confused as the military may have been, the local population was extremely relaxed. The Poles walked about, cold and reserved, as if none of these events would touch them in the least. And they furtively prepared to welcome the Austrians, conferring in secret and waiting for the moment when they could express their ferocious hatred of the Russians. In the Catholic churches, the priests openly spoke about the imminent salvation. An acquaintance told me that his maid had asked him for her salary in advance; she had to buy a new hat because her priest had told his parishioners to greet the Austrian army with flowers and in their Sunday best.

The Jewish mood, however, was very different. Fewer Jews could be seen in the streets. They were scared of a pogrom, which they talked about quite openly. Jews, needless to say, wanted to be rid of the Russians. Nevertheless, they were extremely bewildered as they nervously waited for the Austrians. They did not believe that the Russians would leave Lwow for good. The same events would occur here as in dozens of other towns: the Austrians would reoccupy the place, and the Russians would then return within a few weeks and send the Austrians packing. And the civilians who suffered most from the retreats and returns of the czarist army were the Jews. Moreover, for all their patriotism, a number of Jews had grown accustomed to the Russians and did not feel all that bad under their regime. The Jews who adjusted most readily to the Russians were the shopkeepers and merchants. I heard a few tradesmen say that the Russian officers were terribly crude, that they yelled and cursed, but that they were generally more humane than the German officers. Best of all, they said, the Russians weren't such penny-pinchers as the Germans. They didn't haggle, and they paid decently.

As I later found out, Lwow had several educated Jewish families with pronounced Russophile leanings. They believed that if Russia gained control of Galicia, it would, under the pressure of the peace conference, be forced to grant the Galician Jews the same rights they had under Austria; and having those rights, the Jews would more easily overcome Russian antisemitism than Austrian clericalism, which was making itself felt quite strongly and offensively.

The turmoil affected Jews most of all. Affected the way the authorities treated them. Count Bobrinski, the chief administrator of Galicia, had no influence here because he happened to be in St. Petersburg. The de facto head of Lwow and indeed of all Galicia was Yevstafiy Nikolaiyevich Skalon, the governor of Lwow and the former police commissioner of Kiev. Renowned for his graft, he had apparently been fired several times because of his misdeeds. In Lwow he openly took bribes, fleeced the living and the dead, and victimized both individuals and the whole community. So long as the Russians were entrenched in Galicia and he saw his position as permanent, his treatment of Jews was terrible. But now that his reign was doomed, he suddenly decided to squeeze a fortune out of the Jews. Threatening them with dire punishments, he summoned Lwow's head rabbi, Brauda, and snapped at him: "So far Jews have been peaceful, and we have shown them the greatest benevolence. But now they're acting up again; they're showing their hostility toward Russia. Tell them they're playing with fire. Remember that it's in my power to string up every tenth Jew—every fifth!"

Naturally, his words sparked a terrible panic among the Jews, who were afraid not so much of hanging as of an organized pogrom. They collected several thousand rubles and gave this large amount to Skalon. But he wasn't satisfied. He announced that he would close down the relief committee, and he searched the homes of several of its members, including Rabbi Hoyzner. Two of them were arrested, and Skalon made it clear that he was waiting for a special payoff from the committee. We held an emergency meeting, and the majority thought we should fork over several thousand rubles more on condition that he agree to prevent any pogrom during the retreat of the czarist army. I had little faith in his power to do so—if only because he was bound to run away much earlier. But despite my qualms and my disgust at such methods, I didn't have the heart to oppose this action, to obstruct this precarious way of protecting the Jews against a pogrom. So I allotted two thousand rubles to this measure. The money was to be handed over to Skalon by his acquaintance M., a Kiev businessman. I gave M. only one thousand rubles and told him to convey my assurance that the balance would be provided after the pullout if there was no pogrom. M. went to Skalon and told him that the Lwow Jews, understanding his difficult situation in regard to the Russian withdrawal, wanted to help him with a sum of one thousand rubles and asked him to protect them against a pogrom. And if he succeeded, then he, M., would give him another one thousand rubles.

Skalon calmly heard him out, took the one thousand rubles, and said: "Give the other one thousand to my wife at this address in Petrograd. But send it through a trustworthy person, and he's not to ask for any receipt."

I must confess that the second thousand rubles were never sent to Skalon's wife.

Skalon was not satisfied with this bribe. During the final days before the Russian retreat from Lwow, he warned the wealthier Jews that they would be taken hostage, but that he was willing to cross their names off the list for a good ransom. A few Jews did pay him several thousand rubles each. But at the last moment, he arrested them just the same and deported them to Russia as hostages.

In Lwow, I learned some details about Przemysl. When the Russians marched in, the civilians, especially the Jews, were in the grips of a horrible famine. At Passover, Jews didn't even have enough matzohs for the benediction on the first seder night, so the rabbi allowed them to eat leavened bread. A week or two later, all the Jews—apparently some twenty thousand—were banished from the town. Thirteen thousand arrived in Lwow. To organize the expulsion, the commander allowed (or ordered) the formation of a Jewish implementation committee, with regard to which I have the following Russian document:

To the Jewish Implementation Committee:

By orders of the commander of the fortress of Przemysl, I hereby notify you that the Jews residing in Przemysl and in its environs must leave this area as quickly as possible.

In my desire to facilitate the evacuation, I have set up an implementation committee consisting entirely of Jews. Free railroad cars are being put at the disposal of the departing Jewish inhabitants.

If the Jews refuse to leave willingly and if they refuse to carry out the regulations of the committee, I will be forced to resort to the most drastic methods: a company of Cossacks will implement the evacuation within a few hours, and the rebellious Jews will have only themselves to blame.

Administrator of the Przemysl district, Guard Corporal Kiriakov.

The district administrator has permitted the printing [of this announcement].

Later on, a physician, Dr. Shapiro, who had been in Przemysl during that time, told me that the expulsion of the Jews had taken place on a Sabbath. On Friday evening he had been in the synagogue, where the Jews prayed for the last time. Their bitter wailing was indescribable. After prayers, the synagogue was shut down.

Since there were no Jews left in Przemysl now and there was no one to accuse of espionage, the slanderers turned to the Jewish troops. They spread the lie that Jewish soldiers had cut a telephone line, and supposedly all the Jewish soldiers were then removed from Przemysl.

When the mood in Lwow grew uncertain, it was rumored that all thirteen thousand Przemysl Jews who had found refuge here would be packed off to Russia. Next, it was said that the entire Jewish population of Lwow would be sent away. Naturally, the Jews were terribly alarmed. However, the expulsion decree was never issued—perhaps for lack of time.

4

The very moment the Russians began pulling out from Galicia, the Jewish relief committee was finally constituted in Lwow; presided over by Dr. Diamant, it began to function normally. I must add, however, that it had started operating much earlier. Large sums had been sent from Kiev and Petrograd. Rabbi Hoyzner was the sole contact, and the money was spent almost entirely in Lwow, to set up a few institutions, day-care centers, kitchens—chiefly for the refugees from Przemysl and other places. Now that the committee was official, it broadened its scope, doing more for the surrounding area. With a tremendous effort, it even managed to send large amounts of cash to the nearest villages and towns, mostly through Jewish physicians and orderlies. By the time I arrived, the committee treasury had eighteen thousand rubles—earmarked for the province. The tempestuous events and the precarious situation meant that once the banks were evacuated, Lwow, prior to the return of the Austrians, would be cut off financially from Kiev and Petrograd. Hence, the committee had to secure a great deal of money as fast as possible. Rabbi Hoyzner had already cabled Petrograd, but he was uncertain whether any funds would be dispatched. So I wired Kiev. As a result, we received fifteen thousand rubles from each city within a day.

The committee then asked me to take funds to the surrounding hamlets. Needless to say, I agreed. But since couriers had already been found for the next few days, I remained in Lwow, hoping to meet with [M. G.] Komisarov (the administrator of Dolgorukov's division) and Demidov. The two men were expected in Lwow within a couple of days, and I wanted them to send me on some kind of mission to the towns that I was to check for the committee.

We drew up a list of towns and villages that needed money. I was waiting for Komisarov, the representative of Dolgorukov's division, to obtain an official reason to visit those places. Meanwhile I decided to travel with the state Duma's mobile medical division and stop off at Janow, Javorov, and Krukowjec.

Just as I was preparing to leave, Demidov's assistant came and asked if I could go to Przemysl and bring back a few hundred hospital cots from the tens of thousands left by the Austrians. The city was besieged on three sides and might be cut off at any moment, so we had to hurry since the cots were needed. I had no desire to visit Przemysl, where not a single Jew was left; but since I would lose only two days, I agreed to do it.

I never got to leave, however. Upon going to Demidov's hotel room to discuss the trip, I found him very distraught.

"Przemysl? For the cots?" he answered. "Well, somebody else can take care of that. I have a different request for you, something far more important. Sit down and listen."

And he launched into a detailed report of what was going on at the front. The situation was terrible. The Russians had no shells, no supplies. The orders coming from the chief of staff were muddled and contradicted one another. In short, Russia was on its last legs. And the fault lay not with the army, not with the generals, but with the imperial court, the government, and the general staff. The upper crust in St. Petersburg and Moscow was not acquainted with the catastrophic situation at the front or with the agitation in the army. It had to be told everything and made to realize that now was the time to speak up and demand that the government change its policies and summon responsible members of high society to take power. In regard to all this, Demidov, with the consent of the frontline generals and commanders, had written a letter to the Constitutional Democratic Party, and he wanted me to deliver it to Milyukov in Petrograd and bring back a reply. With the current state of affairs, said Demidov, he himself could not leave Lwow, and there was no one else he could entrust with such a document.

"The army here is helpless and miserable," he said. "It's extinguishing the enemy's fire with its own blood; it's hurling stones at a hurricane. And the general staff is about to embark on a new adventure. We have to save the army and save Russia."

He also asked me to go to the state Duma's committee in Petrograd and request a shipment of canvas tents for the division, because there were no buildings, only ruins, in the places where it was stationed. I agreed, and that same day, May 12, I left for Petrograd.

Before my departure, however, I stopped off at the relief committee, which was discussing the urgent issue of aid. There were dozens of towns that needed help, but it was almost impossible to make contact with them because their inhabitants were not allowed to travel more than half a mile from their homes. The committee had made several requests to Count Bobrinski to allow delegates to go out and distribute money; but he had refused. Now the committee, through me, had appealed to Dovid Faynberg to come to Lwow to handle this matter and try to persuade the count to grant travel permits to representatives of the Russian committee.

5

It took me twelve hours to reach Brody instead of the usual one and a half or two. At every station our train waited for hours as endless military convoys rolled through, carrying troops to the front; several outfits were being rushed over from the Caucasus.

At the Brody depot, I ran into Mr. Mess of Radziwillow; after his father's death, he had been touring the surrounding shtetls, distributing aid. But now, unable to get a new pass, he was forced to stop. He had thousands of rubles, but there was no way to send help to the people starving to death in the shtetls.

"These last few days, banished Galician Jews were shipped through Brody," said Mess. "I asked the station master to let me bring them a little food, but he wouldn't allow it. He did let me give them money, but only through the escorts and not directly to the deportees."

In Vilna I had to spend eight hours waiting for the express. Meanwhile I went into the city, where I learned details about the terrible expulsion of Jews from Kovno Province. When the front had grown turbulent, the commander of Kovno had deported any even vaguely suspicious people. So he was all the more astonished when ordered to expel every last Jew. He promptly wired back, explaining that this banishment was unnecessary and would ruin the entire area. The response was a strict order to implement the operation without further delay. The brutality of the expulsion was such that patients were ousted from hospitals;

the Russians wouldn't even allow a father to remain with a child whose leg had been broken a day earlier by Russian soldiers.

One or two thousand remained in several shtetls in Vilna Province. In the city itself, seven thousand Jews were allowed to stay—but no more. The rest were freighted to the provinces of Yekaterinoslav and Tshernigov. In Vilna, eighty thousand rubles were collected for these homeless deportees on the first day.

Supposedly, the czar's cabinet had opposed the deportations; as a result, the commander in chief had sent a cable: "Stop expulsions. Punish the guilty. Let others go back." However, the military administrator of the Vilna district inferred from this telegram that he should allow the exiles to head home only on condition that he keep a few hostages, who would be responsible for the conduct of the rest. The homeless Jews refused to accept this favor.

I was told that in some villages the peasants brought milk and bread to the deportees, refusing any payment and weeping at the sight of these unfortunates. But in other villages, the peasants saw the expulsion of the Jews in a very different light: "Jews are taken care of," the peasants muttered to themselves. "They're being removed from the dangerous combat zones, but we're stuck here."

On May 15 I arrived in Petrograd and went straight to Milyukov. The letter I carried made a shattering impact on him. He told me that no one here had any idea whatsoever of the chaos at the front. But everyone agreed that things couldn't go on like this. He quizzed me for a long time about my personal impressions and then asked me to wait for several days until he could give me a precise answer.

The mood I encountered in Petrograd was very different, very agitated. The city was rife with rumors that kept changing by the hour. I heard that Grand Prince Nikolay Nikolayevitsh was leaving his post as supreme commander in chief and would be succeeded by Grand Prince Alexander Mikhailovitsh: that Yanushkevitsh was being replaced by General Nikolai Ruzsky and would become minister of war, that Vladimir Sukhomlinov was being appointed administrator of the Caucasus.

More stories were circulating about changes in the government. Both the upper and the lower classes talked about nothing but treason—with which they explained all the frontline debacles. They asserted quite openly that the imperial court was a hotbed of traitors and that the young czarina was in direct communication with Berlin. While the Petrograd authorities were conducting numerous searches for secret radiotelegraphs, people said: "They found out that there's a radiotelegraph linked up directly with Berlin, so they searched every single house with no exceptions, but they didn't find anything. The only building they didn't search is the Winter Palace."

Sukhomlinov and other military personnel were prey to widespread suspicion. The authorities, it was said, had discovered a radiotelegraph in one corporal's place and had arrested another corporal for causing an explosion in Okhta; they had also, supposedly, arrested and shot officers who had blown up a train carrying shells in Gatshine, and so on. The acts of treason were ascribed mainly to Russia's ethnic Germans.

A coachman who was driving me told the following story. A Russian maid was working for a German, and one day, just before going out, he pointed to a machine lying on his table and ordered her to turn on the switch at exactly four P.M. The suspicious maid reported the matter to the police. The police investigated and found that this was an infernal machine, and if the maid had turned on the switch, the whole of Petrograd would have been blown to kingdom come.

Speaking of "myths," let me quote an interesting tale—or, rather, a prophecy—which I heard in Moscow from an elderly coachman, who, it seems, was an Old Believer, a dissenter from the Orthodox church. "Three kings are waging war. The war will last for three years, three months, and three days. One king will die of natural causes, the second will be killed, the third will conquer the entire world, but nothing will come of his victory because there will be three years of famine, and half the human race will perish. Next will come a year with very rich crops, but when they examine the grain, they will see that each kernel consists half of blood and half of sand, and then the other half of the human race will perish."

A common feature of all these rumors and fables about treason was that they almost never mentioned Jews. Suddenly, Jewish espionage, Jewish signals and telephones, and all the other lies about Jews were forgotten. The catastrophe was too enormous and its causes too obvious for anybody to blame it on "Jewish espionage." This was the turning point for such anti-Jewish libel and slander. Later on, there were scattered accusations against Jews, but until the end of the war the dreadful anti-Jewish attitude, which prevailed during the first eight or ten months, did not flare up again. A crucial role in this reversal was played by the expulsions of Jews from Kovno and Grodno, which triggered a worldwide outcry and actually annoyed the Black Hundreds government and even, it was said, Czar Nicholas.

But before that watershed, the Petrograd Jews went through very difficult times. During the expulsion from Kovno, it was rumored that the government was about to deport all the Jews from Petrograd. And right at that time, the authorities, who were looking for a secret radiotelegraph, conducted thorough searches in the huge Petrograd synagogue and in the home of M. A. Varshavsky, president of the Jewish community. This had a terrible impact on the Jews. But they subsequently calmed down a bit upon learning that a lot of churches had also been searched.

Among Jews, every single rumor and conversation dwelled on one thing: the expulsion from Kovno and how the powers that be felt about it. Like all Petrograd tales about the higher authorities, these stories praised the efforts of Jewish lobbyists. To a certain degree these stories reflected the rulers' feelings that they had overshot the mark and that they were dissatisfied with the actions of the general staff. Supposedly, the Italian envoy had called on Sazonov and explained that such persecutions of Jews were offensive to public opinion in Italy, where two government ministers and several military commanders were Jews. Furthermore, it was said, the Russian cabinet had unanimously censured the expulsion, calling it "intolerable" in a report to the czar, who had written "agreed" on that report. Supposedly, Nicholas, confronted with the silence in Kovno during his visit there, had asked for the reason and had been told about the banishment of the Jews. He had then, supposedly, gotten angry and exclaimed, "Why wasn't I asked about this?"

It was also claimed that even military circles were unhappy about the expulsion, and that the commandant of Kovno and several commanders had pointed out that it was impossible to feed the army in that city or obtain provisions from the peasants. Upon seeing the deportees collecting in Dvinsk, the commander in chief of the Fourth Army, Yuri Danilov, likewise sharply criticized the expulsion, and so on.

As it turned out, all these things had an effect on the general staff. Apparently, that lunatic Nikolay Nikolayevitsh realized he had gone too far and started making excuses. He repeatedly maintained that the banishment had been carried out against his will. It was symptomatic of this development that Finance Minister Bark went to the general staff specifically to discuss the Jewish question; and it was even more symptomatic that Nikolay Nikolayevitsh was now trying to exculpate himself, whereas just a few months earlier he had refused even to talk about Jews with Sazonov.

The following account was given of Bark's conversation with the grand prince. The minister explained that such mass deportations turned the civilized world against Russia and devastated the evacuated region. Nikolay Nikolayevtish supposedly replied that he had not desired these mass expulsions, that his orders had been misunderstood, and that there would be no further mass expulsions; instead they would only take hostages. Bark made it clear to him that this too was undesirable.

"Well, that's a bagatelle," the grand prince answered. "Discuss it with Yanushkevitsh." He then claimed he was anything but an antisemite, and as evidence he cited his opposition to the expulsion of the Jews from Warsaw. Needless to say, he did believe that Jews were involved in espionage, but scarcely all of them.

When meeting with Yanushkevitsh, Bark found his attitude toward the Jewish question to be "axiomatic"; but he too promised not to expel any more Jews.

As proof of the government's new Jewish policy, people remarked that Petrograd's Jewish relief committee had petitioned the government for material aid for the Jewish deportees, and the government had allocated half a million rubles toward that end. This was, of course, miserable compared with the one hundred million that the government had granted the Poles for the same purpose. But it did have significance as a matter of principle.

At a meeting of the relief committee, we discussed the Jewish situation in Galicia, and we all felt that it was crucial to send an official community leader to Lwow—someone who could have access to Count Bobrinski. D. F. Faynberg, who was seventy, could not travel because of his ill health. So the committee focused on the two Jewish deputies to the state Duma: Bomash and Fridman. The latter agreed to go. But when he asked Rodzianko, head of the Duma, for a travel permit to Galicia and told him why he needed it, Rodzianko categorically refused, saying that "this is not one of the duties of a Duma member; the Duma cannot allow anyone to go on such a mission." So no one went to Lwow.

Demidov's division was financed by the Duma, and I had promised him that I would ask the Duma committee to send him tents. That was why I attended two of its sessions. The first consisted of some twenty men, including Pavel Nikolayevich Milyukov, Fyodor Ivanovich Roditshev, Yefremov, and Gransky. As it turned out, many of them knew that it was I who had delivered the letter to Milyukov. So instead of discussing the tents, they questioned me for a long time about details of the army's retreat and its morale. At the second meeting (which included Mikhail Rodzianko, Nikolai Maklakov, and Aleksandr Kerensky), Maklakov rejected the appeal for tents. He pointed out that the army, together with Demidov's division, would soon be leaving Galicia altogether and reaching Russian territory, where there were enough houses and buildings. Thoroughly convinced that the southwestern front would soon be shifting to Russian soil, he spoke about it as if there was absolutely no doubt in his mind. And the others concurred. With great effort, I managed to persuade them to issue at least half the requested tents—for the wounded and for the [medical] staff.

On May 25, Milyukov handed me his response to Demidov—or rather to the frontline generals. He also told me about the current mood here. The army could rest easy; measures were being taken to change policies.

"The right-wing parties," he added, "have joined us in demanding a responsible cabinet. Of course, they see it by their own lights, but that makes no difference. The morale in Petrograd has been boosted greatly—it's an oppositional mood, and it's gradually spreading to Moscow."

That same day I headed back to Lwow.

On the train, I encountered Mr. Volf, one of the most respected leaders of Kovno's Jewish community. He gave me some details about the expulsion. His father, together with another community leader, Soloveytshik, had left for Petrograd immediately. There, they appealed to Prince Shekhovskoy, the minister of commerce, and told him about everything that had occurred in the evacuated region. The minister was shocked, almost in tears, but he said there was no way he could help; the general staff would listen to no one.

We sat with Volf in the dining car. The next table was occupied by several elderly professors from the University of Kiev. They were returning home after being presented to the emperor in Petrograd. One of them, in military garb and blue glasses, kept talking about "Yids": they were spies; they were to blame for any and all misfortunes. The only way to rescue the army, rescue Russia, was to exterminate all the "Yids." His voice was very loud. While our train was in a station, a train packed with troops rolled by. The antisemitic professor eyed the train and said in French: "Chair à canon—cannon fodder!"

I couldn't help retaliating. I stood up and snapped, "You called the soldiers 'cannon fodder'?"

Terrified, the professor mumbled something.

I went on: "You've been shooting your mouth off about Jews all day; you say they're unpatriotic, and yet you call soldiers 'cannon fodder'! What right do you have to talk and judge other people? You spread lies; you're a gossipmonger! You're lucky you ran into me! Anyone else would have turned you over to the authorities!"

That was my revenge. He sat there like a beaten cur, soon crept off to his compartment, and never came back to the dining car.

At the Kiev terminal, I met a group of young men from the relief committee. They were waiting for a train bringing six hundred Galician deportees, for whom a supper had been prepared. The young men told me that thousands upon thousands of expelled Galicians had been arriving these past few days. They were forced to walk all the way to the [Russian-Austrian] border; then, inside Russia, the Jews in the shtetls hired wagons for them or bought them tickets for the train to Kiev. The same things—renting wagons, purchasing railroad tickets, supplying food—had to be done for banished Poles and Ruthenians.

The morale in Kiev was very low. The relief committee couldn't possibly cope with the terrible plight of the thousands of refugees, whose numbers were growing daily. Most of them were being sent to the distant

Russian provinces; the rest were divided—more than one thousand apiece—among various shtetls, where there was no place to put them. A few synagogues in these shtetls were so stuffed with the homeless that you couldn't even sit down. And now bulletins stated that the authorities were ousting the Jewish populations from Riga, Radom, Vilna, and a series of other towns. I was also told that thousands of Jews were being ousted from Lwow. No wonder S. A. Grinberg, chairman of the relief committee, and other members were at their wit's end.

6

During my two-week absence from Lwow, the situation there had worsened. The Austrians had taken Przemysl and had advanced so much closer to Lwow that no one could possibly doubt people would have to leave. They calculated the exact day and hour when the Austrians would arrive. Practically no Russian civilians were left. All members of the social institutions were being evacuated, as was the railroad administration. Outside the marvelous palace of the administrator of Galicia, where the governor-general had been living, almost one hundred wagons were standing, piled high with furniture and other articles from the palace. Not only were they trundling off everything that was there; they were also cutting out the silk wallpaper and pulling up the parquet flooring. And the same things were happening in hundreds of civilian mansions, where generals and lower-ranking officers were stealing any and all furnishings that they could and sending them home. As if this universal robbery wasn't heinous enough, the loaded railroad cars blocked the tracks so that the army couldn't evacuate the most crucial matériel. Numerous shells and cannon, not to mention supplies, were abandoned—as were the railroad workshops, which were more important than anything else for the retreating army.

Demidov was in very low spirits. I handed him Milyukov's letter and told him about the mood in Petrograd, but this had little effect on him—

he was too upset. He looked like a man who knows a terrible secret that he cannot reveal.

Demidov told me about the pogrom against Germans in Moscow. Entire neighborhoods were devastated; some four hundred stores had been destroyed; the overall damage was estimated in the hundreds of millions. Subsequently, I learned the exact figures. The damage amounted to half a billion rubles. The rioters had carried off entire wine cellars and guzzled the contents. Other wine cellars had been torched. More than one hundred people had gotten drunk, had choked to death, or had simply drowned in the liquor. Some of these people had been shot. On that day there were forty-eight fires in Moscow.

While making off with booty from the German stores, the mob yelled, "Where's that praying bitch, that German?" They meant the widow of Grand Prince Sergey Alexandrovitsh; he had been assassinated, and she had taken the veil.

The police went easy on the pogromists, following them, saying, "Come on, you've looted enough!" Interestingly, Jewish stores were untouched. Quite the opposite; many Jewish shopkeepers hung out a sign that said, "A Jewish store owned by the son of native subjects of Russia." A few Germans saved their businesses by pretending to be Jews.

Around one A.M., the city Duma held an emergency session. Governor-General Yusupov and Police Commissioner Adryanov were invited but didn't show up. The Duma decided that if those two men didn't come, it would of its own accord cancel their mandates and wire Petrograd accordingly. The threat worked, and Yusupov and Adryanov came. The Duma apprised them of its resolution: if they didn't take the most energetic measures to stop the pogrom within an hour, the Duma would instantly create a popular militia. This ultimatum worked too, and the necessary steps were taken to end the pogrom. Adryanov resigned the next day.

In Lwow, I found Lander, who familiarized me with the situation of the relief committee. During the past few days, it had received fifteen thousand rubles each from Kiev and from Petrograd, so that it now had a total of thirty thousand. Lander had told the committee that when Lwow was restored to the Austrians, neither the city nor the liberated region would require help from Russian Jews or even have any right to it,

just as the Russian Jews would have no right to provide help. He therefore demanded that the remaining money be repaid through us to the
committees in Kiev and Petrograd.

I agreed with Lander. We met with Hoyzner, and he concurred too.
But he said that the other members, particularly Dr. Diamant and Feller
the banker (the trustee), would oppose our idea. They maintained that
once the funds were dispatched to the Lwow committee, they belonged
to it, and the committee was not obligated to send them back. We
decided to demand reimbursement.

In order to stay on and travel through Galicia, I had to join some kind
of division. Demidov's division was going to Volotshisk, and he himself
was so upset and confused that it was hard to discuss anything with him.
So I figured I would join Dolgorukov's division. I had an effusive letter
from him to the division's authorized representative, M. G. Komisarov, a
reputable community leader in Moscow, whom I was acquainted with.

I learned that Komisarov and his division were in the town of Javorov.
Coincidentally, a car was heading there, and so Dr. Lander and I took off.

En route we drove through Janow, which had totally burned down,
except for the church and a dozen Christian homes on the edge of this
small town. A segment of the Jewish population—a few dozen families—
had remained, and they were living in the ruins and cellars of the torched
houses. Not a single shop had survived; but at the entrance to the town
there was a row of small tables where wraithlike figures, mainly women,
were vending bread and cigarettes, while naked, barefoot youngsters
were milling about. The faces of both adults and children were marked
by the savagery of hunger. I gave each woman a few rubles. They gawked
at me with wild, frightened eyes and burst into tears. I was then surrounded by kids, a whole mob of kids, who were stretching out hands,
begging me for a kopek. But when I tried giving one of them a coin,
dozens of hands started grabbing and fighting. I assured them that each
would receive a kopek, and that they shouldn't brawl, but it was no
use—I couldn't give anyone a coin, and I had to leave.

(When I passed through Janow again on the way back, I met with Dr.
Davidzon, who was stationed at the military hospital there. It was overcrowded with wounded men, and he had been working for forty-eight

hours without a moment's rest. He couldn't tell me anything about the local Jews; he had been far away. But he promised to check out their situation and distribute the two hundred rubles I left with him.)

In Javorov, I saw my first dismal tableau of a routed army. The road was jam-packed with vehicles and pedestrians. Some wagons were carrying expelled peasants, especially women and children. They sat there grim, motionless, coated with dust, their eyes lifeless, their faces stony. There were also heavily laden baggage convoys; the exhausted, emaciated horses, which could barely drag them, were goaded on by even more exhausted, dust-covered soldiers. Small clusters of thirty or forty straggling troops rambled along, weary and dejected, carrying a rolled-up flag. They were the sole remnants of whole companies. Most of the soldiers were wounded. An endless line, with bandaged heads, with arms in slings, they plodded along the edge of the road. Some were propped on sticks that they had broken off in the woods. Others leaned on their healthier buddies. On the sides of the road lay tired, feeble, dying men. Not a sigh was heard, not a cry. But all faces were filled with deep suffering and the shadow of death. It was a picture of hell.

I asked a wounded man, "Why are they pulling out?"

"They inundated us with shells," the soldier replied in a faint voice. "We couldn't hold out; we couldn't take it anymore."

A second man said, "Within minutes only two or three men were left of a whole company—they mowed us down."

Javorov, a large town, was fairly unscathed after the earlier clashes. The movements of the withdrawing army were more intense here. The streets were bursting with baggage convoys, Red Cross wagons, and automobiles, with artillery and slogging military units—intermingled with bands of peasants driving cattle and trudging with lowered heads like condemned men.

The endless torrent dragged by in a deathly hush. Suddenly, the stillness was disrupted by a heart-wrenching wail. A peasant woman was bawling because soldiers had taken her cow. She dashed from one officer to the next, wringing her hands, screaming and begging, throwing herself at their feet—and coming up against a numb indifference. The torrent halted for an instant. A funeral procession cut in; a corpse was hurried through. The parted torrent then closed up again and flowed on. Soldiers—tired, gloomy, dusty—dropped out of the torrent, ran over to the mobbed bread tables, tore into the packed shops, hurried back out with a roll, and gobbled it down as they rejoined their units. Jews sat in the stores, unable to keep up with the demands of the customers; Jews walked calmly in the streets, and none of the soldiers touched them. The Jews showed no signs of groveling terror. Nor did any of the soldiers yell any arrogant comments. They were so dejected that they didn't even have the courage to attack Jews. However, they were followed by other units, the last of which would be Cossacks—the annihilators. And they would behave very differently.

But the Jews didn't feel the approaching danger. They didn't understand what was happening. Until yesterday, the town had been quiet, and no one had expected anything.

I went into the side streets, beyond the military torrent, and stepped into the big stone synagogue. There I found several elderly Jewish householders chatting quietly about the Russian pullout. I began conversing with them, and they told me that when the Russians had arrived, they had launched a terrible pogrom, looting the entire town. They had taken thirty hostages, and so far, no one knew where they had been shipped. After that, however, the town had known peace and quiet. The commander was a decent man, who didn't persecute Jews; and he had now promised that no hostages would be taken during the withdrawal. This had calmed the Jewish population to some extent.

The men in the synagogue knew only one thing: the Russians were hurrying away, which meant that soon the Austrians would be coming. These Jews naively asked me, "Can we be sure that 'our' army will get here by tomorrow?"

"It could be tomorrow; it could be a week from now," I answered. "And it's possible that the town will be bombarded before they get here. You have to be prepared for anything. You ought to stock up on bread and water in case you can't go outdoors."

My words upset them, and they began thinking more earnestly about the situation.

In Lwow I was directed to a Mr. Volf, a congregation member and a major community leader. When I inquired about seeing him, I was told it would be difficult. He had been hiding since the previous day. Despite the commander's assurances, he was afraid of being taken hostage.

I went to meet Komisarov's division, which I found together with the mobile medical division of the state Duma. The two divisions were being evacuated across the border to Nemirov and Magerov, respectively. I met with Komisarov and gave him Dolgorukov's letter. Komisarov said that at this critical moment it was hard to talk about any sort of concrete work. For the time being, he suggested that I simply join his division as it headed for Magerov. I got the same offer from the state Duma division, which was bound for Nemirov. I put my answer off till the next day.

Both divisions were leaving, and their hospitals were packed with the wounded. The work was feverish: five or six doctors were bandaging wounds and sending the patients farther along, some on foot, some in small wagons. But more throngs kept pouring in.

"Where's the hospital?"

"They're not accepting any new patients."

The driver and the wounded soldier in the small wagon were flabbergasted. And dozens of such despairing men were gathered around both hospitals.

The booming of cannon was already closer. News came that the Austrians had taken Krukowjec, some ten miles from Javorov. The town commandant had bolted yesterday. All institutions were already gone. Since the leftover supplies couldn't be taken along, the commissariat was distributing them to the passing soldiers and the local Christians—Jews didn't even dare approach. The recipients took as much as they wanted, as much as they could lug. And yet tons of oats, dry crusts, tin cans, and other food would remain and go up in smoke.

Late that night, it suddenly struck Lander and me that we had no place to sleep. After a long search, we found a Jewish inn with two empty beds.

At around five A.M., Lander woke me up and nervously went over to the window. "Look what's happening in the street."

I went to the window and saw lots of Jewish women dashing about, wailing and screaming, followed by half-naked children. We realized that something awful had happened. We threw on our clothes and hurried out. It seemed that around two A.M., troops had surrounded many Jewish homes and seized forty of the more prominent men as hostages.

No one knew where they had been taken, and that was why their wives were rushing helter-skelter, looking for them. Sometime later, a convoy from the town of Sadova-Wisznya rolled through with a large group of Jews, especially old ones and hostages. A group of peasants was standing near the Uniate church; they had been brought here and were being kept here. Not knowing what would become of them, they stood there with lowered heads, silent and servile.

The torrent of the retreating army, which had passed through since yesterday without a moment's interruption, was overflowing into the streets. Wagons and artillery, pedestrians and wounded men—pursued by the thunder of cannon.

The proprietor of the inn and her two daughters, who had been baking bread all night, fell to their knees before us, weeping and begging us to advise them whether to leave or stay. Could the last units, the Cossacks, murder Jews, rape women? . . . What advice could we give them?

Lander drove off to Lwow in a military car. The divisions were also pulling out. But I wanted to try and see Volf. I went to his home. As predicted, I didn't find him. His wife and a daughter were terrified of me. When I calmed their fears and explained why I was looking for him, they told me he was hiding, which was the only reason he hadn't been arrested that night. I questioned them about the local situation. They gave me detailed answers about the conditions, the extent of the plight, and what had occurred during the Russian occupation. The distress had been terrible. Now that forty householders had been seized, many of their families were flat-out condemned to die of hunger, These two women made a good impression on me, but I couldn't decide whether to entrust them with cash for the needy.

The mother, sensing my doubts, was insulted. "If you'd meet my husband, you'd trust him to distribute those few rubles among our poor. But you don't trust me because I'm a woman. Do you think I'll grab the money for myself instead of giving it to people who are starving to death?"

I was embarrassed, and I handed her three hundred rubles.

When I returned to Komisarov's division, it was gone. And most of the state Duma's division had also left. I barely managed to find a car that was heading for Lwow.

7

Within days after my arrival in Lwow, the first sections of the retreating army showed up: baggage convoys, artillery, Red Cross wagons. Masses of wounded men were pouring into the city, and the trolleys were soon used only to carry them to hospitals. It was rumored that Javorov had been taken. People perceived that the end was near, that the Russians would control Lwow for only a few more days.

Dr. Kozhenevsky, chief surgeon of the state Duma's division, came to see me. He was terribly upset. "You haven't heard the latest?"

"What?"

"Come along; I'll tell you."

When we stepped out of the hotel, he said: "The enemy's broken through in Rava-Ruska. . . . He's taken Nemirov. Our division was heading there, and I don't know what's become of them. Either they had enough time to get there and withdraw quickly, or else they struck off and went to Magerov instead. That's the most direct route they could take. We can go and meet them. I've got a car here."

We drove off. This road too was mobbed by the withdrawing army. We stopped in Zolkiew. The town was in chaos. The Jews were terrified. Everyone kept plying me with the same question: "Is it true that the Cossacks are coming?"

We didn't linger, but I managed to see the head of the local Jewish relief committee and give him five hundred rubles, which had already been set aside for Zolkiew.

A few hours later, we were in Magerov. All that was left of this large town was, without exaggeration, its name plus looming walls and chimneys of burned-down, devastated houses. Even the old stone synagogue with walls seven feet thick was half collapsed. Not a single whole building was to be seen—nor a single living soul. As I subsequently learned, Magerov had been under fire for an entire week. A shell had hit the synagogue, killing many people.

We found Komisarov with his division. They were out in the fields and didn't know where to turn. Some of the men were driving through the region, looking for a farm they could use as a garrison.

Komisarov had also heard that Nemirov had been taken. Since the state Duma's division wasn't here, it might have gone on to Sokal. Kozhenevsky decided to head there—and I went along. En route, he attached notes to numerous telegraph poles in case the division passed through.

We again had to drive through Zolkiew. It was late at night. We stopped. The doctor went to headquarters, and I to the train depot. Perhaps the division had come here in order to continue by rail. The station was dark and empty. Wagons carrying the wounded arrived. The train stopped, started again, and headed toward Lwow. And they dragged on. I boarded one of the wagons and rode back to town. Two wounded soldiers and a cholera patient were lying in the wagon. They had been on the road since early morning; no one would take them in.

"These men were moaning a lot, especially the one with cholera," said the soldier driving the wagon. "But now he's silent. He's dead. I think one of the wounded men has died too."

I asked him for news about the war.

"As long as it was the old army, they toughed it out; they weren't scared. But now all the old soldiers have been killed. None of them are left. And the young ones are like calves. They don't understand anything. They get scared by the least little thing, and they surrender or run!"

We continued our trip in Kozhenevsky's automobile; but it was pitch-black outdoors, so we stopped off in a village to spend the night. There was light in one roadside house. We went in. Its two rooms were occupied by a Jew named Horvits and his large family. He and his wife were baking bread. They prepared food for us and beds. Horvits told us that he had been rich, with his own house and land and a lumber business. The soldiers had burned down his home and made off with his lumber. So he had resettled here, in this deserted house, and baked bread for a living.

We went to bed, but we didn't fall asleep. Kozhenevsky was talking about Jews. He had spent practically his entire life in Jewish towns, among Jews, and was so integrated with them that he felt more comfortable with Jews than with Christians.

"During the drive," I said, "I noticed that whenever you had to get directions, you always asked Jews. You never once asked a Christian."

He burst out laughing and replied:

> I've learned from bitter experience. . . . Listen. Jews are suspected of espionage. Do you think that's antisemitic? It's not! The officer who's unacquainted with Jews—which is par for the course—is certain that a Jew "knows everything." And, needless to say, only a spy knows everything. The conception of Jewish omniscience has a very simple basis: "Russians know nothing!" Let's say I'm driving along. I ask a Jew, "Where is the combat going on?" He listens and then pretty much indicates where. He'll tell you how many miles away it is, and how far it's progressed. But if you ask local peasants, one will say one thing and another the exact opposite. . . . Wounded soldiers are coming from the battlefield, and I ask them, "When were you wounded?" "Five or six hours ago." "Where was the battle?" And if you canvass one hundred men, you'll get the exact same answer: "I forget." He's lying. He never knew it to start with; he wasn't interested in the name of the place where he was stationed. So if you want to pinpoint a battle site, you have to see what direction the soldier is coming from, you have to ask how many hours ago he left the battlefield, and you have to check how fast he's been moving and from what direction, and then pinpoint the area on a map. And it's the same with everything else. Russians aren't interested in knowing anything, they have no curiosity; whereas Jews, like any cultured person, want to know what's going on around them. And because of Russian ignorance, hundreds and thousands of Jews have had to pay with their lives in this war.

Around three A.M., after not getting a wink of sleep, we drove on. At seven, we arrived in the shtetl of Mosti-Velki. Since we were running low on gasoline, we stopped to get some. I went to look up the Jews that Rabbi Hoyzner had specified as eminent. (I had lists for a number of towns in that region.) When I found the men I was looking for, I asked them to invite three more prominent Jews. We assembled in one of their homes. They told me that when the Russians had marched in some nine or ten months ago, they had launched a horrible pogrom. However, the town had remained whole, it hadn't burned down; and aside from some scattered looting, there had been no further pogroms. Two days ago, the storm had erupted, the army had started pulling out, and now the Jews were terrified that the Cossacks would come and destroy the shtetl. Hostages might be taken; the Jewish population might be deported. In short, they saw the departure of the Russians as the worst calamity. If only they would stay until peace came.

The economic situation of the Jews had been wretched all this time. They were starving to death. Three or four months ago they had heard about the Lwow relief committee but had been totally unable to send anyone just to request aid. They had had no support whatsoever since the arrival of the Russians.

I gave them six hundred rubles and tried to calm their fears a little. This unexpected help out of the blue as well as my warm behavior moved these poor, terrified, defenseless people so deeply that they burst out crying. It was terrible to see five elderly Jews, two of them quite old, loudly sobbing and weeping like children, hastily wiping away the tears that rolled down their mustaches and beards.

We couldn't find any gasoline in Mosti-Velki, and so to avoid getting stuck somewhere we headed back to Lwow. The road was jammed with the retreating army, and we could barely squeeze through in our automobile. Several hours after we reached Lwow, Kozhenevsky left for Sokal. Late that night, a medic from his division showed up in Lwow and told me that the division was safe and sound in Nemirov, where they didn't even hear the Austrians. There was a regular train from Nemirov, and the division was preparing to transfer to Rava-Ruska. As far as the war was concerned, people didn't know what was happening just half a dozen miles away.

During my twenty-four-hour absence, Lwow had become almost unrecognizable. It was boiling like a cauldron. Every last street and avenue was choked, and the air was filled with voices, the clanging of iron, the pounding of hooves. My hotel was almost deserted. The restaurant was still open, but its entire staff was gone, and there was no food. The shops were open, and the population remained calm, as if unaware of what was happening all around.

It was rumored that the Austrians had already taken Grodek and were only ten miles from Lwow.

An announcement had been pasted on the walls: "All male members of the local population between eighteen and forty-five years of age must be evacuated . . . except for Jews." No one knew the reason for this exclusion, and it made the Jews panicky. The wildest rumors were circulating. Several days later, at the Brody terminal, Lander heard the following when a trainload of soldiers pulled in from Lwow. A corporal had come over and asked: "What's happening in Lwow? Have they already set up cannon?"

"What for?" the troops asked.

"To mow down all the Yids!"

Upon arriving in Lwow, I sought out Lander, and together with Dreziner, a committee member, we went to see Feller, the trustee and banker. We explained to Dreziner and Feller that we couldn't give them thirty-five thousand rubles. Several hundred thousand Jews were homeless, and their number was rising daily, whereas within a couple of days the Lwow committee would be receiving help from the [Austrian] government and from Jewish communities in Vienna and elsewhere. They agreed with us but pointed out that the money was a stopgap to cover their budget until the end of the month. They promised to have the committee meet within a few hours to discuss the matter.

Around five P.M., we went back to Feller's place. The above-mentioned people had been joined by another six or seven committee members. Diamant, the chairman, had not come. Rabbi Hoyzner had predicted that Diamant and most of the members felt that they shouldn't return the money. Lander and I repeated our reasons and stated our categorical demand. Hoyzner gave a fierce, agitated speech, taunting his colleagues for being rude and ungrateful toward their Russian brethren.

After long deliberation, they voted to pay back the funds minus a sum to cover the month's expenses. Someone raised the question of whether the issue could be settled without the chairman; and they concluded it could. We figured out how much was needed that month for all the institutions supported by the committee: soup kitchens, day-care centers, Jewish elementary schools, and so on. The calculation came to 10,000 rubles, and they said they would return the remaining 25,000. However, the trustee had only 20,000 at hand, and it was all in one-, three-, and five-ruble pieces—ready to be distributed. The entire amount, weighing around forty pounds, was in a big carton. I didn't know what to do with this load. The bank had already quit the city, and there was no place to trade the small change for large bills. Nor would it be very convenient dragging a huge box around in this bedlam. Furthermore, I already had 6,000 rubles on me. If I were found with all this cash, I would have a hard time explaining why I was carrying it. My only choice was to transport it to Kiev.

Once the money issue was resolved, we had a long talk about the overall situation. Dreziner told us that he had been visited by Dudikjevic, the famous Russophile, who played a major role in Galicia, orchestrating the devotion of the masses to Russia. Now, of course, he was leaving with the czarist army. He had calmed Dreziner's fears, assuring him that no pogroms or other anti-Jewish violence would be permitted. But he *had* offered some advice: Jews should send a delegation to Count Bobrinski, thanking him for his kind treatment of the Jews of Lwow. Dreziner had conferred with other members of the community, and they had vetoed the idea. For one thing, it was inappropriate in the eyes of the Austrian authorities. Second, who could say how the count would receive the delegates? He might have them all arrested!

Next we came to the most unsettling topic of all: the hostages. We had already seen the list of hostages that the Russians planned to take along. Forty-two or forty-five men, including the entire committee. At the top: Rabbi Hoyzner and Feller. They all said they would hide; however, it was difficult to find a safe refuge. A Polish priest had offered to conceal Hoyzner, but he had a better place. He would go to a friend, a physician in charge of a mental institution, and spend a few days among the lunatics. No one would hunt for him there.

We very warmly said farewell to one another, farewell for a long time—who could say how long? And our hearts were burdened with the dire question: What would happen to all these people tomorrow—would they all survive?

I hurried to my hotel with my carton of twenty thousand rubles. On the way, I saw three airplanes hovering over the city; they dropped three bombs.

Back in my room, I looked out the window. From all sides, people were dashing to the water faucet in the square. Everyone was clutching a bucket, a pitcher, or some other receptacle. They had found out that the water system would be shut down within the hour.

I ran into V. Ton, a journalist, who had been in the war zone all this time, writing for *Birzheviye Vyedomosti*. He was very pessimistic. The Russians, he said, would be driven and driven all the way back to Kiev. "This place is no longer interesting. Now Russia is interesting. Great events are going to take place there." (He repeated those words several days later, when I bumped into him in Kiev.)

"What great events do you expect?" I asked him.

"Events so great," he replied with deep conviction, "that by comparison the fall of the Romanov dynasty will be a bagatelle! The blame for the army's huge defeat lies not only with the ruling classes but with all of us. There's no way out. A separate peace would be awful. Germany would crush Russia. But Russia is doomed all the same. She'll lose her historic place as a great empire. Russia is about to crumble and fall apart. History has forgiven Russia a great deal. But now it's time for her to pay."

I wanted to get to Sokal, where one of the divisions was supposed to arrive. I was told that a car belonging to Demidov's division would be coming to Lwow from Volotshisk and that it would be going on to Sokal. I decided to hitch a ride.

The next day, June 5, the army was gone. The streets were empty. All the institutions had pulled out. The final trains were chugging off, but they were so packed that it was impossible to squeeze in. And the automobile I was waiting for still wasn't here. If it didn't show up by evening, I planned to hop any train heading for Kiev. I didn't care to stay on till the last moment, unable to account for what I was doing here with a big pile of cash.

In the morning, I ran into the famous war correspondent Vladimir Nemirovich-Danchenko. He had been in Lwow all this time, surrounded by high-ranking officers, who kept cajoling and flattering him. A few words by him in *Ruskoye Slovo* could make a career. He always went around like a bridegroom, holding his head high, talking loudly and with authority and self-assurance. Though nearly seventy, he was constantly on the move, traveling everywhere, seeing everything.

Even now, he was lively, active, and talking a blue streak. He invited me to join him; he was visiting a friend, a journalist named Pankratov. En route, he told me he had just returned from the front, where he'd been under fire the whole time. He was preparing to go back to the front, to Grodek, and was trying to coax Pankratov into accompanying him.

"They're bombarding the entire route to Grodek," he added.

"Why should I court danger?" exclaimed Pankratov. "It's so easy to get killed."

"You're scared? I'm not scared! Very interesting. Listen!" And he bragged about his heroic feats. Then he lashed out against General Alexei Brusilov, blaming him for everything. His incompetence and criminal recklessness had annihilated the army. "After the war I'm going to expose secrets that'll make your hair stand on end." He turned to me: "At the front just four miles from Grodek, there are only two battalions in the trenches. And they're supposed to stop the enemy!"

And he talked on and on, cursing everyone and boasting. I stopped off to say good-bye to Mrs. Reichenstein, the organizer and administrator of the day-care centers, which she had done a good job of setting up.

"You know what?" she said. "The Russians are leaving, but I'm not overjoyed. I know all about the atrocities that their army has committed in Galicia, but I don't harbor any hostility toward them. Savage as they may be, they're a lot simpler, more generous, and more humane than the Germans. It may sound bizarre, but during these past ten months I've grown accustomed to the Russians, and I've developed a positive feeling for them."

The car I was waiting for was still nowhere in sight. Perhaps something had interfered, and it wouldn't show up at all. So I figured I might go to the station and catch a train. As I was leaving the hotel, a young man stopped me. We had already met at some point, but I couldn't remember where.

He asked me, "When are you pulling out?"

"I don't know. I'm waiting for a car."

"Travel with us. We've got our own train, and we'll be heading out for Brody at seven P.M."

"Very good!"

Taking the money and my belongings, I got into the young man's auto, and we drove to the station.

Inside my compartment, I learned that this was a division of the Bessarabian Zemstvo [district council]. Its hospital, which had already transferred to Brody, specialized in contagious diseases, especially cholera. The hospital had 480 patients. The train, which was carrying the entire storehouse and all the personnel, consisted of eight cars and was attached to a freight train. Although the train was scheduled to depart at seven P.M., we didn't get going till two A.M.

I left Lwow on June 6, and the Austrians entered the city on June 8. I still haven't found out what went on in Lwow during those two or three days. There were rumors that a pogrom had taken place, that a traditional rabbi or a government rabbi had been shot; but all this was nothing but vague hearsay. V. Ton, who left Lwow on June 7, during the day, has told me that there was no time to evacuate the civilian population. Nor did they have time to blow up anything but the railroad terminal— one of the most beautiful buildings in Galicia. The final retreating units plundered all the wealthy shops on the great boulevard, especially the jewelry boutiques. They also smashed into a wine cellar, guzzled their fill, and poured the rest into the streets. The later troops crawled along the ground, slurping up the liquor from the mud. When the police were pulling out, the inhabitants booed them from their windows.

Someone else has told me that many of the drunken soldiers remained. The Austrians found them and shot them as marauders.

Another characteristic feature. Throughout the occupation of Lwow, the Russians published a newspaper, *Tshervonaya Rus.* I stumbled upon the last issue, which appeared on June 6. It didn't contain the slightest allusion to the withdrawal. The tone was cheerful and victorious. The gazette listed a whole week of productions at the Russian theater: "Saturday, June 8, *Cavalleria Rusticana;* Sunday, June 9, *La Belle Hélène.*" But the most interesting thing of all was a decree put out by the administrator of Galicia: "All Jews are to be excluded from all juridical institutions in Galicia." The province was slipping through Russia's fingers, but the persecution of Jews was still going full-throttle!

8

Like all Bessarabian divisions, the one I stumbled into belonged to the Black Hundreds. On the way to join it, in my railroad car, I happened to meet Makar Ivanovitsh, a Duma delegate (I've forgotten his last name), a physician, Dr. Zhelebovsky, and a Pole named Rychlewski, as well as nurses and orderlies. . . . The conversation turned to the war, the hopeless situation at the front. The Austrians were shelling us, and we had nothing to fight back with. The doctor knew of instances when our soldiers had responded by throwing rocks. "Russia can only be saved by the people now. And the government is doing nothing to motivate them—it doesn't trust Russian society. . . . When Lwow falls, there will be serious disturbances," the doctor said.

"The army is coming apart. The officers and generals only think about medals and rewards and are obsessed with their petty fights about corps and divisions. And things are no better in the rank and file. *Ruskoye Slovo* says that soldiers are rushing into battle, but actually they're rushing away from it. They're surrendering in huge numbers and looking for any possible way to get out of serving. You know what they're doing? Deliberately infecting themselves with VD. There's a brisk business in gonorrhea pus—they're charging a ruble a drop."

A bit later, they came to the subject of Jews. Talking of Warsaw, the Pole said, "The Jews there are very happy; there are three times as many of them now."

"They haven't gone there for fun," I objected. "Warsaw has one hundred thousand homeless Jews from all over Poland. They've either fled there or been forced from their homes."

"No wonder," replied Rychlewski. "They're all spies."

"Can you prove that?"

"I don't have the facts, but everyone says so."

"And they all probably have as many facts as you do."

"I'm not an antisemite," the doctor joined in. "But it is true that the Jews are celebrating our defeat."

"In general, Galician Jews mean trouble," Rychlewski continued. "They take terrible advantage of the peasants. But the Jewish intelligentsia in Galicia is very different; they're very decent and respectable. Some of my best friends are Jews, and they're truly devoted Poles who work for the benefit of the country. They could really be useful if our Polish deputies stopped persecuting them and gave them a chance to prove themselves."

It took us eighteen hours to travel thirty-five miles from Lwow to Brody. We spent hours at every station, letting freight trains through from Lwow. It was amazing—the goods being shipped from there. Shattered barrels, broken furniture, rotten tires, and other totally worthless junk. We reached Brody around eight P.M. Some three hundred feet from the depot our train came to a standstill in this thick, suffocating smoke. The cholera patients' bedding and clothes were being burned near the station.

In Brody I planned to transfer to the special train for Kiev. I went to find a cart to transfer my belongings. But when I got back with the cart, ten minutes later, my train was gone. Makar Ivanovitsh and several nurses who had also gotten off started looking for the train with me; we looked on all the tracks, but we couldn't find it—it had been swallowed up. We went to the station master; who refused to answer us. When we insisted, he began to shout:

"What train? Leave me alone! I've got enough trouble! What number was the train?"

"We don't know."

"You don't know? Well, neither do I. Leave me alone. Hundreds of trains pass through here."

We went to the town commander. He was no more helpful than the station master; he couldn't tell us anything. He went to the station master with us, but they were promptly at each other's throats.

"I'm going to drop everything and walk out," the station master yelled. "You can do the work without me."

"I can drop everything too, you know," the commander retorted. "I'm fed up with this garbage—damn it to hell!"

After a lot of yelling, the station master asked us, "Which track did you come in on, the wide one or the narrow one?"

"The narrow one."

"Why didn't you say so? We send all the narrow-gauge trains to Dubno."

"What do you mean Dubno?" We were beside ourselves. "The train had eight cars for the Bessarabian division."

"Who cares?"

"What kind of nonsense is this?" shouted Makar Ivanovitsh. "The train's got our entire hospital on it—480 cholera patients and all our staff and supplies, and you up and send it to Dubno? I'm lodging a complaint! I'm going to wire the commander in chief!"

"You can wire all you like," the station master replied. "I follow my orders, and my orders are to send on 140 trains. They all go to Dubno. I dispatch a train every five minutes. And you threaten me?"

Makar Ivanovitsh hurried off to complain somewhere and demand the return of our train. I realized this was useless and went to the platform to catch the next train to Dubno. I was very worried about my case of twenty thousand rubles, which had been left lying open in the railroad car.

The platform was seething. Workers were milling about, shrieking, quarreling, making a racket. And every few minutes, trains were coming in and pulling out. I caught the first one to Dubno and spent three hours in a car full of railroad workers eating, drinking tea, and trading stories about the war.

"This general got killed in Galicia, and they put his coffin on a train for Tver, where he was supposed to be buried. The train arrived, the priests were waiting at the station, they rang the bells and had a parade, and then they opened the doors to the car. Instead of the general they found dried fish. The car had been switched!"

"Ha ha ha!"

"When we were at the front," said another man, "a whole division was sent to the wrong place—the Caucasus instead of the southwest. There were loads of blunders like that."

Barely half a mile beyond Radziwillow, the train ground to a halt. The jolt was so sudden that we fell on the floor, with bags and bundles raining down on us. We jumped out of the car. The night was pitch-black. At the end of the train we saw lanterns bobbing and heard shrieks. A second train had rear-ended ours, smashing two cars. A few people had been killed and some injured. We were sure to be stranded till daylight. A few passengers returned to their cars and went to sleep; others broke off the wood from a fence and built a fire. All at once, we heard a shout from the back of the train: "Everyone get the hell off! There's another collision coming! A third train's charging toward us!"

More turmoil. But this time we felt nothing. I don't know whether the train braked in time or whether the impact failed to reach our car.

The train didn't reach Dubno until dawn. And not even Dubno proper. It halted at a whistle-stop three or four miles away. The track leading to the town was packed with dozens of earlier arrivals. The narrow-gauge line ended here, and there was no place to send these trains on. I got out and walked. The third train was the one I had ridden from Lwow. I found my case and my other belongings intact.

9

The Russian retreat from Galicia, especially from Lwow, came soon and interrupted my plans for traveling in the occupied area. Now there was no question of my doing any kind of systematic work to help the Jews there. I couldn't even settle on a destination.

I wondered whether it made any sense to go, but the Kiev relief committee insisted that I should. Russia still controlled hundreds of towns and villages that would receive no aid from Lwow, still being under the czar's rule, so they had to be provided for. Since it was impossible to stick to an itinerary, I would go wherever I could. Every last village needed material assistance and also morale boosting in the critical moments of the Russian pullout.

I agreed to head back to Galicia, joining either Demidov's or Komisarov's division, and tour all the Jewish communities I could reach. Since Dr. Kozhenevsky had agreed to set up the mobile medical unit for Demidov's division in Sokal, I went there via Kovel, where I visited the Jewish relief committee. Its chairwoman, Dr. Faynshtayn, supervised the work with great devotion. The chief task was to prepare food for the hundreds and thousands of expelled Jews transported through Kovel. The committee was at war with the railroad administration, which prohibited any contact with the deportees.

I found several dozen Galician Jews sitting on the ground in the station courtyard. Some were praying in their prayer shawls and phylacteries. The guard wouldn't let me go over to them.

"Where are they from?" I asked.

"From Sokal. Thirty-five of them."

"What happened in Sokal?"

"They beat up the Jews and ransacked their stores. The commander ordered his men to take the merchandise. No one else was bothered."

"You're sure the commander ordered it?"

"Tak tetshno, absolutely, sir."

Through great effort, the committee obtained permission to bring food to the Jews.

The committee told me a story about Ivanov, the supreme commander of the southwestern army. Ivanov had received a delegation of four rabbis from Chelm, who had brought him a Torah scroll. He was very moved; he hugged them and gave the eldest a silver snuffbox. After they left, he sent someone to fetch them back and then handed them six hundred rubles for the poor.

The story sounds apocryphal. I heard many legends about General Ivanov. Many people believed that he came from a Jewish background, that he himself or his father had been forced as a child to serve in the czar's army. His patronymic, Yudovitsh, seemed to bear out the story.

In Kovel I met a member of Komisarov's division, who told me that the troops were stationed at Kristanopol, some ten miles away. We traveled there together, and I stopped off at Sokal.

Sokal is a large town and was apparently once rich and beautiful. I arrived on a Saturday. There was a deathly hush, the stores were all closed, and I couldn't tell whether that was because of the Sabbath or the recent pogrom. On closer inspection, I saw the battered doors, the smashed windows, the twisted, ripped-out metal doors. The interiors were all in shambles—torn, gutted, riddled with bullets.

I couldn't find any Jews. I turned off into the side streets, one after another. No troops to be seen; just poor Jewish homes. A bit farther, a huge, ancient stone synagogue from the seventeenth century—one of the most beautiful I had seen. Women, children, and old people were sitting all around it, with drooping heads, as if they were mourning the temple.*

An old Jew with a thick gray beard and a handsome face emerged from a side lane; he was wearing a *shtreymel* [fur hat] and a satin caftan. He trudged slowly and calmly toward the synagogue. I went over to him and said, "Good shabbes."

He stopped and gazed at me for a while, cold and distant. Then he curtly replied, "Good shabbes."

Not knowing how to break the ice, I asked, "Did a pogrom take place here?"

"Yes."

"Shops were looted?"

"All of them."

"Was anyone killed?"

"No. . . . Wait, yes, one person. . . . A lot were injured."

"No damage to the synagogue?"

"No damage."

His answers were clipped and dry. Then he turned away and entered the synagogue.

I had counted on finding Dr. Kozhenevsky in Sokal, with the mobile medical unit in Demidov's division. But no matter how hard I looked, I couldn't find him. I went into a hotel, rented a room, and questioned the elderly Jewish proprietor about events in the town.

"They destroyed Sokal. They spent the whole week looting, smashing, beating. They didn't leave one home or store untouched. Maybe a few hundred Jews were slaughtered or mutilated. The clockmaker was murdered, leaving a wife and eight children. . . . That much we know, but how much don't we know? There are orphans in the woods, and no one knows what happened to their mothers. . . . A Cossack hacked my daughter's arm off with his sword." She spoke in a monotone, but with tears streaming from her eyes.

---

*Refers to the destruction of the first and second Jewish temples in Jerusalem.

"They began by rounding up all the Jewish men in the square, about a thousand, and they said they would shoot them all. Then they said they would send them to Russia. . . . The Jews collected a few thousand rubles and brought the money to the commander. So he took just seventy-five men and packed them off to Russia, and the rest he let go."

I had a few people to look up. I asked the hotel owner to send for the men. She said they would probably be too scared to leave their houses, but she agreed to try to bring them. She put on a colorful babushka so people would mistake her for a peasant, and left. A couple of hours later, she returned with the news that all the men were in hiding. I had a large sum for the needy, but no one to give it to, so I left seventy-five rubles with the woman.

Then I went back into the town, where I heard that the mobile medical division was in Belz. So I went to the train station and asked the telegraph operator to send a message to Belz. He replied that the town had stopped responding at 3:37. Apparently, it had been taken by the Austrians.

With this news, Sokal was evacuated. The commander had departed. Only his division staff was left. At night the town was encircled by the fire of towns and villages burning nearby. After that, I saw the same fiery rings almost every night, wherever I happened to be with the retreating army.

I spent the night at the depot, and in the morning boarded the train for Kristanopol.

The Jews in the town, which wasn't very large, didn't seem to have suffered too much. The stores were open, but the Jews were terribly frightened. The streets were choked with the army in retreat. I walked into a small shop and struck up a conversation with the owner, an elderly man with an intelligent face. I told him I was coming from the Lwow committee and asked him what had happened in Kristanopol.

"When the Russians marched in ten months ago, they destroyed the town and looted everything. They killed five Jews—shot three and slaughtered two. They raped eight girls and twenty women right in front of their menfolk, who were tied up. . . . And when it quieted down, we were left naked and impoverished. We didn't dare leave town even to buy a little bag of flour; it was forbidden. We were starving. No help came from anywhere. And now worse is coming. God only knows what's in store for us."

At my request, the storekeeper summoned four men from the community, and we met in his back room. I discussed the situation with them and gave them five hundred rubles for the poor. I visited the synagogue with one of them; it was filled with crates and baskets. Jews from all over town had concealed their valuables here, reckoning that it would be the safest place. The synagogue itself had many precious items, especially brass chandeliers. I suggested they store all the valuables in the attic and then chop up the ladder. I also advised them to place barrels of water inside the houses in case of fire. They should expect fires. Throughout the day, Sokal was surrounded by pillars of smoke from the burning towns and villages. The people tried to pinpoint their locations: Mosti-Velki? Belz?

That evening, I met with Komisarov and heard that the Russian army had pulled out of Mosti-Velki. But first the Cossacks had perpetrated a terrible pogrom. Now the town was being shelled by the Russians and was burning. The retreating medical division, headed by Dr. Shapiro, a woman doctor, was now in Porkhatsh, a village some five miles from Kristanopol. That village was being shelled as well, and Dr. Shapiro and the nurses were working under fire, performing surgery, bandaging the wounded, sending them off. At two A.M., her staff reached Kristanopol. The Austrians were already approaching Porkhatsh. The rear guard was holding back the enemy, but the division would have to move on during the night or at the latest by morning.

I hurried to the station. It was a mess. Everyone was being evacuated. Only the explosives trains were being left behind. The line running south to Lwow had been demolished; rails had been removed, the sleepers torn out and heaped in pyres. I spent the night at the station. The rings of fire grew closer and more intense. I saw a large fire nearby and I headed over. The mounds of sleepers and other wood were blazing around the depot. It was a clear night, with a full moon shining in the starry sky. I turned to go back and saw something fantastic: hundreds of stone slabs, red, burning, with Hebrew letters glowing. At first I couldn't understand what I was seeing. But then I realized: this was a Jewish cemetery. The glowing gravestones were reflecting the flames. It was an extraordinary spectacle, as if generations—centuries—of Jews had returned from the past to the mystical moonlit night, to gaze with fiery eyes at the horrors closing in on their shtetl.

I didn't sleep long, waking at around eight. A soldier marching by told me, "There's a pogrom in town. Cossacks arrived an hour or two ago, and they're smashing everything, beating up the Jews."

I ran out. The street was in turmoil. Women were dashing about, screaming, wailing. Small groups of elderly Jews were shuffling from one place to the next. Piles of broken merchandise were lying outside many of the stores, surrounded by clusters of people. I could see no soldiers or Cossacks.

I learned that at six o'clock a Cossack detachment had arrived. Within two hours they had destroyed the shtetl, plundering half the stores. Now a few Cossacks and soldiers were left, hauling off the leftovers from the shops. The soldiers were followed by peasant women, who were collecting merchandise in sacks.

I strode into one or two stores and drove the soldiers away. In one basement, I pulled a Cossack out by his ear, threatening to shoot him. Turning white, he emptied the loot from his pockets. When the Jews saw I was actually managing to force the thieves out, they came over, yelling: "Come to my store! Have pity! They're looting my store!"

Little by little, the shtetl settled down. Once more I gathered the men I had spoken to the previous day. They were tearful and shaken. We tried to assess the damage. It turned out that some hundred families had been ruined during those two hours. I left another eight hundred rubles for the victims, with the proviso that a precise itemization be submitted to the Lwow committee once the Russians were gone.

During the mayhem, notices had been put up throughout the town: All males from eighteen to fifty were to be evacuated. In contrast with Lwow, the proclamation included Jews. This put the Jews in an even worse position. While I was meeting with the community leaders, someone came with the message that the town commander had summoned the mayor and one of the most prominent Jews to discuss the proclamation. Should they obey or not? I advised sending someone to discuss it with the commander.

At noon the turmoil began again, with crowds in the street, shouting and weeping. A Cossack officer and two others were going through the undamaged stores, looking for guns. They were also taking an inventory of the flour, sugar, kerosene, candles, which would be requisitioned. As the three Cossacks came nearer, people watched, turning white, wringing their hands.

A pale Jewish woman with roaming eyes came over to our group. In a soft, desperate voice, she said: "Oh, my! I'm done for! They're heading for my place. . . . They're going into my cellar."

I tried to calm her. "They're not taking anything for now; they're only making a list."

"You don't know what I've got in my cellar," she whispered.

"What?" I asked nervously.

"Better not ask!"

"Guns?"

"Guns? Nonsense! No, several hundred rubles and my widowed sister's jewels—everything we own. They're going to take it all."

A couple of hours later, more running and crying. Thirty Jews had been grabbed in the street or in their homes and were being herded into the marketplace. The guards said they would be sent to do forced labor. One of them was a sick, pallid young man. I talked the guards into letting him go. The moment they released him, people on the side started to whisper to the guards, offering them money, haggling, ransoming the prisoners.

By now, the booming cannon were quite close. The last units passed through the town. A medic came to inform me that our division was pulling out at eighteen hundred hours. I would have to join it. Dr. Shapiro would stay behind with several orderlies and treat the wounded. She would be the last to leave—when the Austrians reached the edge of town.

The Jews asked me to stay until the last minute. I could only stay if Dr. Shapiro agreed, but she didn't have room in her automobile. I told the Jews that if anything happened, they should go to her. I also asked her to take one hundred rubles in case she had to help someone. She was annoyed and said she wasn't getting involved in Jewish affairs. . . . An intelligent woman who displayed extraordinary heroism under fire didn't have the courage to show that she was Jewish to help the persecuted. And she wasn't the only one to respond this way.

IO

Komisarov's division had been unable to do any real work because it had spent the last six weeks packing and unpacking. So Komisarov decided to move to the rear where things were calmer. From Kristanopol, he traveled via Sokal in the direction of Lutsk and finally took over a farm near Poretsk.

Since it made no sense for me to stay with Komisarov's division far in the rear, I figured I would head back to Galicia and look for Demidov. An officer passing through told me he had seen the troops in Sokal. So back I went.

The railroad track was being destroyed. At each wooden bridge, the poles were wrapped in straw, waiting for the sentry to strike the match. Dynamite had been planted under the iron bridges. The Sokal station had been evacuated, aside from the explosives train. New barracks half a mile away had cost half a million rubles, and now they too were to be torched.

The town itself was still the dismal wreck it had been a few days earlier. Not a shop was open. However, there were two or three small tables with bread set up in the street. Troops clustered there, buying up the bread. Others, wandering around, were angry because they could find nothing to buy. So of course they cursed the Jews.

I went back to the hotel where I had stayed before. The proprietor told me the pogrom had kept raging these past few days.

I was intent on speaking to people from the Jewish community. Rabbi Hoyzner had suggested I find a man named Shmutser, and so I asked the proprietor to arrange it. Going on ahead, she led me through an alley to a house filled with troops who, as usual, mistook me for an officer. They jumped up from their seats surprised, wondering what I was looking for.

I summoned the lady of the house, an old Jewish woman, and sharply ordered her to give me a clean room and tea and a snack. I would wait for Shmutser without the soldiers wondering why I was there. In the room there were about fifteen people, all of them homeless women and children from Magerov. The Russian army had plundered the entire town, then torched it. One woman's husband had died of fright. Her daughter had also died, leaving six children. And now she was there with her grandchildren and family, all of whom were famished. When I gave them twenty-five rubles, they were astonished and loudly burst into tears.

The hotel owner returned with the news that Shmutser was afraid to go out. I didn't want to leave without providing some kind of aid, so I asked her to summon two elderly people. She called in her husband and another old man. They didn't inspire much trust in me, but I gave them two hundred rubles for the local relief committee.

I went to town, searching for any clues to Demidov's whereabouts, but found nothing. . . . All at once, I heard someone shouting my name. I whirled around. People in a car were waving handkerchiefs and calling to me. I recognized the nurses and orderlies from Demidov's division. Delighted, I hopped in. The division, it turned out, was at a burned-down farm some two and a half miles from Sokal, having come from Belz. Before their retreat, there had been a pogrom and almost the entire town had gone up in flames. The marauders had carried off whatever they could, particularly copper. They had removed four brass domes from the old synagogue.

I drove to the farm with the nurses and orderlies. The property was very large and rich, but so utterly destroyed, burned down, that the division had to settle in the stables. The division was preparing to retreat farther, but first it had to get food in Vladimir-Volinsk. I volunteered to go.

The road was flooded with fleeing Ruthenian peasants—hungry, dejected. A few had been trudging for two weeks without help, without bread. No one cared about them. Some formed groups and stole into the fields, carrying off the grain and whatever else they could lay their hands on. They even got into fights with the local peasants.

I stopped off in Poretsk. The town was in an uproar. The prefect came dashing over. He told me he had been at the district police commissioner's office and had seen a circular ordering the entire population, regardless of nationality, to be deported beyond the Volga. Some people wanted to leave on their own, but the police chief refused to issue passes, and anyone caught traveling without papers was sent back.

"What should we do?" he exclaimed. "The town's in a turmoil. Some are saying we should flee as soon as possible, but others say that when the Austrians marched in at the start of the war, the ones who stayed were well off, while those who fled became paupers."

When I set out for Vladimir-Volinsk, I took the prefect along. I wanted him to get a clear idea of the situation from the district police commissioner and to ask him to order the police chief to hand out travel permits. Upon arriving, I found the same agitation and turbulence. A dark cloud was hovering over the town: fear of expulsion. No one knew what orders had been given. Would everyone be deported or only able-bodied men? Would the decree apply to everyone or only to Jews? And how long would the district police commissioner prohibit anyone from leaving? He wanted a bribe of two thousand rubles, but the town didn't have a kopek to its name.

His office was mobbed by people wanting passes. The Cossack sentries were yelling, cursing, driving away the Jews. Before my eyes, a Cossack gave a hard shove to an old man. When I threatened to have him court-martialed, the Jews were flabbergasted, and the old man followed me, thanking me over and over.

Instead of sending the prefect of Poretsk to the district police commissioner, I went myself. I explained that our division was stationed near Poretsk and that the townsfolk had asked me to have the commissioner clarify why the police chief refused to grant any travel permits.

"So far," he replied, "I've received no details about the expulsion. But I see no reason to hold up people who want to leave of their own accord. So I'll order the police chief to issue passes without further delay. If you like, you can deliver the written order to the police chief yourself." And he gave me the document. Since I didn't know whether I would have time to stop in Poretsk, I entrusted it to the prefect.

When I had left Demidov's division to get provisions in Vladimir-Volinsk, I had planned to meet up with it again in the hamlet of Versin. But once there, I was told that the troops had been ordered to travel farther, to the village of Vatin, via Goroshkov, Milyatin, and Bobyatin. So I started after it, but en route ran out of gas. I left the car with the driver in a village and hopped a military wagon. We moved very slowly, and at three A.M. the drayman dropped me off at an army hospital. Everyone in the building was asleep, and nobody heard my knocking. So I found a stable, climbed up to the hayloft, and lay down. The instant I dozed off, I heard terrible, heartrending sobs and moans from below. I trembled. Lighting a match, I saw a young donkey. It had been braying loudly. I had never heard a donkey braying before; it sounded like bitter human weeping.

In the morning I went into the hospital, where I drank some coffee and listened to the doctors talking. Ignoring the presence of a stranger, they made some strongly revolutionary comments against the government and the czar. I had never before heard such things in the army.

The doctors gave me a small wagon, which brought me to Vatin.

The division had halted here and established a triage clinic to bandage wounded men and send them on. I wanted to remain with the division because it enabled me to visit the surrounding towns. As it turned out, deportees from places close to the front passed through Vatin. From dawn to dusk, wagons transporting homeless Jews, chiefly from the shtetl of Horokhov, rumbled past the division building. Wagons were packed with all kinds of household goods, and in the middle of these belongings, like birds in a nest, were children and women. Men trudged behind each wagon, and the whole convoy looked like a funeral procession.

They were leaving because they feared pogroms and a general expulsion order. The police chief was demanding huge bribes for travel permits. For now, these Jews were going to Tortshin, less than twenty miles from Horokhov. They didn't want to go too far from home; perhaps they would be able to head back soon.

II

During the past few weeks, ever since I had cut back across the old Russian border, I'd come to realize that this vast area, with its dozens and dozens of Jewish towns and villages, was afflicted by the gloomiest terror and despair. Even though the battles were hundreds of miles away, the overall mood here was the same as among the Jews in Galicia. Hour by hour these frightened Jews were waiting for two plagues: a pogrom and a mass expulsion. Normal life had stopped; a panic had broken out; Jews were scurrying helter-skelter, trying to save themselves as fast as possible.

I decided to go to Kiev, inform the relief committee about the current situation, and urge it to take any measures whatsoever to prevent the deportation of the Jews. I also wanted to propose that the committee send funds to the shtetls that were poorest and closest to the fighting, so that the Jews could have vehicles ready in case of a sudden expulsion. Since I had run out of cash, I planned to ask the committee for a large sum and then tour all the communities near the front lines. For this purpose I was hoping to obtain an automobile in Kiev.

On June 19, 1915, I set out for Lutsk. The railroad station, where I was forced to spend several hours, was in a complete uproar. Trains were anywhere from twelve to eighteen hours late, and the place was mobbed by thousands of travelers. They were waging a war for tickets and seat reservations, which were being sold at astronomical prices. Jews were not allowed to enter the depot, and so they stood or sat outside with their boxes and bundles. The policemen and the railroad employees were shoving them around, cursing them, punching them. It was both a dreadful and familiar tableau.

The Jewish druggist told me that the dozens of Jewish families living by the station had formed a relief committee to help the thousands of Galician Jews—refugees or simply evacuees—coming through in troop trains. Until a day or two ago, the Russian commander had not allowed anyone near these Jews. But now he took pity on them and permitted their local brethren to approach them. They brought any food they could to each train, but the committee had little of its own. I promised them that I would obtain help in Kiev.

But in Kiev the mood was even worse than during my last visit there. The flood of Galician evacuees and refugees was never ending. They came streaming into Kiev—1,000, 2,000 Jews a day, and they were sent on to the province of Voronezh. Two thousand homeless Jews were shipped here from Riga. A few days later, evacuees started pouring in from Podvolotshisk, where the entire Jewish population—some 4,000 or 5,000—had been expelled without warning. As I subsequently learned, the sole reasoning behind this action was that the military and the social organizations needed lots of places to live in that town. The instant the Jews were booted out, peasants began thronging in from the countryside, plundering the deserted homes and shops, stripping them bare. Some 2,000 evacuees arrived in Kiev. The rest scattered among the surrounding towns and villages.

To make matters worse, Kiev became hysterical. The enemy had stormed so close to the Russian border that it was feared he would reach Kiev. The wealthier and more nervous people started fleeing the city, thereby triggering a panic.

In Kiev people already knew about the pogroms and expulsions in the towns and hamlets near the border, and the news had likewise gotten to St. Petersburg. But as with the previous decrees, no one could help. The Jews tried to get government permission to send an authorized representative around the various shtetls in Russia and provide relief. But even this appeal was denied.

As for a car, I was unable to obtain one in Kiev. Four automobile requisitions had taken place, leaving none of the rich Jews with a car that would be useful to me.

After receiving five thousand rubles, I took a train to Vatin, first stopping in Lutsk. Here too an expulsion order had been issued to the Jews, but then rescinded, so that minds were put at ease. Jews lived moment by moment, and if the knife was removed from their throats for even an instant, they would calm down. In the shtetl as well as on the train, I heard both soldiers and civilians claim that a twenty-one-day truce had been agreed on. Who could have been spreading this rumor, which was told to me by dozens of people?

In the street I was stopped by a young man from Poretsk, who spoke to me tearfully. He said that on the eighteenth of June, part of the retreating Eighth Division [of the Russian army] had launched a pogrom, which had raged for an entire day. The Jews had dropped whatever they were doing and had escaped into the nearby forest. Meanwhile peasants had come from the surrounding villages and cleaned out all the Jewish stores and houses. The next day, the pogromists left, and when the survivors returned and tried to regain their property from the looters, the police chief expelled all the Jews from the shtetl. Some 150 families scattered over the surrounding hamlets, while several hundred families went to Tortshin or Rozshishts. Wherever they settled, they were starving to death.

I handed the young man a few rubles and told him to return to Rozshishts and to ask the rabbi and the mayor to meet with me in Lutsk so that we might discuss the situation.

I went to a local Jewish householder and invited the official rabbi as well as several community leaders. From them I learned that Lutsk had until recently been in good shape. The town had managed to support all the homeless Jews fleeing here; furthermore, it had collected money and sent it to the relief committee in Kiev. But now things had changed drastically. Lutsk was practically a ghost town. The richer Jews were scampering away in all directions. No one knew what tomorrow might bring; no one could tell whether the Jews would be thrown out. They knew only one thing: all the authorities, from the district police commander down to the village police chief, were badgering the Jews, demanding bribes.

During our meeting, the rabbi of Poretsk and the village elder arrived from Rozshishts. They repeated the description of the pogrom. We decided that the rabbi and the village elder should invite four or five prominent congregants to Rozshishts. They would form a committee, draw up a list of casualties, and hand the list to the Lutsk committee, which would then provide aid. The Lutsk committee, which was more familiar with the local people and their circumstances than I, advised me on the distribution of the funds. For now, I gave the committee seven hundred rubles for the Poretsk Jews and one hundred rubles clear to the rabbi. He wasn't happy about this arrangement, but he put up with it.

The Lutsk community gave me a trunk containing rare articles from its old synagogue. I found an ornamental Torah crown from the eighteenth century and two rare hammered silver candelabra with sculpted figures—dating back to the late sixteenth or early seventeenth century. There were several other silver objects in an old artistic style: a Levite pitcher, a myrtle branch, a pointer for Torah reading, and a plate. And there were also two ancient gold-embroidered items: a tablecloth and a curtain for the ark. The overall value of these treasures added up to some twenty or thirty thousand rubles. I brought the trunk to St. Petersburg. Later, in 1918, when the Soviet authorities were about to dismantle the

Jewish Museum, I took the trunk with all its contents, plus four crates of other rare articles, to the Alexander III Museum; I was given a receipt for the entire lot, which is still in storage there.

In Lutsk I met the wagons of our division. They were bringing the wounded here. One of the drivers gave me a lift to Vatin.

I spent more than a week in Vatin, which had been receiving a nonstop torrent of wagons carrying Jewish refugees from many of the surrounding hamlets.

The division of the state Duma included a dozen top-ranking medical orderlies and nurses—all of them more or less intelligent. There were also: a physician named Kuptshikov (a Social Democrat) and Pavel Ivanovitsh, a fourth-year medical student acting as a full-blown doctor. The top officer, Dr. Kozhenevsky, was currently in Kiev. All his subordinates were very angry at him for his despotic ways, and they said that if he returned they would all transfer to a different division. But then he came back from Kiev with news, with money, with everyone's pay, and he said a few nice things—so they put their differences behind them.

Along with the food I brought from Kiev, there were five bottles of cognac, and everything was packed on a small wagon bound for Vatin. The vehicle was stopped overnight in Lutsk. Ivanovitsh, the medical student, who had brought some wounded men to Lutsk, was supposed to travel with the wagon. Unlike us, he did not sleep at the inn; instead, he caroused the night away with a company of officers, and by the time he left in the morning he was dead drunk. In Vatin, they noticed that three bottles of cognac were missing. The entire staff—nurses and high-ranking orderlies—convened on a square near the church and put the student on trial. He was accused of stealing the three bottles, getting drunk, and also getting a simple soldier, an orderly, drunk. There was a suggestion that the culprit be remanded for a court-martial. Ivanovitsh burst into tears, confessed his sins, and begged for forgiveness. He said he was a sick man, an alcoholic, and couldn't resist the sight of liquor. He promised to return the stolen cognac. We voted. I was in favor of forgiveness, and if it hadn't been for my vote, he would have been turned over to a military court.

During our trial on the square, the church was surrounded by the local peasants—men, women, and children—who were watching the removal of the bell. Soldiers were taking them down throughout the region to keep them from falling into the clutches of the Germans, who needed brass. I couldn't tell about other areas, but I did know that several wagonloads of bells had remained in Vladimir-Volinsk, where the Germans had grabbed them.

The men now removing the bell worked earnestly and silently, while the villagers surrounding them were grief-stricken. The women were weeping softly because their church would stand hushed for a long time. When the bell was lowered to the ground, it emitted its final clang, a pitiful moan that sounded like a prayer. And then the bell went mute. Perhaps forever, perhaps until it was melted down and recast as a cannon, which, instead of summoning the faithful to worship would send a tempest of death and destruction over the fields.

The village had two Jews, shopkeepers, whose customers were all peasants. I got to know both men. The first, a simple rustic, practically a peasant, was decent and guileless. He was not happy that the war was drawing closer. Whatever happened to all the peasants of this village would happen to him. He was on good, even brotherly terms with them. Furthermore, the landowner had given him a horse and wagon in case he was expelled. The second Jewish shopkeeper was less of a peasant. He was something of a religious scholar with a dignified demeanor and a fine face with sad, good-natured, black eyes. When he spoke about the troubles afflicting his people, his voice trembled, and tears came to his eyes. He never complained about his own situation; things weren't so bad. He had eleven sons—God preserve them—seven of whom were in Brazil, working their own farms. They consistently sent him money, urging him and the remaining sons to join them; but he didn't want to leave his home, his roots, his familiar environment and move to some foreign place where there were no Jews.

This shopkeeper offered to put me and the physicians up in the two best rooms in his house. He knew that so long as we stayed there, no one would touch him. The day after my arrival I rode over to Tortshin, which had also taken in most of the refugees from Horokhov and other places.

Tortshin was an old, destitute village consisting of a single long street with poor, tiny stores. Women and children were standing by each house, as if it were so overcrowded that it had no room for the people outside. And indeed, that was pretty much the case. One or more refugee families were living in each house. Moreover, all the granaries were filled with people, and many stables had been turned into shelters.

While I was in Tortshin, I heard the story of a Jewish officer who was stopping passersby, questioning them in Yiddish. He would treat them to tea, give candy to the children, and hand out money. One woman traveling with her children was offered five rubles. She refused to take it, so he handed the money to some other woman. No one knows who he is.

I was traveling with a medic who turned out to be an ethnic German—one of the many German colonists in the province of Volhynia. He told me that the czarist government was deporting them all to Siberia, but not allowing them to sell their land or their homes. The colonists were hawking their furniture and their grain, practically giving them away. Later, some Jews informed me that the expulsion of the ethnic German colonists was devastating the area. Their farms were the finest and most productive.

The medic also told me that the fifteen year old daughter of a German colonist had died in the district hospital. She had been raped by an entire squad of Cossacks.

In Tortshin it was rumored that the Russians had won a great victory: they had taken back Lwow, and supposedly two Japanese artillery outfits had arrived. This kind of rumor was repeated wherever the Russians were withdrawing.

12

Dr. Kozhenevsky brought back an order that the entire division, with its two units, was to be thoroughly restructured—that is, drawn out along a single line. One unit would be stationed at the front, the other some twenty or twenty-five miles inland, and the division with the hospital even farther away, so that the wounded arriving at the first group would be sent on to the second. They would rest, get food, and then be dispatched on to the division hospital. To adjust to the new arrangement, the two units would move back to the rear, purchase horses and wagons, and a full inventory.

Since it was now pointless for me to remain with the group, I decided to join up with the engineering division. Several weeks earlier, F. I. Preobrazhensky, its delegate, had invited me to join. The engineers were supposedly stationed in Vladimir-Volinsk, and so I left for there on July 1.

Some forty miles before Vladimir-Volinsk, I stopped off in Lokatsh, an old Jewish shtetl with a brick portal and the ruins of an ancient castle. Upon driving into town, I promptly noticed that something unusual was afoot. The inhabitants were all tense as if expecting a pogrom. Most of the shops were closed, but the owners stood at their doors, sad and disheartened. In the middle of the marketplace, small groups of householders were standing, peering about, conversing softly. Any pedestrian walked swiftly as if carrying important news.

I didn't know whom to question; so I told the drayman to take me to the biggest house in the market square. I entered. The mansion was rich but half-empty, as if the tenants were moving out. Few furnishings and household articles were left. I walked through several rooms but found no one. It was only in the last room that I came upon a poorly dressed elderly Jew named Shvarts, who worked for the owner. His employer, a wealthy Jew called Atlas, was out, and his family had already driven away. Shvarts was a bit scared of me. I eased his fears and asked him to send for the owner.

Meanwhile Shvarts told me about himself: "I had three sons. Two of them went off to war. One got killed; the other was seriously wounded. Now the third's been drafted. I myself worked in a mill for fifty rubles a month. But now the mill's closed down, and I have no livelihood." He spoke calmly, quietly, and added: "Am I the only one? Everyone's lost a family member in the war, and here we're all starving to death."

Mr. Atlas arrived. He told me that for several weeks now it had been rumored that the entire Jewish population would be booted out, and this had created a terrible mood. Earlier, it had been said that the expulsion would take place on St. Peter's and St. Paul's Day. The Jews were already preparing. In the meantime peasants from the surrounding countryside were already driving up "to get the Yids' belongings." But no decree was issued. Just today, however, the police chief had come and announced that the commander in chief of the army had ordered the expulsion of all Jews from the region within twenty-four hours. His exact wording: "Deport the entire Jewish population south of Hrubieszow." Although Lokatsh was east of Hrubieszow, the district police commissioner had ordered the expulsion of the Jews. A large bribe had persuaded the police chief to put it off for one day. Atlas's wealthy partner, Mr. Zusman, had immediately gone to Vladimir-Volinsk and given the district police commissioner five hundred rubles to try to have the edict rescinded or at least to delay its implementation as long as possible. For every day was a boon for the town and for these two businessmen, who had to transport the thousands of sacks of flour from their mill.

The situation was sad enough even without an expulsion. There were a lot of homeless Jews here from Poretsk, Milyatin (thirty-one families), and other shtetls. And there was no money to help them. Cholera was more and more rampant, and there was no doctor at hand. One week earlier, a crew of homeless Galician Gentiles had passed through, and they had started a pogrom. The local Jews had appealed to the police chief, who angrily snapped, "And you've paid me nicely for my protection?"

They paid, and he sent the rioters packing.

I asked Atlas to call several prominent householders together. They founded a relief committee to assist the homeless and, in case of an expulsion of the Jews, to obtain bread for the needy and wagons for the sick and the children. I gave them four hundred rubles toward those ends and another twenty-five for medical supplies. Zusman's son, a university student, volunteered to go and procure them in Vladimir-Volinsk, so I took him along.

En route he told me several stories. In Lokatsh two officers were billeted in the home of a Jew whose two sons were students. The officers got drunk, hollered that all Jews were spies, and they yelled at the householder, "They oughta massacre all you Yids!" And they even threatened him with their swords. The women were terrified, and the two students began saying that they should go into hiding. But the father stayed calm. "I'm glad, children. Now you know how hard it is to be a Jew and how high the price is for this honor. You'll learn to appreciate being Jews all the more."

A Jew whose boy was in the army wrote to his corporal and asked how the son was. A few days later he received the following answer on a numbered sheet of official stationery: "Dirty Yid! Your son's in captivity."

In Vladimir-Volinsk, I stopped at a hotel. Young Zusman brought over his father, who told me he had spent the four hundred rubles persuading the district police commissioner to delay the expulsion from Lokatsh. The commissioner had then wired the commander in chief, asking whether Lokatsh was part of the area "south of Hrubieszow." An answer would not arrive for several days, and perhaps it would say that Lokatsh should not be evacuated.

I learned that the police chief of Poretsk was prohibiting the return of any Jews who had fled the shtetl during the pogrom. One Jew had come back expressly to recover seven Torahs remaining in the synagogue, and the police chief had threatened to arrest him; he had refused to let him salvage the scrolls and had ordered him to leave town immediately.

According to the government rabbi and a community leader named Yakhinzon, the commander in chief's instructions to deport all Jews from places "south of Hrubieszow" were causing dreadful turmoil, especially because of their vague wording. The Jews in Vladimir-Volinsk and dozens of other towns were panicking. I advised the rabbi and Yakhinzon to immediately send a deputation to Petrograd and try to get the order canceled. To that end, they appointed the rabbi of Vladimir-Volinsk and the rabbi of Ustilug. They were to leave the very same day, but they didn't start out until four days later because the rabbi of Vladimir-Volinsk had to officiate as sandek, the godfather, at a circumcision, and he refused to get going any earlier.

In Vladimir-Volinsk, I found the Russian engineering division. It turned out that Preobrazhensky, the division's plenipotentiary, was leaving and handing it over to the newly arrived delegates from Moscow: N. V. Tulupov, a famous pedagogue, and Ivanov, an instructor at the University of Moscow. Preobrazhensky introduced me to them, and I joined the division as a clerical administrator. Promising to start work in a couple of days, I headed for Vatin to pick up my belongings.

On the way, I stopped off in Lokatsh to inform the Jews that the expulsion was temporarily suspended. I visited Zusman's home, where I met his wife, a rich provincial with "aristocratic" airs. She launched into "noble and elegant conversations" with me, explaining how cleverly she had argued with Cossacks, who demanded that she sell them mead. All this time, it seemed, despite the terrible dangers afflicting the Jews, black marketeers had been peddling mead to the Russians and the Cossacks. The previous day had brought a whole squadron of Cossacks, who, upon hearing that their buddies had drunk mead here, demanded some for themselves. Mrs. Zusman had talked and talked to them, saying that today the mead was all sold out; but she promised to get hold of more.

I scolded this intelligent woman thoroughly and insisted very sharply that steps be taken to pour out all the mead in town. (I'm anything but certain that this was done.)

While telling me about the mead incident and other episodes, Mrs. Zusman kept looking around as if expecting somebody. Just as I was ready to leave, several poor people filed in. Each one described his plight and requested help. Next there was a whole throng of homeless Jews from Poretsk, who complained that their rabbi had given them none of the money I had left for the pogrom victims in their shtetl. I instantly realized that Mrs. Zusman had deliberately held me up while spreading the news about "the officer who distributes money" and advising people to come and ask me for aid. I sent the individual paupers to the committee, and I gave the Poretsk Jews a note for the rabbi, directing him to assist them together with others.

13

The division I joined had a mobile medical unit with a hospital employing two doctors and more than ten nurses, plus some orderlies. It also had a second hospital with three doctors and a staff of about thirty, as well as its own train for transporting the wounded. Right away, I noticed the internal friction and head-butting. Each doctor, especially the head surgeon, Dr. Moskvin, wanted to be totally autonomous. As for the delegates, they wanted everything done their way. Several days after my arrival, Dr. Moskvin had a fight with Ivanov, a delegate. Ivanov gave an order—and the physician responded with an obscene gesture.

A bit later, the plenipotentiaries started locking horns among themselves. Each insisted that his orders be carried out. Ivanov was uninterested in the work. He spent hours getting dressed, doing his nails, and he loved strolling and enjoying himself. Tulupov, in contrast, devoted all his time to working and was very earnest about it. A grim and gloomy man, he enjoyed needling people with sarcastic remarks. He was especially incensed at Ivanov and kept seeking ways to jab at him. Ivanov easily put up with it. He was interested in the more beautiful nurses and kept looking for excuses to go to headquarters and "present himself" to some general or other. In this climate, the work obviously couldn't proceed as smoothly and harmoniously as it might in a friendlier atmosphere.

I spent the first few days here doing clerical chores, which had been dreadfully neglected. One of my tasks was to sort out the personal effects of patients who had died in the hospital. I inspected several hundred of these packages and sent them to the appropriate heirs. Only one package contained a wad of money (seventy-eight rubles). All the others had minor sums: a few dozen kopeks, at most three to five rubles. Nor was there a single object of value; just a torn pouch, a small knife, a comb. I might have concluded that most of the regular troops never did any looting. But I knew that the orderlies who carried the wounded, especially the critical ones, emptied their pockets.

Most of the deceased left no correct address for their parents, wives, or children. However, a soldier's ID card did note his native province and sometimes his district or village. I could therefore send a package only to a district or town, requesting that it be forwarded to the relatives. For some men who died without regaining consciousness, there were no documents indicating so much as a name; so they were buried anonymously. Typically, a Russian soldier going into battle, often to certain death, wouldn't bother keeping his name and address on a slip of paper.

I once found an interesting document in the division archive. After lying in the hospital for only two days a soldier, brought straight from the trenches, had died of pulmonary gangrene. A day before his arrival he had gone to the evacuation hospital to complain about his symptoms. There he was accused of malingering. The commandant sentenced him to twenty-five lashes and ordered him back to the front. By the next day, when the soldier was hospitalized, he was unconscious. And this attitude toward the rank and file was not unusual.

Our division occupied a portion of the large brick barracks that made up a separate community outside the town. Along with our hospital, the barracks now contained two other hospitals and also official apartments of Komisarov's division as well as the evacuation point. The army had laid a track connecting the barracks to the station in order to transport the wounded directly by rail. The day I joined the division, our train of wounded men was slated to leave for Kovel. The doctors of all three hospitals separated the lightly wounded from the seriously wounded and helped put the latter into the railroad cars. This triage was very primitive. Anyone who could walk was classified as lightly wounded and had to go on foot; those who couldn't walk were put in heated freight cars. As a result, a few men who had been badly wounded in their heads or chests but had enough strength to drag themselves along had to trek a distance of sixty miles.

The train also had passenger cars for wounded officers. One of them had endured severe head and chest wounds two days earlier. He was running a high temperature and was greatly agitated; he kept talking, giving the doctors his impressions of the most recent battle, while laughing loudly and drily. It sounded like the guffaws of a skeleton. With that sepulchral mirth, he described the death of his friend, a second lieutenant: "It tore him to pieces . . . Ha! There were just bits of flesh flying every which way, ha!" He went on: "We expected an attack, but they told us, 'No need to hurry. We're going to prepare for this with a storm of fire.' Okay, so we wait—ha! And the Germans keep shelling us. A day goes by—and there's no storm of fire from our side. All at once we hear, 'Pop, pop, pop!' And then again: 'Pop, pop, pop!' Six shots—and then silence. That was our storm of fire. Ha! Then we were ordered to attack. . . . Ha!"

He suddenly blacked out. Half-dead, he was carried into the train.

I visited our hospital. What dreadful wounds, what inhuman agonies! How do people go on living with half their heads torn off, with their chests ripped out? But worst of all were the gangrene cases—men decaying while still alive. I stopped at the bed of a young Bessarabian Jew with a face as black as soil and the tormented gaze of a wounded animal. His spine was broken, and the lower half of his body was paralyzed and rotting with gangrene. He was unable to speak, unable even to tell me his name, although he understood my questions.

Next, I saw a young peasant who lay on his bed there, sighing. He too had gangrene. I gave him a lit cigarette. He greedily took several puffs and thanked me with his eyes. Several minutes after I moved on, he feebly called out: "Nurse! It's the end. . . . Write to my family. . . . Send them the two rubles eighteen kopeks. . . . Tell my friends I'm sorry if I did them any wrong. . . . Let them remember me in their prayers."

And then after a while: "Nurse! . . . I'm dying! . . . Give me a kiss."

She kissed him, and he died.

A couple of days later, I went to Gribovets. Here, some twelve miles from Vladimir-Volinsk, our medical unit had its hospital closest to the front—only four or fives miles from the battlefield.

The peasants were wandering about, lost and dejected. Aside from the proximity of the war, there had been a pogrom here several days earlier. An Uhlan regiment had ridden in, plundered the village, and raped all the women.

Cannon were booming interminably. All around, you could see the pillars of smoke from the burning villages. The road through and beyond Gribovets was packed with retreating second-class transports. Endless streams of wounded men were barely managing to limp toward the hospital, hopping, straggling, leaning on friends. The hospital was located in a large building on a nobleman's farm. The eight rooms were bursting with patients. In one room they lay side by side on the floor, critically wounded and mostly unconscious, too far gone to be transferred any farther. In the other rooms they lay, sat, or stood, waiting for surgery. Instead of heads, arms, legs, there were piles of blood-soaked gauze. And everywhere, on the clothes, on the walls, on the floor—blood, blood, and more blood. The pungent stench of blood was sickening. The bandaging was done in a separate room, on five or six tables. And what ghastly wounds! Torn bodies, arms and legs cut off!

In the operating room, two Jewish doctors, a man, Rozentsveyg, and a woman, Kantsel, had been working without rest for twenty-four hours.

During the four or five hours I was there, they performed twenty-three operations.

Amazingly enough, in that hell of blood and inhuman anguish, no shouting or weeping was to be heard. The physicians ripped the dried gauze from living flesh, they probed deep into the wounds, and some patients were treated without chloroform. But I heard no shouting, no weeping from anyone. They bore their pain with gritted teeth and with cold sweat on their brows.

A fortyish soldier sat, naked, on the operating table. He had four wounds. The surgeons were operating without chloroform. They had just removed a piece of shrapnel from his back. The wound was fearful, as wide as the palm of a hand. The man endured the operation without a sigh, though his entire face was drenched with sweat. The female doctor handed him the small, sharp piece of iron that she had taken out of his back. Without so much as glancing at it, he threw it under the table.

"Why don't you keep it as a memento?" the doctor asked.

"Worthwhile keeping that filth?" he responded indifferently. After a pause, he added, "When I recover and go back to combat, I'll keep it." And he even cracked a smile.

The large courtyard and the surrounding square were overflowing with patients waiting to enter the hospital. Those who could move crowded around the supper cauldron. Groups of men were discussing the events on the battlefield, which they had left just hours before. Off to the side stood a young soldier cleaning and polishing a whole stack of medals while crying his eyes out. He was the orderly of a seriously wounded colonel to whom the medals belonged.

In a small circle of patients, one man was talking excitedly: "We waited all night long, then all morning. At noon, our officer led us in an attack. Straight into the fray. The area was wide-open, we were right in front of the enemy, and he was blasting away at us. . . . And then the officer called, 'Forward! Forward!' All at once we were in mud, in a swamp. But we had to go on. So we crawled through the mud. It came up to our waists. And the enemy mowed down every last one of us."

He showed us his overcoat and his pants, which were still wet and caked with mud.

Among the wounded there were a few POWs, especially Magyars, none of whom knew a word of Russian. They sat or stood in the distance like frightened animals and were more pitiable than the Russians. A wounded Russian soldier went over to a Magyar, put his hand on his back, and, in a sympathetic tone, asked him, "Magyar, why don't you have some soup?" And he used gestures to get his invitation across.

The POW caught his drift, said something in Hungarian, and motioned with his hands.

The Russian understood. "You don't have a spoon? I'll get you one right now, my friend!" And he hurried off to find a spoon for the foe, who had been riddling him with bullets just hours earlier.

The torrent of wounded men swelled and swelled. From dawn till two P.M., eight hundred passed through the hospital. All the available wagons took patients to Vladimir-Volinsk. Now the rooms here were full, but no vehicles were left. And then we heard the news that our army was pulling out, and an evacuation order might come any moment. The older surgeon, Dr. Rozentsveyg, asked me to go to corps headquarters and request wagons.

Headquarters, in a village six miles from Gribovets, was in an unscathed, wealthy farmhouse. It was calm and quiet. In the courtyard, troops were grooming horses or sitting in clusters, chatting and laughing. I asked to see the corps physician. He had me ushered into the large, richly furnished parlor. The door to the dining room was open. There, on a long table covered with shiny white tablecloths, I saw wine and fresh flowers. Music was coming from the next room: someone playing a Beethoven sonata. Staff officers were walking through, quiet, elegant, self-assured. After the scenes I had just witnessed, I was surprised by the hush, the calm, the sheer peacefulness. It was a different world.

An old physician with the rank of a general came over to me. He listened to my report, was filled with pity for our division, and promised to give us anything we required. He immediately went to the phone and peremptorily ordered someone to send us fifty wagons without delay. Next he rang up someone else and ordered that person to move a military hospital closer to ours. Then he invited me to supper and offered to introduce me to the corps general. I begged off, explaining I had no time. But seeing how well disposed he was toward me, I asked the doctor to ask the general whether the army was going to expel the inhabitants of Vladimir-Volinsk and other towns, and if so, whether it was only the Jews or everyone.

He left and brought back the following answer: "The general says that no definitive decision has been reached as yet. But he's almost certain no one will be expelled."

Several days later, our division was told that all the members of the hospital staff in Gribovets were being awarded St. George medals. That same day I returned to Vladimir-Volinsk. Late one night, as I was working, there was a knock at the door. I said, "Come in." And in walked Dr. Levis, the head surgeon at the evacuation hospital. Extremely agitated, he asked to see the delegates.

"They're asleep," I replied.

"Wake them up. We've just received orders to evacuate the hospitals on the double so we can get going in the morning. We're retreating in a big hurry, and we're leaving Vladimir-Volinsk."

I woke up the delegates. And they in turn woke up the entire staff, causing a great ruckus. Most of these people, who were quite experienced, claimed this was a false alarm. Dr. Moskvin was the most annoyed. He flatly refused to evacuate the hospital: "It's the usual nervousness of the rear division. The evacuation division can run to wherever it likes, but I'm not budging. Behind us we've got our corps headquarters; our hospital closest to the front is twelve miles from here—it hasn't stirred an inch, but we're panicking here!"

Most of the personnel agreed with him. They went back to bed and refused to evacuate no matter how furious the delegates got. And in the morning, it turned out that this had indeed been a false alarm. Dr. Levis received orders to prepare the hospitals gradually for evacuation. Headquarters excused him for starting a tumult. But for a long time, the physicians and the higher-ranking orderlies kept making snide remarks to Dr. Levis and the delegates.

14

The moment I reached Vladimir-Volinsk, I asked Mr. Yakhinzon to gather some community leaders so we might confer on the local situation and plan what to do in case the Jews were booted out. Some twenty people showed up. In conversing with them, I saw that the Jews were in a state of turmoil only because of the possible expulsion. Still, they hoped to stave it off until the arrival of the Germans—something they were optimistic about. I felt duty-bound to describe what had happened in most places that had changed hands. If a town wasn't shelled and burned down, the withdrawing army torched it and launched a terrible pogrom. Often, at the last moment, the troops drove out the entire population or rounded up hostages. Naturally, my report made a great impact. The locals had a very different image of the coming of the Germans. Nevertheless, nearly all these community leaders opposed a voluntary evacuation. Some even argued that the Jews should ignore any deportation order or at least, if possible, hide out for the few days until the Germans marched in.

"Look," said one of the householders. "Let's say there's a fire. It won't destroy the entire town. And if there's a pogrom, something will remain. If, say, ten or twenty people are killed, then so be it. But if we all leave town, we'll be impoverished and lots of people will die of starvation and other hardships."

I proposed setting up a committee, which, in the event of a pogrom or a sudden expulsion, would provide food and wagons for the poor. Such a committee, I was told, would be difficult to organize. If all the Jews were forced out, it would be every man for himself; no one would have time for community affairs. I replied that this attitude was scandalous—more precisely, sinful. My comment hit home. Seven or eight people volunteered to take on the work.

We founded a committee and drew up an outline. We reckoned that at least six hundred rubles could be raised in the town; I promised them one thousand more. They would be able to buy several tons of flour. Furthermore, they should look at some horses and wagons with the goal of purchasing them in time. To avoid having them commandeered, I promised to keep them in our division.

I learned that the Jews here, and several Christians, were digging trenches in their yards in case the town was bombarded. The local authorities knew about it and had no objections.

On July 12, Yakhinzon came to me, deeply upset; the "leader of the aristocracy" had told him that they had just received an order to oust the entire population of Vladimir-Volinsk and that this order would be made public at any moment. The next day, the rumors kept growing. I handed the committee members the one thousand rubles I had promised them. They bought over five tons of flour, gave it out for baking bread, and set their sights on twenty horses and ten wagons for transporting the poor, the sick, and children.

Aside from the fear of expulsion, the Jews were in dire straits because of a typhus and cholera epidemic sweeping through the town. Not a single doctor was left, and the only pharmacy was being evacuated.

I asked Tsukerman, the Jewish doctor in our division, to spend a few hours daily visiting the local patients. He agreed. So did the delegates. But Moskvin, the head surgeon, thought there was no way that Tsukerman could abandon his hospital work for several hours a day. I called for a meeting of the doctors of all three divisions (ours, Komisarov's, and the evacuation division), and they were willing to provide medical care in town one day a week. Their decision was approved, and the doctors treated the townsfolk until the final day, when the hospitals left.

I suggested that the community leaders entrust me with the rare and precious synagogue articles, as had been done in Lutsk. They replied that all these items, including the ancient chandeliers, had been taken by the beadle, a dubious person, who had great pull with the district police commissioner. The beadle was supposedly in the secret police, and the town was scared of him. So they had given him the silver and the other articles without protesting.

Two representatives from Ostilye said that five Cossacks had galloped into their shtetl on the eleventh and ordered the entire Jewish population to leave the town. The Jews quickly drummed up 250 rubles for the Cossacks. But the Cossacks demanded 500, and they took the 250 on condition that they receive the balance within a day. The representatives now asked me to give them the 250 rubles. I dug in my heels and stated that they shouldn't have paid any money to the Cossacks; they should have gone to the district police commissioner and asked him whether such an order had been issued. They heard me out and agreed with me, but added mournfully, "What if the Cossacks start a pogrom in the meantime?"

There were also representatives from the shtetl of Ozdiutshi, where four hundred homeless Jews had wound up. I gave the local committee four hundred rubles.

The Kiev central committee of the Association of Towns had invited Tulupov, the delegate, to come to Kiev on the eighteenth [of July] for a conference of the delegates of the association's divisions with the mayors of the provinces of Volhynia and Podolia. The goal was to discuss the issue of help for these populations. I asked Tulupov to take me along to the conference so that I might report on the situation of the local Jews and the homeless in the frontline towns and townlets. He agreed, and on July 16 we motored to Kovel, where we caught the train. I stayed in Kiev until the twenty-ninth, but was unable to return to Vladimir-Volinsk because it had been occupied by the Austrians and our division had fallen back to Kovel. In Kiev I also heard that before leaving Vladimir-Volinsk the Russians had launched a pogrom, burning down all the houses on the street leading to the depot.

Later on, I heard all kinds of rumors about Vladimir-Volinsk. Several people said that before the Russian retreat someone had spread a rumor that Jews had fired at the Russian military and concealed Germans in their homes. So the Russians had started killing Jews, mowing down some two hundred. Other people told me that the Russians had shot down a German airplane, and inside it they had found not only the aviators but also a Jewish cobbler from Vladimir-Volinsk or Kovel, who had told the Germans where to drop their bombs. As retribution the Cossacks had burned down the entire town. So far, I had received no solid information about what had happened there. However, the withdrawal of the Russian army had not gone smoothly.

At the Kovel railroad station, we ran into Dr. Rozentsveyg, the physician of our hospital, which, stationed in Gribovets, was closest to the front. He was coming from the headquarters of the army commander in chief to determine the new location of the hospital. It was almost decided that he should move it to Trisk.

We were so engrossed in our conversation with Rozentsveyg that we didn't notice our train leaving right under our noses. Rather than waiting twenty-four hours for the next train, we figured we'd drive the three hundred miles to Kiev. After spending the night in an empty railroad car, we left at dawn.

At first, we were terribly cold. But when the sun rose, the trip became a real pleasure. The Lutsk-Zhitomir highway is one of the best in Russia. I haven't found such a wonderful road even in Galicia. It was as smooth as a parquet floor. Our automobile ran swift and easy, doing some twenty-five miles an hour. If we hadn't stopped to eat supper or change flat tires, we would have reached Kiev by six or seven P.M.

Given the horrible state of the rail system, I was surprised that the authorities weren't using the highway at least to carry provisions and matériel. During our trip, we never once encountered or overtook any transport, any artillery, any detachment. All we met were homeless travelers—mainly deported German colonists—riding or walking. You could recognize the Germans' huge, solid covered wagons half a mile away; they were practically tents. Their horses were powerful and well fed. A German strode alongside his wagon, calm and self-assured, his face revealing neither confusion nor despair. This was in glaring contrast to the poor, forlorn, and despondent homeless Galicians, Russians, and especially Jews in their small, open drays, which, brimming over with a mishmash of household items, were pulled by dejected, moribund nags.

Somewhere along the way, men were building fortifications, digging trenches, and putting up barbed-wire barriers. I particularly noticed a field of high grain, where soldiers and expelled peasants were working in tandem. The peasants were cutting the grain; the soldiers were putting up barbed wire. The two groups, whether doing peaceful or martial labor, were interwoven.

In need of a minor repair, we halted near a small bridge spanning a ditch. Glancing into the ditch, I was amazed to spot an elderly Jew and a younger one, both without jackets. The elderly man lay there, reading a holy book; the younger one was pensively crooning something. I climbed down and asked what they were doing. They said they had been sent here to guard the telephone lines—in fact, Jews had been assigned to guard the phone wires throughout the area. These two men were shopkeepers in the nearby village.

We spent roughly an hour in Rovno, which gave me time to see a few acquaintances. They told me that ever since the headquarters of the supreme commander had been transferred here, life for Jews had been hell. They were not allowed to leave town; they were oppressed and persecuted at every turn. Kulikover, a local Jewish leader, had asked the commandant to let them feed the expelled and arrested Galician Jews who were passing through. The commandant refused.

Kulikover retorted: "You might as well lay all the homeless on the tracks and run a train over them. That way you'd at least put them out of their misery on the spot."

Because of his brash comment he was arrested and would be transported to Siberia.

Not far from Rovno there was a camp of about one thousand homeless Galician Jews and Russian peasants. They were not allowed to go through the town. These refugees were dying of hunger, cholera, and typhus. No food or medical help was organized for them.

In Novgorod-Volinsk we found many homeless people from Kremenits, Dubno, and Astra.

We had supper in Zhitomir. The deeply agitated town was bristling with wild rumors. People were scared that the Germans would march in, and the richer ones were leaving en masse.

We reached Kiev at four A.M. The conference of the association's delegates, slated to begin on the eighteenth, was postponed to the twenty-second because many participants had not yet arrived. Prince Mikhail Aleksandrovich Urusov, chairman of the Kiev committee, and Andrei Ivanovich Shingarov, a Duma member (who later joined Kerensky's cabinet and was tragically killed), took advantage of the delay. To familiarize themselves with the plight of the homeless, they went to Vladimir-Volinsk. Tulupov headed to Moscow for a couple of days.

At the Jewish relief committee, I gave a report on the places I had visited. I pointed out that in the dozens of frontline towns and townlets that Jewish delegates were allowed to enter—or in any case move far more freely than in Galicia—I had found no delegates, no traces of organized help. I was now told that the committee was trying to get travel passes for several members but was having a difficult time of it. Moreover, the committee had no data on where assistance was needed. A few days later, the Zemstvo Alliance committee voted to have the alliance admit several representatives of the Jewish relief committee so they could freely tour the areas near the front. The committee told Dabin, the writer, to go to Vladimir-Volinsk, but before he could leave, the town was occupied. The committee also agreed to send aid to Poretsk and Ostilye.

Mikhail Alexandrovitsh Kishkin came from Moscow; this man (subsequently, minister of the interior in Kerensky's last cabinet) was vice chairman of the central committee of the alliance. I met with him and offered to address the delegates about the Jewish homeless. He found my idea interesting and invited me to the conference.

The conference began on the evening of July 22. It was attended by delegates from some twelve to fifteen divisions and ten mayors from the provinces of Podolia and Volhynia. There were talks, reports, and papers about the sufferings and deprivations endured by the traveling homeless, for whom no help was arranged. Suggestions were voiced for organizing food and medical aid, food centers, cauldron centers. But none of the speeches and debates ever so much as mentioned the word *Jew.* Their stock phrases were "People of all nationalities," "Christians and others."

I was the last person to take the floor. When I used the word *Jew,* they all glared at me as if I had broken a verbal taboo.

Underscoring and welcoming the fact that the Zemstvo Alliance, as a social institution, did not discriminate among ethnic groups, I pointed out that administrative activities and everyday conditions had left the Jews in a unique quandary, which necessitated specific forms of aid. Homeless Jews, I said, were in a very different predicament than homeless Christians:

1. The Christians from the front line had left voluntarily or been expelled from the provinces of Galicia, Volhynia, and Podolia. They needed help as transients. The Jews, on the other hand, came from

a range of provinces, including Kovno and Grodno, and were remaining in their places of transit or were expelled a second or
third time.

2. In each location the Jews had chiefly been expelled, as Jews, from
the frontline towns of Volotshisk, Satanov, Karitnitse, Tarnarude,
Horokhov, Milyatin, et cetera. These deportees had spread through
the surrounding towns and were waiting for a new expulsion decree.

3. Many of the homeless had fled pogroms (e.g., in Poretsk and
Krilov) with only the clothes on their backs. They had settled tem-
porarily in the surrounding towns and villages such as Rozshishts,
Ozdiutshi, Tortshin, Ostilye.

4. Most Jews were expelled in haste, allowed at best two or three
days, more frequently twenty-four hours, which left them no time
to take their possessions.

5. It was harder for a Jew than a Christian, especially a farmer, to
move to a different town with his possessions. Jewish property
consisted of merchandise; Jews had no livestock. Since the railroad near the front was off-limits to Jews and even the highways
were unsafe, they had to rent wagons from the Christians. Furthermore, in these panicky times it was often impossible to obtain
wagons, and the owners charged outrageous fees: fifty or sixty
rubles for a distance of thirty miles. Nor could a Jew buy horses
because they would be requisitioned.

6. Christian transients could eat at army messes and at the food centers of any division. Jews, of course, were afraid to approach a division, nor could they eat nonkosher food.

7. In the summer, a homeless Christian could hire on as a farmhand.
But Jews were inexperienced in such work and could not get these
jobs anywhere.

When I finished my report, Kishkin said, "Your information is very
interesting. Can you please tell us in what way the alliance can assist the
Jews?"

"First of all," I replied, "the alliance should establish food centers in
all the towns containing homeless Jews."

"I think we can accept that," said Kishkin. "Anyone opposed?" No one objected, and the motion was carried.

"Second," I continued, "wherever Jews are expelled, the alliance must help them obtain horses and wagons. Third, we have to create an employment agency for homeless Jews."

"That we cannot take upon ourselves," Kishkin broke in. "It would mean favoring homeless Jews, and our alliance cannot do that. All we can do is ask the authorities if they would be willing to provide free lumber from state-owned forests to construct barracks for homeless Jews."

"I would also suggest," I went on, "that the conference advocate the elimination of the Jewish Pale of Settlement."

"No, no!" Kishkin cried out, almost terrified. "We can't do that! Our conference is a local one. The Moscow conference voted for the elimination of the Pale. And that's enough!"

My report took roughly an hour. Responses came only from Kishkin. No one else said a word. They all kept a cold and grumpy silence.

The next day I visited Kishkin and thanked him for his support and for gaining approval of the food centers. I then added, "I must tell you that yesterday's session made a great impression on me."

"Why is that?"

"To be frank, the attitude toward helping the refugees was cold and officious. I had expected that the delegates, at least you as chairman, would be concerned about these poor people and think of ways to help them. Instead, you just said, 'We cannot discriminate between Jews and non-Jews.' In other words, it's none of our business. I'm being candid with you because your organization may be the only one we can appeal to without risking an antisemitic reaction. And if you behave so officiously, where can we go?"

My words apparently affected him. At a loss, he argued, "But the Jewish Relief Committee is organizing aid, and it's accomplishing a lot more than we can."

"That's not true. I've just toured numerous towns in Lutsk and Vladimir-Volinsk and aside from the small sums I left there, no help has been organized by any Jewish committee."

"But you have to understand that we can't deviate from our principles.

All we can do," Kishkin added, "is subsidize the Jewish committees so they can organize the necessary aid."

Our conversation took place in the alliance committee building. When I left Kishkin's office, I was approached by a delegate who had attended yesterday's meeting, Dr. Yevseyev, the representative of a Siberian division stationed in the Galician town of Tarnopol, who wanted to hear more about our relief efforts.

I spent a few more days in Kiev to obtain food and medical supplies from the Red Cross. Before leaving, I met with Dr. Lander, who had come from Galicia. He told me that only twelve places were still in Russian hands, and that the local Jews were in a terrible state, suffering from hunger and a cholera epidemic. Worse, they were shackled to their shtetls and not allowed to take even a few steps beyond the town limits.

15

On July 30, I rejoined my division in Kovel. We were occupying a house but not yet functioning—we hadn't even unpacked. It was uncertain whether we would stay here for long. All sorts of dreadful rumors were circulating. Planes were flying overhead dropping bombs, while baggage transports and artillery were retreating.

I looked for Dr. Faynshtayn, the chairwoman of the local Jewish committee. She told me that during the past few days three railroad cars filled with deportees from Lyubomil had passed through, but that a larger number of the homeless were traveling in wagons or on foot. Some Jews were afraid of going by rail; it was rumored that homeless Jews were being kicked off the trains in the middle of nowhere. More than one thousand homeless Jews had gathered in the shtetl of Holobl, and the Kovel committee was organizing aid for them.

Since Kovel was a central point in the movements of the homeless, I gave the committee one thousand rubles.

Dr. Faynshtayn told me that several days earlier the townsfolk had panicked because of a rumor that the post office had been evacuated.

Now they had quieted down. All sorts of food was being confiscated in the stores. Bread was scarce, and there was no sugar. They had appealed to the commandant to permit several boxcars of sugar to come in. And he had retorted, "Let the Jews put salt in their tea!"

I arrived at seven P.M., and that same day, our division was ordered to quickly retreat toward Kobrin. According to gossip, the Germans had smashed through the front lines, and on the previous night the Russian Thirteenth Army had pulled back some twenty-five miles and was about to fall back another twenty-five miles. The town was in a state of chaos and terror.

We spent the whole next day preparing to depart. The physicians and the delegates ran over to headquarters a dozen times, questioning everyone: "Where are we going?" But no one could answer. The people at headquarters were no less agitated. Softly, with frightened faces, they announced shocking news to one another: Kiev and Zhitomir were being evacuated, and the population of Dvinsk was being expelled.

Since headquarters was retreating to Kobrin, our division decided to follow suit. At six P.M. our train took off, going via Brest-Litovsk. We advanced very slowly, letting by the trains carrying troops to that city. In Malarito we spent several hours in the station. Walking into that small, poor shtetl, which had some one hundred Jewish families, I tracked down Aaron Savtsits, a prominent member of the congregation. He told me that the town commandant was a brute, who had instituted corporal punishment against the civilians irrespective of age and sex. People received twenty-five lashes for the mildest offense. By the same token, he was very strict with his men and would brook no pogrom.

At the synagogue I chatted with a group of worshipers. Their cheeriness was quite typical. The large towns located several hundred miles from the front were panicking because they were sure the Germans would march in, but the small towns, including those nearest the front, were fairly certain "they won't get this far." And why not? "What's so special about our shtetl? What do they need it for?" And the notion of the German arrival was permeated with the same optimism here. For weeks now, this shtetl had been ringed all day by columns of smoke and all night by the glow of fires in the surrounding towns and villages. Yet these Jews were confident that everything would work out fine: "Even if the Russians go and the Germans come, life will go on in peace and quiet."

Homeless Jews kept passing through; they were poor and hungry, but the shtetl couldn't help—it was much too poor itself. I left one hundred rubles for the refugees.

We reached Brest-Litovsk on the third day, the morning of August 2. Our train halted several miles from the station, so I transferred to an automobile. In town I got hold of the local newspaper, and the first thing to catch my eye was an order issued by General Leming, the commander of the fortress city: "The entire civilian population of Brest-Litovsk must leave the city within the next three days, the third, the fourth, and the fifth of August. To facilitate the evacuation, the city will be divided into three sections, whereby one section will leave each day. Thirty trains will be provided, ten per day, to carry the evacuees."

I was, of course, shocked. I went on into the city, where the streets were packed with retreating baggage convoys and military personnel. I stopped an old Jew and asked him where I could find the Jewish relief committee. He gave me the last name (I've forgotten it) and the address of the chairman, who lived very far from the station. The only nearby drayman, a Jew, had refused to take me, claiming he was busy. But now, hearing me speak Yiddish and learning that I had to reach the committee, he volunteered to drive me.

The committee chairman, an old, venerable man with an intelligent face, was delighted that I had come at this critical moment, and he sent for several members: Dr. Shapiro, Mr. Mints, and two others.

They told me that no pogroms or even lootings had occurred during the past few days, thanks to General Leming, a thoroughly decent and kindhearted man. He never took a kopek in bribes; he fought against the lies about Jews and throttled even the slightest attempt to start a pogrom. Unfortunately, the second in command, Sokolov, was utterly corrupt. Two months ago, in order to squeeze money from the Jews, he had begun grabbing them for forced labor and sending them to dig trenches some five or ten miles away. When told that he was disrupting the overall functioning of the city because people were afraid to go out, he proposed that Jews hire Christians to work in their stead. However, he himself pocketed the cash. After lengthy debates, the Jews collected thirty thousand rubles to pay four hundred Christian laborers. But this was not enough for Sokolov, who continued nabbing Jews in the street. His men seized about one hundred Jews, kept them in the courtyard of the police station from seven P.M. till morning, and then sent them to work near the village of Straditsh, twelve miles from town. They were not allowed to spend the night there "because Jews have no residence permits for the villages." Now that General Leming had ordered the entire population to leave Brest-Litovsk, Sokolov was doing everything in his power to evacuate the Jews separately, before the Christians. But with strenuous efforts the Jewish leaders managed to prevent this.

After the committee told me all these things, we tackled the economic issues. So far, the economic condition of the Jews here had not been bad. The townsfolk had aided local paupers as well as thousands of homeless who had passed through or remained here. Moreover, they had sent donations to Petrograd's Jewish relief committee. But now, of course, the situation had changed radically. During the past few weeks, when people had been worried about the possible evacuation, all the richer Jews had departed. Those who had stayed on were ruined, so there was little chance of obtaining money from them. It was difficult just getting people to commit to the work of a relief committee. At this point, it was every man for himself.

Nevertheless, several people expressed willingness to forget about their own problems and volunteer. They formed a new committee. As for money, the previous committee had 2,500 rubles left of the 30,000 collected for hiring Christian proxies. The new members also pledged to gather another 1,000 rubles in these final days. I promised 1,800 rubles. They voted to use 5,300 rubles to buy eighteen tons of flour, bake bread for the poor, and distribute the rest of the cash among the needy, who would be registered the next day. The committee members would have to go to each and every train, supplying bread and money for the trip and making sure that at least one intelligent person was aboard to look after the evacuees, and so on.

The Zemstvo Alliance likewise promised to arrange help. I then went over to the Association of Towns. The delegate, Dinesman, reacted coldly to my request for organized help: "It's a fire—every man for himself!" He said he could let me have ten medical students to accompany the trains, adding that they were from the Warsaw committee of the Association of Towns. I already knew that the members were all Poles with an antisemitic attitude. Several days earlier, Dr. Malinowski, the committee delegate, had fired the only ten Jewish orderlies on the committee. Naturally, I turned down Dinesman's offer of Polish escorts.

I went into town. At first glance there was no hint of what was happening. The shops were open and seemed to be doing business as usual. The streets were thronged with pedestrians. The houses were bustling with everyday life, and smoke was curling from the chimneys. But looking closer, I noticed that "life" and "movement" were not very normal and already had a moribund tinge. The merchants were packing up their wares, and the larger stores were shutting down, one by one. Wagons filled with domestic items stood outside many houses, and some people were walling up the doors and windows of their cellars, where they were storing the articles and furnishings left behind. The faces of the passersby were gloomy, disheartened, and despairing.

The big and beautiful city, which, just yesterday, had been alive with all its senses, was now fatally wounded, as it were, and dying. Brest-Litovsk was like a huge, healthy animal whose veins have been opened, releasing a hot torrent of blood. Minute by minute the city grew paler, weaker, and soon it would lie there, cold and dead. The houses would be deserted and boarded up, the shops bare and closed, the streets mute and snuffed. For now the city was still living, but these were the death throes, the feverish convulsions of a dying creature. The city's tragic appearance was emphasized even more sharply by the planes, which were circling like black crows over a mortally injured man. The large birds of prey seemed to be waiting impatiently for the wounded giant to breathe his last so they could pounce on him and rip off pieces from his still-warm body.

And here was the channel through which the blood flowed from the murdered city, the major thoroughfare leading toward the highway to Kobrin and Pinsk. Baggage transports, artillery, and military divisions were retreating incessantly, and the gray iron stream was joined by more and more civilian vans, wagons, and pedestrians. These refugees, who distrusted the gratis trains, were primarily Jews.

The wagons were piled terribly high; they were towers of crates, bundles, tables, and dressers. Children and elderly women sat in the gaps. Other wagons had a couch attached in front, and on it four or five people were squeezed together with their backs to the horses. These bizarre vehicles reminded me of the ones used fifty or sixty years ago for carrying criminals through town; amid drumrolls, they were brought to the punishment site. On his chest each miscreant bore a sign announcing his crime: "Thief," "Murderer," and so forth. The faces of these condemned Jews were like those of criminals being taken to their execution. Each wagon was followed by the younger family members—it was virtually a funeral procession. And the single worn-out horse, with its protruding ribs, deployed its last ounce of strength to drag the precarious tower.

I was frightened by the sight of the crammed wagons joining the vast military pullout. I had seen such retreats, especially hasty ones: the width of the road filled with vans and drays, cars and wagons, slowly dragging along side by side in three, four, or even more lines. So long as the procession flows unhampered, movement is mechanical, each vehicle depending on all the others, which are virtually fused into a single entity. But if there is any impediment, if a horse tumbles, a wagon capsizes, then confusion takes over. One vehicle after another has to stop quickly, or else they clamber atop the preceding one like floes of ice in a debacle. There is yelling, turmoil. But it's even worse when the mechanical stream is followed by a new and faster torrent, when a swift auto carrying an important person tries to pass to the front or, even more dangerous, when an artillery division has to get ahead in order to protect the baggage vans against the arriving enemy. The results are catastrophic. Drays and wagons fly apart or squeeze and huddle together, and if they don't move fast enough, they are turbulently hurled aside, on top of each other, turned over, or knocked from the road. And if the road rises, they tumble and scatter, crippling both man and beast. It's easy to picture what happens to the high "Jewish towers," with women and children squashed into every nook and cranny, when they're whacked by a surge and shoved aside or into a ditch.

I went over to a few such wagons and talked with the men who were walking behind. For now, they were heading to Kobrin, almost twenty miles away. Beyond that—they'd see where others were going. Many realized the danger of joining the military torrent, and they figured they would strike off into side roads beyond the town. They had taken along bread, but no water, and when I reminded them, they went to fetch some.

I entered the large synagogue. It was forlorn and deserted. The distraught beadle was packing his belongings. What would happen to the synagogue, to the holy books? He had no idea. No one had thought about it; no one could speculate. I went to the committee and offered to take along the more than eighty Torah scrolls. The trustees joyfully agreed. With great effort I managed to find a carpenter willing to build ten crates by the next day.

I drove over to our train, which stood outside the city, on the track leading to Kobrin. I decided to stay in Brest-Litovsk for three days, spending the nights at Dr. Shapiro's home.

The next morning the newspapers ran an announcement by the town commandant: "Today, the third, there will be no free trains available. Tickets must be purchased. Instead, fifteen trains will be available both tomorrow and the day after tomorrow."

Apparently, the inhabitants had little faith in the trains and were resorting to any vehicles they could get hold of. The stream of wagons grew bigger, virtually forming a strand like a military baggage transport.

The town was eerie, almost frightening. Many homes were already empty and boarded up. The passersby were gloomy and despondent, sometimes tearful. The catastrophe was gruesome, but nowhere so harsh, brutal, and humiliating as the specifically Jewish expulsions. Tragic as the situation might be, both rich and poor, Jew and Gentile saw it as a disastrous misfortune of war, a harsh civic duty. No one felt that the authorities were booting out suspicious elements, traitors, like mangy dogs, with drooping heads. Jews were not being subjected to disgrace, to laughter and derision from the soldiers and the privileged inhabitants, who would then normally loot the property of the deportees. This calamity did not distinguish between Jews and Christians; it brought them together. People were looking for help universally, pouring out their bitter hearts to one another, packing their possessions, sharing wagons, huddling together like neighbors, like human beings. Dreadful as this adversity might be, Jews thought and said that it could have been far worse if it had been limited to them.

Planes had been flying overhead since dawn, hurling bombs. Heavy explosions boomed here and there. Whenever terrified pedestrians spotted an aircraft, they would leap into doorways, into houses—and for a moment the streets were deserted.

I went to the hospital, where the needy were being registered. The vast courtyard and the surrounding streets were filled with one thousand people, mostly cripples, professional paupers, crowding the door and the windows, pressing, shoving, yelling, asking to be registered faster. The cripples were flaunting their deformities, insisting on being registered first. Two committee members had been drudging since daybreak. By evening, they would be able to supply help.

Next I went to the railroad station. It was a nightmare. The huge structure was jammed ceiling-high with tens of thousands of crates and baskets, valises and bundles. The platform and a broad surrounding area were likewise chock-full. Lost and agitated, exhausted and quasi-insane, people were roaming about, scurrying from place to place, swooping down on the porters and employees, who likewise had no idea of what was happening. Screams and prayers, sobs and curses—everything was mixed up in an endless, thunderous uproar.

On a sidetrack far from the station, I found an evacuation train. But it required tickets. And it was swamped. Hundreds of people were jostling and shoving, trying to squeeze in. A few women came rushing over, asking me what they should do. They had been unable to buy tickets—could they board the train? I told them to do it. I questioned the passengers, gave some a few rubles, showed them how to arrange themselves in the heated cars. Noticing some turmoil at the end of the train, I went over. Five or six Christians had settled in the last two cars and were letting no one else aboard. Dozens of Jews were standing around, brandishing tickets, begging for mercy, weeping, pleading to be allowed into the nearly empty cars. I shouted my lungs out at the hooligans, and within half an hour both cars were packed.

At the station I was told that our division's train would be leaving Kobrin the next morning, taking wounded men to Pinsk and farther. To make sure I would catch my train in Kobrin, I had to leave Brest-Litovsk at night—to my great sorrow.

16

Kobrin is a small shtetl surrounded by many parks and sporting a monument to the first victory over the French, in 1812. And now Kobrin was the center of the retreating military and the evacuees and escapees. The streets were choked with soldiers and baggage transports. All squares, courtyards, vacant areas, riverbanks, and parks were occupied by the homeless, especially male and female peasants, who could be identified from afar by the loud colors of their clothing. These throngs were everywhere, cooking food and drying laundry over campfires or feeding cows and horses. These thousands of people looked like nomads wandering with their herds from place to place.

Despite the dense flow of troops and refugees, the local inhabitants were calm and confident. All the shops were open, and the people were engrossed in business. The fear of war had not yet reached them; they did not yet feel the danger that was approaching their town. No one thought of leaving, escaping; no one figured they might be ousted. How could they be? Just two days ago Kobrin had been quiet, silent—how could they be evacuated out of the blue?

The shtetl had a Jewish relief committee. Its chairman, the local government rabbi, told me it had been formed several months ago and was supported by whatever it got from the town. Practically all the young Jews had worked for the committee. Earlier, there had not been enough for them to do; but now that many of them had departed, and the workload had increased, the committee was terribly understaffed. During these past few days the influx of the homeless had greatly swollen. One thousand or more were arriving daily. Nevertheless, the committee was managing with its own funds, distributing bread and hot meals, for which it received only 120 rubles a day from the Zemstvo Alliance. However, there was a shortage of bread; none could be obtained for love or money. Furthermore, there was no place to lodge the newcomers. Each private home already had one or two families, the great synagogue and a few smaller ones were full, while troops were billeted in the rest. And more refugees were expected, thousands, perhaps tens of thousands, especially from Brest-Litovsk. Where could they be housed? Nor did the committee have the means to send them any farther. Every train was grabbed by Christians.

The rabbi accompanied me to the synagogue, a huge, ancient stone building. The large courtyard was lined with many smaller houses of study, brimming with homeless Jews. Virtually every square yard was occupied by an entire household. The sick and the healthy were thrown together pell-mell, and all were marked by the bitterest want, poverty, and desolation. I was instantly deafened by the clamor from all sides: children crying, adults yelling, cursing, sighing loudly—and through the cacophony I made out the plaintive crooning of psalms.

I was told that two days ago a homeless woman had given birth to a pair of boys and then succumbed to cholera. The husband had lost his mind and vanished. The twins were being looked after by the committee.

Our division stopped at the railroad station and promptly began loading wounded men in order to transport them to Pinsk. The division removed a total of 113 patients from the military hospital. Since four train cars remained empty, I asked Tulupov if I could fill them with homeless Jews, whom I would take to Pinsk. Having already visited the synagogue with the rabbi and seen the dense throng, he granted my request. I then informed the committee that I could take along one hundred people, but they and their belongings would have to be at the station within three or four hours. The members promised to take care of it.

A few hours later, however, one of them notified me that the police were not allowing the homeless into the station. They had managed to drive the wagons circuitously across parks, farmland, and ditches, toward where the train was standing by the other flank of a hill. But then night had set in; the wagons had heaved from side to side through the darkness, losing crates and bundles. The Gentile draymen had cursed and scolded and wanted to dump all the baggage in the middle of nowhere. The women and children had cried and screamed. And now I was informed that the wounded soldiers were aboard and the train had to leave. Upon reaching the hill, the homeless Jews dashed to the train and started climbing in. But then a new snag. When the homeless Christians in the nearby field saw refugees clambering onto the train, they all

began doing likewise. Nothing helped—no amount of coaxing or ordering. The Jews might have to stay in the field. With great effort, I talked
the Christians into sticking to one train car, leaving the other three for
the Jews.

Swiftly, calmly, quietly, the Christians loaded their belongings and got
in—sixty-four people in one railroad car. But things were different with
the Jews. Every family had a huge amount of luggage. And what luggage!
As much as ten feet long! A wig maker had four tall mirrors in one crate; a
tailor had two sewing machines; someone else had a bureau, a bed. People
dragged it all uphill, ten lugging one item. Shouting and hollering, expend-
ing their last drop of strength—but hard as they strained, they couldn't do
it; they didn't know how. They struggled nervously; they talked; the
women yelled out whole Yiddish prayers; they were all sickly and powerless. . . . And around them stood Gentiles, guffawing at these ghastly
scenes. Finally, I hired a few soldiers, and they transferred all the luggage.
The three Jewish cars were so clogged that only one hundred people could
jam in—but a lot more had shown up. I couldn't leave them in the fields
with their children and their belongings. So I went to the station master,
and, difficult as it was, I wangled two more cars out of him. The rest of the
homeless Jews scrambled in—and at one A.M. off we chugged.

Watching these refugees board the train, Tulupov and Ivanov felt so
sorry for them that they made me a promise: once the train was back,
they would turn it over—all twenty-odd cars—to homeless Jews: "Now
the battles are going to be fought in and around Brest-Litovsk, and the
wounded will remain there. In any case, we'll be cut off. For a while,
we'll have no one to transport, so you'll be able to use the train for your
homeless."

At eight the next morning, August 5, we arrived in Pinsk. I went to
see M. Khayfets, chairman of the Jewish relief committee and head of the
section of the Ozov Bank. From his very first words I gathered that the
mood in Pinsk was not affected by the war. The town was still and calm;
there was no movement, no military presence. The Jewish leaders had
gone off to their summer homes. The previous evening, there had been a
cheerful amateur show with a patriotic, charitable goal, and Khayfets
had been there till late at night. In short: ordinary provincial life. The
Jewish relief committee was almost inoperative. No homeless were

allowed into the town, nor had the municipal administration originally permitted the Jews to establish a food center at the depot for the refugees passing through. By now, permission had been granted, but no food center had materialized.

When Mr. Khayfets convened the committee, I suggested leaving the homeless Jews in Pinsk. The members, though willing, were uncertain whether they would be allowed to take them into the city. When I got back to the station, I learned that the wounded were not being unloaded. They, together with us, were being sent on to Homel. I talked to the homeless Jews, and they agreed to go there.

I've already mentioned that in Brest-Litovsk I had ordered ten crates for the synagogue's Torah scrolls. However, the carpenter built only two crates, and so I packed sixteen scrolls in them. I shipped one crate off to Kobrin and took the other along to Pinsk, where I left it with the synagogue trustees.

Unbeknownst to me, several dozen homeless Christians entered our railroad cars during the few hours we spent in Pinsk. Nor did we realize that at some station or other, three cars containing expelled German colonists had been coupled to our train. I had brought bread and sugar along from Kobrin, and I now distributed them equally among Jews and Gentiles. For the children I had white bread, and I also purchased milk for them at various stations.

Among the Jewish refugees from Brest-Litovsk there were several dozen Jewish families from Vlodava, from Poland. Throughout the trek, the Brest-Litovsk Jews argued with the Polish Jews, especially the women, who kept cursing one another. I reproached them, saying that whether they were from Poland or from Lithuania, they were all Jews, and neither ancestry was superior to the other. Both sides ardently agreed—and within an hour they were fighting again.

In one car, there were two sick females: a terribly emaciated girl, who was unable to eat and just lay there, moaning; and an adult, who kept having convulsions and shrieking hysterically. At every stop, the other women asked me to remove the convulsive one because she was frightening the kids. But where could I put her?

At our first stop after leaving Pinsk, I was told that one of the homeless, Lando, an elderly Jew from Vlodava, had suddenly collapsed and blacked out. I went over. He looked seventy but was only forty-eight. A shopkeeper, he had been robbed of his entire fortune, one hundred rubles, at the synagogue in Kobrin. This had shattered him. Today, while eating bread and jam, he had suddenly lost consciousness. When I reached him, he was lying motionless on the floor, with closed eyes. His lips were trembling feebly, spitting out seeds that had remained in his mouth. Dr. Shapiro, the female physician on our train, was less interested in medicine than in finding out how to convert to Christianity as soon as possible so she could marry a wounded pilot, whom we were taking along. She felt the old man's pulse and said he was dozing, so we should let him rest. That night, he died without coming to.

In the morning I found his body on the floor of the car. He was surrounded by his wife and four children, all of them weeping softly. The rest of the passengers in that car were likewise crying. A day earlier, as I recalled, I had been pestered to move the sick woman, who had been getting on her neighbors' nerves. So now I decided to have everyone in the dead man's car transferred to other cars. But to my surprise, no one wanted to leave. "We rode with him while he was alive, and we're not going to desert him in death."

In Homel, the authorities refused to accept the wounded and told us to travel on to Rohotshov, where a lot of military hospitals were concentrated. But I decided to leave the homeless in Homel.

The local Jewish relief committee proved to be very active. Not only had it organized help for the three thousand homeless Jews in town; it also fed the tens of thousands who were passing through. As in other places, the authorities had originally clamped down on providing food for these Jewish transients. But now they permitted it, and committee representatives were on hand at the station to greet every trainload of refugees.

They swiftly got the Jews and Christians out of our cars and notified the Jewish burial society to pick up the corpse.

Before we could even finish, the town commandant notified us that a regulation banned the admittance of homeless people here. Our passengers would have to be sent farther on: Christians to the province of Tshernigov and Jews to the province of Penz. The Christians—Ukrainians and German colonists—took the news calmly. If Tshernigov was their destination, then so be it. I turned them over to the commandant. The Jews, however, were in the throes of despair. They had counted on staying in Homel or its environs, which were closer to home, in case they were allowed to head back soon. They were also terrified by the prospect of going to a totally unfamiliar region where there were no Jews and where they might not find any suitable work. I pleaded with the commander to let them remain in Homel, but he wouldn't hear of it. Meanwhile a committee member informed us that a train of homeless Jews would be going to the province of Taver that evening and it might be able to take along my refugees. The passengers clustered around me, asking for advice. The train for Taver would be starting in a few hours, but if they chose Penz, they could spend a couple of days resting in the station. I advised them to choose Taver. They could find jobs there more easily, and the area was Jewish. The latter argument tipped the scales. Come what may, they wanted to be among Jews! And they all agreed. "We'll obey you like a father," they tearfully said. "We're going to Taver!"

All told, we had 128 homeless, including 53 children. The sick women were soon brought to the Jewish hospital. Their families and Lando's widow and fatherless children—a total of 21 people—got out in Homel. The remaining 107 went on to the province of Taver.

Our train with our wounded soldiers lumbered off. At that instant, we heard heartrending shrieks from one of the cars. Jumping out, I saw that the dead man was still inside. He was lying on the floor with a candle at his head. His widow and children stood around him, yelling bitterly. We stopped the train. The Jewish burial society hurried over and carried away the body. The weeping and shouting Jews, the terrified members of the burial society, who were dashing along with the corpse— the soldiers and the Gentiles lingering on the platform found it all strange and funny. A few wanted to roar with laughter. But they restrained themselves; the mystique of death won out.

We reached Rohotshov late at night and left the wounded there. Our train was sent back via a detour through Minsk, Baranovitsh, and Zhabenko. In Minsk I found the same calm mood as in Pinsk. I went looking for one committee member after another, but it was no use. They were all in their summer homes. Unlike Pinsk, however, Minsk had thousands of homeless.

When I returned to the station, Ivanov, the deputy, who had just gotten back from headquarters, told me that the general staff was moving from Rovno to Mohilev, that they were expecting the czar to pass through, and that the headquarters of the Thirteenth Army was shifting from Kobrin to Vilna. During these transfers, no other movement was permitted on this line, and so our train would be delayed for several days, perhaps a week.

Ivanov was boiling. "Those people at headquarters! They didn't so much as glance at my papers; they didn't even ask who I was—and they promptly blurted out all that top-secret information! It's maddening!"

And yet Ivanov himself was blabbing out all this top-secret information in front of the entire personnel of our division.

That night I was sitting with a soldier—one of our orderlies. He was describing his very interesting experiences in the Russo-Japanese War. His words were quite poignant. "I was on sentry duty. The weather was glacial. I was frozen to the ground. In a while it would have been over for me! But then someone came, thank God, and I was broken loose."

In Minsk we were likewise "frozen to the ground." But on the third day, our train was "broken loose."

I was unable to obtain any bread here for the Kobrin refugees. The town commandant advised me to telegraph the commissary bakery in Baranovitsh. I asked for 7,200 pounds of rye bread and 900 pounds of wheat bread.

In Minsk I was told what had happened in Brest-Litovsk. Instead of the thirty evacuation trains that had been promised, only three had been provided—and on the last day to boot.

As for my bread, I was sent only 3,600 pounds of rye bread and 540 pounds of wheat bread—all of it poorly baked.

17

At ten A.M., while approaching Zhabenko, our train was suddenly shaken by a loud boom. It was instantly followed by a second and far more thunderous explosion. Our car lurched sideways, then forward, and ground to a halt. The small window was shattered; there was a hole in the wall. Before we could even collect ourselves, someone hollered, "Fire!" Across from us, on the other track, a gasoline tank was enveloped in red flames. Our train hastily pitched forward, chugged several dozen yards, and then halted by the station.

We quickly jumped out. Someone instantly popped up, claiming, "I saw it with my own eyes!" He said a soldier had carried something and thrown it, and it had blown up. Actually, however, the explosion was caused by two grenades tossed from German planes.

Two gasoline tanks were burning, and they threatened to ignite the other seven on the same train. In addition, four nearby boxcars containing shells and explosives might catch fire any moment. The railroad employees scurried to and fro, looking for a locomotive to haul away the fuel tanks and the endangered boxcars with their precarious freight. By the time they found a locomotive, some fifty people had rushed over to the burning tanks, arduously unhooked five of them, and shoved them away. An arriving locomotive pulled off the cars containing explosives.

The first German grenade had hit a passenger car filled with railroad employees. Several dead or injured people were removed from the wrecked and burning car. An elderly man was dragged past me. His arms were tattered, and blood was pouring from the back of his neck. He was desperately shouting: "I beg you! Save my jacket—it's inside the car. It's got my pay, which I just received—175 rubles."

By now the raging blaze had engulfed all four tanks. An incredible panorama! Huge billows of tinder-red fire tumbling thick and solid, churning out equally huge, fiery billows strewn with black dots and streaks—and more black billows over them, making the flames look like crimson splotches against an ebony background. Dozens of thick billows came rolling out of one another, becoming all black and fat and turning into columns of smoke that zoomed high, bending, spreading, and drifting for miles around like a black cloth.

Suddenly, a new boom, stronger than the earlier ones. Nobody knew where it came from. When the panic subsided, we saw what had happened. Because of the gases, the first tank, where the fuel had burned up, had flown off the platform and landed one hundred yards away. Two people were killed. I went over to the tank. Two corpses were lying nearby. One was an elderly man—almost naked because his clothes had burned off. He lay facedown in a pool of blood. Singed intestines were spilling from a broad, gaping injury in his side. One leg and one hand had been severed as if with a knife and flung nearby. A bit farther away lay a boy with half his head ripped off. I noticed that the old man's hair seemed gray and kinky. Taking a closer look, I realized that his hair had been burned in a split second, and the ashes had twisted into curls.

At around three P.M., we started out for Kobrin, but then stopped after three miles. We learned that several dozen trains were lumbering ahead of us, inching slowly toward that town. It took us five or six hours to cover each mile—and a whole day and night for twelve miles. Kobrin was still three and a half miles away. So I set out on foot. The entire road ran past what looked like a migrants' camp. Thousands of troops as well as male and female peasants were sitting on either side of the road, cooking supper. In an area one third of a mile wide, where the rails descended into a trough, there were wrecked, charred, shattered train cars, and whole piles of telegrams and official documents were scattered about. Two days earlier, a mail train had collided with an army medical train, killing thirty-five people and injuring many more.

At the Kobrin station, I met Tulupov. He told me that Panovka, the government rabbi, had visited him, and the two of them had gone to the committee of the Association of Towns and requested aid for the homeless Jews. Tulupov had also gone to the synagogue with the rabbi and had been deeply shocked by what he had witnessed there. Thousands of refugees were squeezed into the building and the courtyard. Many had cholera, and the sick and the dead were lying together with the healthy. A living hell.

Since Tulupov also told me that for now no wounded men were coming from the front, I asked him to lend me his train so I could transport a group of the homeless.

"You know very well," he replied, "that I always go along with your suggestions, and I don't foresee any obstacles. But you will, of course, take along not just Jews but also Christians, like last time?"

"That goes without saying," I said. "But bear in mind that the expenses are paid with the money from the Jewish relief committee, which I can spend only for homeless Jews. If I also take along Gentiles, you'll have to try and get funding from some institution to cover these expenses."

"Ohh! Why do you discriminate between Jews and Christians?" Tulupov exclaimed sorrowfully.

"I don't discriminate; others do. Dozens of trains carry refugees daily, and there's not a single Jew among them. Jews aren't allowed on board. The local commandant won't let any Jew near the station."

"That's all true! But that's what *they* do, and we feel it's wrong, inhumane. Why do you want to imitate them? Jews, Christians—they're all the same homeless and unfortunate human beings."

"The issue here isn't the homeless themselves, whom I too find equally unfortunate," I said. "It's a question of who should be helped by which relief committees. I haven't seen any Russian relief committee—and they exist—helping any Jews. And besides, even if I agreed with you, I would need permission from the Jewish relief committee to spend its money on Christian refugees."

The state rabbi was supposed to meet Tulupov at the station, but since he didn't show up, I went over to his place. A tremendous movement filled the streets. It was the normal picture of a hasty military pullout.

Together with the rabbi, we went to the synagogue. It was a nightmare. There were several dozen Holy Arks containing Torah scrolls from all the large and small synagogues in town, and there were dozens and dozens of crates, packs, bundles, parcels. And among them all, standing or stretched out on the floor, there were hundreds of people, old and young, crammed together, shoving and yelling, with children weeping. The building was filled with pungent odors and was terribly unclean. I was instantly dazed, and sickened by the stench.

In a corner of the eastern wall, a girl of about ten was lying on the floor. Her little face was all blue. Next to her stood an elderly woman, crying.

"What's wrong with her?" I asked.

"Her tummy," the mother tearfully replied. "Could we get a doctor maybe?"

"Cholera," the rabbi whispered to me, and he pointed to a whole row of stricken people lying near the girl. On some the covers were drawn over their heads. They were dead. Nearby lay a child, its face red with fever: measles.

"Isn't there any place we could move the sick people to?" I asked the rabbi.

"No," he answered. "The hospital is occupied by the army. There's no place that will take private patients—especially if they've got cholera."

"Couldn't they be transferred to a study house?"

"The study houses and the small synagogues were occupied by the military. They've been liberated, but now they're filled with the families of Jewish cobblers and leather workers, who are employed in the commissary workshops."

Upon learning that I was from the relief committee, dozens of people thronged around me, each person with his plea.

"A number of the homeless should be settled in the town," I told the rabbi. "Can't we dig up a few apartments?"

"There are apartments," a homeless man said. "But we can't go outdoors."

"Why not?"

"They beat Jews up; they kill them! The army's drafting the kids who are supposed to report in 1917. The recruits roam the streets, getting drunk and thrashing any Jews they find. They even beat up the Jewish recruits. People complained to the military commander, and he issued an order prohibiting the beatings. But it hasn't helped."

The large synagogue courtyard presented the same tableau as the interior. There were several thousand people here. Some were cooking over small fires. It was truly a nomadic camp.

Everyone knew I was supposed to bring bread, and people kept pressing me: "Where's the bread?" No bread or flour was to be had in town. With great effort, the authorities managed to obtain one thousand pounds of bread on the previous day. But how far would that go for three thousand people? It came to one third of a pound per person.

Several Jewish war veterans came over to me. "This is the second day we've been arguing to build some kind of barrack for the sick here in the courtyard, to keep them apart from the healthy. We've got a couple of boards, and there must be a few carpenters among us. We could pull it off in two days."

"Well, then, what's holding it up?"

"We need money. For material and labor. At least a few hundred rubles."

I told them to get to work right away, and I promised to pay for anything they required. In my presence, they organized a group of workers and agreed to start immediately.

I had already been told that one of the homeless was a young rabbi whose pregnant wife had contracted cholera. After giving birth to two little boys, she had succumbed. The bewildered father had disappeared several days ago. The twins were now under the supervision of the homeless, and they needed a wet nurse.

My cash was almost gone, and I was faced with many expenses. I wired the Petrograd and Kiev committees to send me three thousand rubles each in Pinsk. I then had to go to Pinsk, get the money, find a wet nurse for the twins and a doctor for the homeless, then return and get as many of them as possible into a train. Since my bread transport was still some two and a half miles from the station, I asked Rabbi Panovka to have the young committee members transfer the bread to the synagogue once the train arrived in town.

At the depot I was told that the shtetl of Drohitshi had several thousand homeless in a terrible plight. I decided to go there from Pinsk. The train I took was carrying artillery, and the only passenger car was mobbed.

All along the way, a young, agitated ensign talked about the chaos in the army. He openly made revolutionary statements and menacingly argued: "Don't worry! Their turn will come! The Siberian soldiers say, 'We won't go home till we get our demands!' The Siberians will show them!"

In Pinsk, the atmosphere was very tense. Many public buildings were being evacuated. People were fairly certain that the Germans were about to march in. On my first day there, I heard rumors that Leming, the commandant of Brest-Litovsk, had been unmasked as a German spy and hanged, and that the fortress city was being hastily evacuated and abandoned without a fight. Nobody wanted to believe these rumors, but they had a terrible effect.

There were lots of refugees in Pinsk. The Jewish committee was organizing help for them, for which purpose it received 120 rubles a day from the Association of Towns.

Several days earlier, the local transport commandant had summoned the Jewish representatives and repeated all the wild slander about Jews: they were spies, they shipped coffins containing gold instead of corpses, and so on. Jews, he added, were agitating among the peasants, telling them to withdraw their bank savings. The commandant threatened to put up warnings everywhere describing these crimes. The representatives knew what he wanted, but couldn't even decide whether to grease his palm, much less on the sum.

The funds I had wired for still hadn't come, but Mr. Khayfets lent me several thousand rubles on account. I met a female doctor who was working at the Association of Towns, and she agreed to go to Kobrin, as did a Jewish nurse. They promised to go the next day and bring along a wet nurse for the twins. I wanted to leave the same day, so I went to the station and boarded a medical train for Kobrin. Several hours dragged by, but the train didn't budge. Meanwhile the doctor showed up and told me that the train would not be going to Kobrin—in fact, no more trains would be going there. The authorities had issued an order to that effect.

Upon getting out of the train, I ran into a physician I knew from the Twenty-fifth Evacuation Hospital. I questioned him about the order.

"Why must you go to Kobrin?" he asked me. "Your train left Kobrin. It passed through here several hours ago with your entire division; they were heading toward Luninets."

"What are you talking about? You're sure you're not mistaken?"

"You don't think I know the engineering division train?"

I went to the station master, and he confirmed that the engineering train had just left the Porokhonsk station.

I took the next train to Luninets—I was hoping to catch up with my train. There were several homeless Jews in my car. One family was from Veliko Litovsk, a large shtetl with five hundred Jews. Cossacks had ransacked the entire town, driven all the people out of their homes, poured kerosene over the houses, and set them on fire. The whole shtetl had burned down.

18

In Porokhonsk, I found our train. It turned out that while approaching Kobrin, it had not even been permitted into the station. So it had promptly come here instead. Despite all the pleas and protests of the deputies, the train hadn't been permitted to take any homeless or wounded aboard. They couldn't even unload the bread I had brought. The answer was the same every time: "We've got orders to prohibit any train from entering Kobrin and to send them all back to Porokhonsk." Here in Porokhonsk the train had been shunted to a sidetrack, and nobody knew how long it would remain there; maybe a few days, maybe a few weeks.

The reason was clear. The line was monopolized by retreating trains. All day long, another would charge through every ten minutes—especially trains with battering cannon. There was no doubt that the army was hastily evacuating Brest-Litovsk. According to the passengers, the enemy had broken through in Malarito, Zhabenko had burned down, and airplanes had dropped countless bombs on Brest-Litovsk, killing over thirty troops and setting the whole town ablaze.

I was beside myself. Not only had I lost the possibility of transporting some of the homeless from Kobrin, but I had failed to give them the bread I had brought for them. It had been in its car for five days now and was starting to turn moldy.

I went to the station master and promised him a nice gift if he coupled the bread car to any train bound for Kobrin. He promised to do it. But on the first day, not a single train was heading there. The next day, medical train no. 2240 arrived; destination: Kobrin. It took a lot of effort, but I managed to talk the senior physician into letting me load the bread into one of the cars and accompany it to Kobrin.

We arrived in the morning. The station was feverish with movement. The platforms were clogged with thousands of crates and bundles. People were evacuating everything they could. Near the depot, several dozen trains filled with refugees and the equipment from local institutions as well as merchandise were waiting to be dispatched. Homeless peasants were camped for several miles around the station. The nearby military hospitals were overflowing with wounded men, and an endless line of wagons kept bringing more and more from the front. A loud cannonade resounded from the direction of Brest-Litovsk.

The medical train I had ridden on immediately began loading these wounded. Since this task would take many hours, I had time to visit the town, see what was happening there, and find wagons to transport the bread.

The movement of the retreating army was extraordinary. Baggage vehicles were slogging along three or four abreast. It was impossible to squeeze through. With great effort I succeeded in finding a small van. But it had to halt at every corner to let the baggage wagons pass. At one crossing, my drayman, a Jew, was struck sharply across the back by an officer's stick.

"Listen," he said to me in Yiddish. "I know I'm going to have a lot of trouble. They're going to confiscate my horses; my home may burn down because they're going to torch the town before leaving. And God knows what will happen to my wife and kids. But still, it's a holiday for me when these Russian soldiers get their comeuppance. An eye for an eye! They're drenched in our blood. Why did that butcher have to whip me? Why?"

I went to the synagogue. Things were the same as three days ago, except that the sick had been carried to a small prayer room in the courtyard. No one had even started building the barrack. I asked the young committee members to send wagons for the bread. I also learned that the doctor, the nurse, and the wet nurse who were supposed to come here from Pinsk had not arrived.

"We don't need the wet nurse anymore," one woman told me. "One of the twins has already died, and the other is going the same way."

And she took me to see him.

The baby lay in a trough, a skeleton covered with a thin membrane of flesh. His tiny arms and legs were like scrawny twigs, his delicate features had a bluish pallor, and his two black eyes seemed to fill out his whole little face. I will never forget that gaze. The eyes were deeply aware and dreadfully sad, like the look of an old man who has seen everything and forgiven everything. Those sad eyes stared at me and pierced my soul, not with a child's sorrow but with a quiet thoughtfulness. The boy's tiny mouth was round, without lips, the size of a small coin.

The baby was dying. For two days now he had taken no food and was fading silently and painlessly like a tiny candle at the Holy Ark. My heart filled with tears at the sight of that tiny victim of the war. I felt as if my own child were dying.

"What can we do? How can we save him?"

The woman standing next to me shook her head sadly. "Save him? Let the poor thing die in peace."

Perhaps if I had promptly found a woman who could nurse him, he might have survived. But in all that chaos I had no solution, and so I walked away with a grieving heart.

I had assumed that the refugees would be surprised and depressed by the news that the train had already gone and that it was impossible to evacuate any of them. Not at all. Very few wanted to leave. They were certain that the Germans would be here within a day or two and that they would then be able to return to their homes in Brest-Litovsk and other towns. The young committee members told me that prior to departing, Rabbi Panovka had called on the Third Army's commandant, who had been in Kobrin with his headquarters. The commandant had cordially promised not to torch the town during the withdrawal. He had also made sure the rearguard unit was comprised not of Cossacks but of regular soldiers, who would march quietly. He had put up posters throughout the town: Anyone caught stealing or looting would be court-martialed. This calmed the refugees.

The committee went off to find wagons for the bread. I headed for the station. Since the bread car had to take in wounded men, I unloaded the bread while waiting for the vehicles, and it spent several tragic hours on the open platform. The retreating soldiers and the hundreds of lightly wounded men trudging through the depot were drawn to the mountain of loaves like moths to a flame. Every minute, I was approached by an emaciated, often bandaged soldier, who begged me pitifully, even tearfully: "Sir, please have mercy, give me a piece of bread. I haven't eaten for two days; I've got no strength left!"

How could I refuse? I handed out bread. At first large chunks, then smaller and smaller ones. Finally, I began saying no, explaining that the bread wasn't mine, and I had no right to give it away. But I was surrounded by dozens of starving, fainting men with outstretched hands and hungry eyes, and they kept pleading in trembling voices. And so during those hours I reluctantly distributed 100 to 150 pounds of bread. And if the loaves had been stacked there for a few more hours or my heart had been softer, not a crumb would have remained.

At last the wagons arrived. It took us some four hours to struggle through the baggage vehicles and reach the synagogue. The bread on the wagons was well covered so that no one would see it; but some people did snatch a few loaves even though I yelled and waved my sword.

The bread was poorly baked. Plus after five days it was starting to turn moldy. But when I delivered it in the synagogue courtyard and the homeless saw it, their joy was indescribable. We began doling out the bread immediately, but it was difficult holding back these famished people. They lunged at the scales; they yanked it out of our hands; they gathered the crumbs on the ground. Most tragic of all was the distribution of the white bread to the children, the old, and the sick.

"Are they that hungry?" I cried out to the committee members.

"Indeed they are. But mainly you can't get bread or flour now for any amount of money. These three thousand people will have to live on your bread until the Germans arrive. That's why they're so desperate for it."

Earlier, while leaving the station, I had run into Rabbi Panovka, who was already in a railroad car with his family. He told me he had had 308 rubles left for the homeless and had handed the money to the local committee. I added another 800 rubles, gave the members some instructions, exchanged warm good-byes with the refugees, and went to the depot, planning to catch up with my division in Porokhonsk.

At the station, I quite unexpectedly ran into Dr. Tsukerman from our mobile medical unit. It turned out that the mobile hospital, led by Dr.

Rozentsveyg, had been in Malarito and had just escaped from there. Now the hospital was here and had joined the main hospital, and they would remain as long as possible. There was more than enough work here, said the physician. Wounded men were pouring in from all sides.

Rumor had it, he continued, that the Russian army had left Brest-Litovsk because the Japanese had sharply criticized the fortress for its ancient cannon.

Tsukerman also promised to stay in contact with the relief committee and help protect the refugees if necessary. I gave him four hundred rubles in case he needed to aid the homeless locally or wherever he went.

All the public buildings were evacuated by now. At the depot two trains were left: the commandant's and the one carrying explosives. There was also the medical train, which had taken in roughly six hundred wounded and was about to chug off. I boarded my train. Before it could start, several planes flew overhead, dropping bombs on the refugees in the fields and around the station. Some thirty men, women, and children were killed or injured.

One of my fellow passengers was a member of the Kobrin judiciary. He told me that the order to evacuate all public buildings had been issued on January 6 by the governor of Grodno Province but had not reached Kobrin until six days later.

"This morning, they appointed a committee to requisition all the cattle. I was a member. But within several hours they ordered us all to leave town on the double."

When I brought up Brest-Litovsk, he said: "There were rumors that Leming, the town commandant, had turned out to be a spy. I heard he'd been arrested and even shot. But I spotted him this morning; he was motoring through Kobrin."

When our train had advanced some five or six miles, I looked through the window and saw our engineering train heading toward Kobrin with the entire division. I had no reason to go back; I decided to stay in Pinsk until the train returned.

In Pinsk, the tension was growing by the hour. The town was panicking; normal life had ground to a halt. The banks had stopped operating; they were not paying out any money. All coins had suddenly vanished. The rich were struggling to leave, but there were no trains. And this was eighty or ninety miles from the fighting! The reason for the panic was that during the evacuation from Brest-Litovsk all the routes had been choked, blocking all movement. The panic was intensified by the news that the Germans had broken through in Malarito, hemming the Russians in on two sides.

There were over three thousand refugees here, from Brest-Litovsk and other places. The authorities had promised to evacuate them, but no railroad cars were available, and the homeless were famished and stranded out in the open. The relief committee did not have the wherewithal to help them. Its appeals to Moscow and Petrograd had gone unanswered.

I spent the entire day at the station, waiting for the train from Kobrin. We heard that airplanes had bombed out the depot there.

19

The division train arrived in Pinsk around eight P.M. It was packed: some six hundred wounded men, dozens of them injured by bombs; women and children; over sixty people stricken with cholera; and twenty-odd refugees. The cholera patients were in a dreadful state. A few were crawling around in the flatcar, vomiting and dying there. During the eight or ten hours since the train had left Kobrin, six people had died.

Around midnight we took off for Homel. The train was very slow. It spent five or six hours at the stations and in the countryside. The next day, we paused in a dense forest for several hours. On board were two corpses that had to be buried. A grave for both of them was dug along the way. Soldiers chopped down a couple of saplings for a cross. We had a priest and also a few singers among the wounded. And so a funeral took place with all due rites. The dead men were soldiers. One had succumbed to his wounds. His face was black with gangrene. The other man, a cholera victim, had a blue face with white foam on his mouth. They were laid to rest side by side, in their overcoats. The priest celebrated them, sang "Remembrance Everlasting," and promised forgiveness for their sins, "both spiteful and involuntary ones." The grave was surrounded by tall swaying pines, and a dismal chanting came from the cars. The grave was filled in, the big, white cross erected. The soldiers were supposed to inscribe the men's names, but the wounded soldier had neglected to leave his name. A pencil was used to write the other soldier's name on the cross and to add "and an unknown soldier." Their friends wanted to include some kind thoughts about their comrades in the forest, even though the first rain would wash everything off. Recalling a poem of Nekrasov's, they wrote out an excerpt:

> *Go and die for the honor of our fatherland,*
> *For your conviction, for your love.*
> *Go and give your life without complaint,*
> *You shall not die in vain, for a thing is everlasting*
> *If blood flows underneath.*

They read the inscription aloud several times, sang "Remembrance Everlasting" once again, and then the train moved on.

Many refugees were plodding alongside the tracks; some were Jews, and I took several aboard. They turned out to be cobblers, who were considered government employees because they worked in the commissary. Their families and their belongings had been evacuated to Vitebsk. Now they too had been sent there. Their train had been stuck in the countryside for several days now, and they had no bread. They hadn't eaten in three days. To avoid starvation, they were hiking toward any depot. I gave them food and let them sit on the train steps. In the evening, I took seven more Jews aboard, and they managed to squeeze in between the cars. Then some Christian refugees came along and drove away the Jews, but I brought them back. An hour later, a squad of soldiers routed them. To make a long story short: the Jews were driven off four times, so I finally had to let them into the car.

Our train waited in Luninets all night while doctors and nurses bandaged the wounded. What dreadful injuries, especially the ones caused by bombs. They treated an eight-year-old, a Galician peasant boy. One foot had been totally blown off; the other was so badly hit that it would have to be amputated. While they were bandaging his open wounds, the pain was so intense that he nearly passed out. I handed him a small box of chocolates. It affected him so deeply that he forgot his agony, and while they were digging around in his injuries and broken bones, he wolfed down one bonbon after another, his eyes sparkling—with pain or delight? When they finished and carried him out of the bandaging car, he suddenly cried out in despair, "My candy!" He had forgotten the box.

The next morning we spent hours at the Klimovitsh station. Jewish boys, with the ribbon of the Zemstvo Alliance on their arms, were going about, working as medical orderlies. This was the first depot where I found Jewish orderlies. I learned that the local Jewish, Russian, and Polish relief committees had joined forces. Over one thousand homeless were coming through here daily, and they were given food and aid.

The Jewish orderlies told me about the Jewish situation. In the nearby town of Mazir there were lots of refugees—and more were expected.

"You know," one boy frantically broke in, "the head of the Lid yeshiva, Rabbi Reynus, has died, and the entire school is being transferred here!"

We remained in the countryside all night. The doctors used the time to perform operations in a special surgery car, with a sheet over its wide door. The medics carried wounded men over from the other cars and then carried them back after the operations. While waiting, they lay amid torches on the grass near the tracks, swapping tales. I sat with them.

Many of the wounded had gangrene. One man, whose gangrene had spread from his arm to his chest, was suffering terribly. To calm him down and make him believe he would be saved, the physician decided to amputate the gangrenous arm. He was brought to the surgery car, where it took the staff a while to chloroform him. Suddenly, they heard him blithely singing an off-color military ditty under the chloroform. The orderlies lying on the grass burst out laughing. One of them exclaimed: "He must be having fun under the knife!"

"He probably thinks he's about to attack the enemy," somebody added.

"If he thought so, he wouldn't be singing like that. An attack isn't all that much fun."

"Why not?" said a brash orderly with a naive face and kind eyes. "It's a lot of fun. We were involved in a skirmish with Germans. We started lunging, and I stuck my bayonet right into a German's heart. He gave me this astonished look. Then he meowed like a cat, meeooow! And then he keeled over. As our boys ran past him, they each stabbed him with a bayonet, and he flipped over each time." The narrator burst into good-natured laughter.

At the door of the surgery car, one edge of the sheet was lifted up, and someone held out an object wrapped in white, bloodstained linen. An orderly took it and unwrapped it. We saw an amputated arm. It had a large gaping wound and was as black as coal. It gave out a terrible stench.

"We have to bury it," said the young orderly who had told us about bayoneting a German.

He dug a deep hole, made the sign of the cross three times over the arm, placed it in the hole, filled in the hole, and, using the shovel, drew a cross on top. All the orderlies doffed their caps and earnestly crossed themselves.

In Retshitse, our cholera patients and a few badly wounded soldiers were taken away. As for the rest, we had to carry them farther.

On the fifth day of our trip, we reached Homel. Several posters in the depot warned that "nefarious persons are spreading rumors that Jews are hoarding coins and are therefore responsible for their disappearance. An investigation has shown that Jews are not the culprits, and that this disappearance is caused by other factors." The reasons were listed, and the announcement was signed by the commander.

I couldn't believe my eyes. A proclamation defending Jews—it was completely unexpected! I asked several acquaintances in Homel, and they told me that the commandant was a tolerant man but would never have dreamed of issuing such a statement on his own. The local Jews had gone to great lengths and apparently buttered him up with a present. But then, supposedly, he had been severely rebuked for this action and was being transferred.

I was no less surprised reading newspapers after not having seen any for some two weeks. What was happening in Petrograd and Moscow? Clearly, a thorough upheaval. *Novoye Vremya* had revolutionary articles. The writers were calling openly for a committee to save the society, a coalition cabinet, the appointment of Lvov as prime minister. They sharply attacked the government. A revolution had also taken place in the attitude toward Jews. Refugees were now allowed to settle outside the Pale, and its abolition seemed practically inevitable.

In Homel, the authorities refused to take our wounded. All the barracks and hospitals were overloaded. Our train was sent on to Oriol. But having no reason to go there, I, together with Tulupov, boarded the passenger train for Kiev. I found everyone there very nervous, certain the Germans would arrive within weeks. It was rumored that the authorities had decided to evacuate the city. Anybody who could was leaving.

Kiev too had an acute shortage of coins. Hundreds of people were lined up at the bank, trying to exchange paper money. The bank was changing only one ruble per adult.

There was a tremendous amount of vital news. Ruzsky had been appointed commander in chief of the northwestern front. That terrible Yanushkevitsh had been removed as staff administrator and was being transferred to the Caucasus. According to rumors, even Grand Prince Nikolay Nikolayevitsh was being relieved of duty as supreme commander in chief and replaced by the czar himself. This news, spoken softly, was received with smirks and amazement.

The mood in Kiev was also revolutionary. A meeting of the Association of Towns was shut down because of "revolutionary statements." Tulupov told me that all institutions had received top-secret orders to check whether they had any members of the various underground organizations, considered defeatist. If identified, these people were to be taken directly to the constabulary.

Tulupov shrugged. "Such arrogance." He was agitated. "Ordering social organizations to take on the job of spying and policing. And what kind of fantasy are these defeatist groups? Who are they? The authorities have made them up to distract attention from their own crimes. If they want to find real defeatists, they ought to go to our beloved empress and her lover Rasputin."

Despite all these shifts, the Jewish situation in Kiev had not improved. Thousands were pouring in—Jews who had been driven out, deported, arrested, or otherwise made homeless. And news was coming in about dozens of pogroms and other persecutions.

Several days earlier, General Murinov, the commander of Kiev, had summoned Hurevitsh, the state rabbi, as well as the Protestant pastor.

The general yelled at Hurevitsh and stamped his feet—he accused the Jews of hoarding coins and threatened dire punishment. He asked the pastor, "How many Protestants are there in Kiev?"

"Roughly five thousand."

"Too many! Too many!" he screamed at him.

I ran into the Zionist activist Yisroel Razov, who had just returned after being detained abroad. I assumed he had come to Kiev from Petrograd on Zionist business. But taking me aside, he confided that he had been forced out of Petrograd.

I was dumbfounded. "Why?"

"Right after I came back, I was investigated. Needless to say, they found nothing. Two days later, I was given twenty-four hours to clear out. Why? Because the government received 'precise evidence that the Zionists have joined forces with the Muslims against Christians.'"

On January 23, 1916, the newspaper *Kievlanin* ran an editorial calling for the gradual evacuation of the city. The civilian population, it said, would do best to leave in an organized way. This article hit the city like a bomb. It was viewed as the voice of the authorities. The city panicked. Thousands of families made a dash to get out. Hundreds of stores and public buildings began evacuating. It was as though Kiev were three miles from the front, rather than three hundred. People acted as if the Germans would be marching in tomorrow. When I left a few days later, the scene at the station was indescribable. The terminal and all the platforms were jammed with thousands of crates, baskets, and bundles. The crowd of travelers was so dense that it took me several hours to push forward to the ticket window. My mind was numb from the din. And then I heard that two or three people had died of strokes in the bedlam.

20

The Russian pullout from Galicia and southwestern Russia was swift and systematic; during that time, the frontline medical divisions and mobile hospitals endured a great deal and were of little use. No sooner did they manage to set themselves up than they were forced to pack up and move elsewhere. Often they had to escape quickly under fire, leaving the wounded and some equipment. A few divisions and their hospitals had even been captured. Although the divisions were formally responsible to military headquarters the connection was very loose; when fleeing, they never knew exactly where to go, so they resettled wherever they could. As a result, most of the medical divisions decided to move far to the rear. These included the Duma's division as well as Dolgorukov's. The engineering division also resolved to pull back its two hospitals and set up the train to carry wounded men between points in the rear.

Under these circumstances, I had no reason to stay with my division. I planned to join the central organization of the Association of Towns and work in its refugee department, but the government then turned over all refugee matters to the Red Cross, eliminating any participation by the association and the Zemstvo Alliance.

Thus there was no job for me in the Association of Towns. And the Kiev relief committee had obtained permission for several members to tour the frontline areas and organize assistance for the Jewish refugees. So my work in those regions was not crucial, either.

There were only a few places left for me to visit, the few Galician areas still in Russian hands. But everyone was convinced it was merely a matter of days before they would be evacuated. Besides, there was no division there that I could formally join.

For these reasons I left the front and went to Moscow and Petrograd to obtain a passport. New goals and missions awaited me.

VOLUME FOUR

I

For over a year, until the end of 1916, I was cut off from Galicia and its problems. . . . I spent most of those months in Petrograd, dealing with other affairs.

During that year, Russia's situation changed radically. An end to the fighting was nowhere in sight; no one believed in a Russian victory, yet the war had exhausted every last ounce of strength, creating an explosive situation in both the population and the army. Throughout the empire and especially in the two major cities, the deprivation increased day by day, turning into a famine with its first clear symptom: huge lines outside the bakeries and groceries. Discontent passed all limits, and people were starting to express it in revolutionary statements. The moderate progressive bloc in the Duma demanded a responsible cabinet. The press took on a menacing tone, and everyone felt that catastrophe was imminent and inevitable.

The autocratic government, losing its sense of survival, was rushing blindly toward an abyss. Our Russian Belshazzar didn't see, didn't want to see, the fiery handwriting on the wall—the prophecy of his downfall. Under the influence of the drunken Rasputin and his gang, he laughed at the nation's pessimism, annoyed the moderate opposition, and even broke with the Black Hundreds, who were his only supporters. Eventually, the grand princes formed a conspiracy, their first act being the assassination of Rasputin.

But quiet prevailed in everyday life, as is normal before a storm. Gone were the panic and confusion of the retreat of 1915. The enemy had stopped its advance. During the winter lull, the Russian army reorganized, obtaining enough shells and artillery so that it was ready for battle by the summer of 1916. In June and July, Brusilov swept into Galicia, and within five or six weeks he captured a large portion of eastern Galicia and the whole province of Bukovina. The invasion of the Carpathians began anew.

In August and September of 1916 several wires from Kiev's Jewish relief committee and from Dr. Lander urgently asked me to go to Galicia and Bukovina and organize help. I headed for Kiev.

A year earlier, when leaving the front, a piece of Galicia, including the town of Tarnopol, was still in Russian hands. It had been incomprehensible that the Russians could hold out there. Everyone assumed then that the Austrians had strategic reasons for ignoring this region and that it was only a matter of days or at most weeks before the Russian army would have to retreat. Later, when the enemy stopped advancing, everyone— including me—believed that this remaining part of Galicia consisted of only a few towns and villages, so there had been no point in my visiting.

Now, however, upon reaching Kiev, I realized my mistake. Two entire provinces, Tarnopol and Czortkow, several dozen towns and villages, and approximately one hundred thousand Jews had remained in Russian hands. Brusilov's campaign had added an area twice that size, including the towns of Buczacz, Kolomyja, Stanislavov—and all of Bukovina. The overall territory, covering tens of thousands of square miles, had a vast Jewish population.

Dr. Lander had stayed in Tarnopol and organized a committee, which he linked to the one in Kiev. Ever since May 1915, he had been working tirelessly: visiting towns, distributing aid, constantly calling on the Kiev and Petrograd committees, demanding help for the ruined Galician communities, isolated from the rest of the world. Working with Dr. Lander all that time was S. Homelsky of the Kiev committee.

Tied to his army hospital as part of his military service, Dr. Lander was unable to reach all the necessary places and give regular support in response to the overall emergency. So the brunt of the work had fallen on Mr. Homelsky, who had managed to accomplish a lot. For sixteen months preceding my arrival and many months after, he plugged away in Galicia with great devotion, or, more precisely, self-sacrifice. It was purely thanks to him that the plight in these towns had been carefully noted and that all sorts of necessary aid had been provided. Committees had been set up everywhere and money allocated, so that every town, large or small, had received steady help—not the haphazard kind of contributions I'd handed out randomly but systematic assistance that had saved hundreds, even thousands, of people from starvation.

Brusilov now occupied dozens of destitute towns and Homelsky could hardly do all the work alone. To make matters worse, Dr. Lander had fallen ill, which forced him to return to Russia indefinitely. As a result, the Kiev committee believed it was urgent for me to go to Galicia and take on part of the burden. Apart from the normal relief business, it turned out that I had a further mission. From Homelsky:

> We're on the verge of a financial crash. Our Galician budget is climbing from month to month—it's up to sixty thousand rubles. And at the same time, our income is shrinking; during these past two years our donors have grown tired of giving. They've become immune, jaded. It would take some hideous catastrophe to rouse them to donate large sums. The emergency in Galicia has become the normal state of affairs, and no matter how dreadful it is, it leaves them cold. They say they've got enough paupers in Russia. So their contributions keep dwindling, and it's getting harder and harder to pry money out of Petrograd. We haven't seen a kopek in two months, despite our telegrams. And now we're facing a deficit of almost a one hundred thousand rubles.
>
> At the same time, we have to change our whole welfare system in Galicia. So far, we've been limited to philanthropy. But now the authorities are allowing many refugees to return home, so our structure has to be thoroughly revised. We have to get the needy to stand on their own two feet and organize their communities, so that little by little they can take care of their poor. That way, people will stop living on handouts and we can gradually reduce its budget, perhaps eventually close down altogether. Granted, at first we need much larger sums, but it'll be easier to get money toward an ultimate goal. If we can show our donors an estimated decrease in our budget, they might even boost their donations.

So I was charged with developing a new system of help, and I agreed. But then I unexpectedly got sick and was unable to leave until early December. In the meantime, however, Dr. Lander had resumed his work.

"I have spent two and a half months traveling around Galicia and Bukovina," he wrote:

> The plight of the Jews is critical. We need a minimum of forty
> thousand rubles a month. Kiev's relief committee has no money, so
> it refuses to provide any further help. In September, in Petrograd,
> I delivered a report on the Galician situation and received a
> promise of ongoing help. I beg you and the other members to take
> all the essential actions to provide help for the next few months. I
> beseech the Petrograd committee not to abandon the population,
> which is cut off from the rest of the world and which has been sup-
> ported solely by Russian Jews for the past three years. I urgently
> implore you to answer me c/o the Kiev committee.
>
> Dr. Lander

2

I traveled through Galicia from early December 1916 till early March
1917, visiting various places, a few of them several times.

By now, the overall Jewish situation had been transformed. The Russian army's defeat in 1915 and Poland's severance from Russia had put an
end to the stories of Jewish espionage. Grand Prince Nikolay Nikolayevitsh and Yanushkevitsh had been transferred to the Caucasus,
which brought an end to the mass expulsions of Jews from the front line.
Many of the deportees had been allowed to return to their homes and
Jews were admitted into Russian towns that had previously been off-
limits. Soon the Pale of Settlement would be abolished altogether. The
government itself was now doling out funds to aid the deportees. This
new spirit was reflected in the way the local authorities and even the
army behaved toward the Jews in Galicia.

After the fiasco of 1915, there had been new disclosures. Despite the
rigid censorship, people learned the truth about Russia's cruelties and
atrocities in Galicia. Both the people and the press were greatly upset,

especially because Russia's barbarism sullied the country's image among its allies, who had endured much criticism for their alliance with Nicholas II's savage regime. The Russian government, realizing that Nikolay Nikolayevitch and his troops had gone too far, adopted a new policy regarding the occupied population. The Russians introduced a civil administration in the segment of Galicia that remained in their hands. Instead of sending the most criminal and unsavory element, the government installed educated and relatively decent people. This move gradually brought an end to the systematic terror of the population, especially the Jews.

At the very least, the new authorities were formally made responsible for the local population's welfare. In several places, they relaxed or even rescinded the travel ban, which had afflicted Jews almost exclusively. Some refugees returned to Sokal, Kudrentsy, Tarnarude, and, later on, Husiatyn and Zaleszcziki. Earlier, civilians dealing with the military were at risk of being branded traitors, and assistance efforts were seen as aiding the enemy. But now the authorities established direct relations with all the relief institutions. In fact, the civil authority often took its own measures to supply medical aid and food, and enable people to rebuild their homes. Officially, this was motivated by the fear of epidemics, which could spread to the army.

Of course, the situation was still far from ideal. Jews were still being dragged off to forced labor, bribes were still extorted, and hatred was openly displayed. And there were still bizarre notices being circulated about expulsions. An order to halt the deportations inspired the following notice:

A telegram from the staff of the Thirtieth Army Corps

The corps commander has ordered the corps to accept, through appropriate orders, the telegram from the supreme commander regarding specific directives to the army:

The supreme commander in chief has ordered a complete end to forced deportations during retreat. Refugees who leave Galicia voluntarily and flee to our provinces as well as populations on the borders are to be sent to Volhynia and Podolia Provinces. Those refugees who wish to return to Galicia should not be prevented from so doing if it can be determined that they come from there. All homeless people must be settled in the abandoned [German] colonies. Galician Jews are not allowed to cross into Russia, and those who have already done so must, as far as possible, be returned to Galicia. Currently, the Austrian border is lined with camps of Jews who were deported from the Galician war zone but not permitted to enter Russia. During our army's retreat, it is imperative that officials examine, that is, tour, the camps to forestall any outbreaks of epidemic and take energetic measures to prevent Jews from aiding the enemy. The ultimate goal of these evacuation directives is to keep the enemy from finding bread, forage, copper, cattle, horses, or other live animals useful to the enemy army. Our military may not destroy any agricultural buildings that do not interfere with its work. Furthermore, all looting and violence must be severely punished. Given the abolition of forced deportations, local populations must be informed that the enemy will undoubtedly draft all males between the ages of eighteen and fifty, so that we ask them to leave voluntarily.

No. 19125. Signed: Mavrin. Husiatyn 4873 Sannikov 2477. Commander of the Tenth Corps, Colonel Stavrakin.

A second order, dispatched to all corps and units, stated:

The commander in chief of the Western front has ordered the removal, from the corps region, of all people of the Jewish faith who are working for the Red Cross, the Zemstvo Alliance, the Association of Towns, Northern Aid, and any other voluntary organizations for medical help, except for physicians. Physicians of the Jewish faith are to remain wherever they are stationed, performing the duty of corps physician. G. Kari. March 1917, no. 837.

Nonetheless, even with these notices, the authorities had revised their attitude. During the time of occupation, the Russians and Polish Jews had grown accustomed to one another. The Jews had shown that there was no reason to suspect them of collaborating with the enemy. Bit by bit, the Russians had watched them and grown used to their faces, their clothing, their behavior, and had started appreciating their abilities. For the Jews' part, they had likewise been watching the Russians, gradually adjusting to them, often learning to speak their language. This led to greater mutual understanding and a fusion of interests.

Still, while the libels, pogroms, expulsions, and arrests had abated, the Jews were beset by economic, moral, and psychological ruin.

The war itself caused mass devastation, exacerbated by the destruction of farms and expulsion of peasants. Because of the general insecurity, two-thirds of the soil had been left fallow. The lack of raw materials, the paralysis of business and commerce, and the decrease in the population led to the closings of factories—and even craftsmen had no work. The intelligentsia that had remained after most professionals had run away or been taken hostage and deported had absolutely no means of support. The complete isolation and the ban on traveling even to the next village had wiped out all trade.

In short, all levels of society were ruined and without any income. During the early part of the occupation, the impact wasn't felt so deeply. Large stores of grain and all kind of merchandise still existed. For a time, many jobs and businesses were kept going by sheer inertia. The professionals and even the craftsmen had their savings, which covered their expenses for a while. People didn't regard the situation as critical, believing as they did that the occupation would be short-lived; no one expected the war to drag on for more than a few months, at most a year. They saw it as a temporary disaster. Many dramatic and tragic events occurred, but during the initial period the mental state, the overall mood of the population, remained unaltered.

However, a very different picture developed after two years of occupation, which exhausted all provisions of grain and goods. And most people had spent whatever capital they had. Day by day, the number of the needy and the hungry increased. Like a chronic illness, poverty invaded all parts of the collective organism. Shoes and clothes became threadbare and tattered; homes were dilapidated. People were physically weakened. The endlessness of the war and the occupation undermined all faith and hope in regard to speedy aid. Morale was low and pessimism rife. There was a forced isolation from one's own—indeed from any— cultural life. For two years, educated people had not laid eyes on a newspaper or a new book, had not been able to attend a play or a concert, had been cut off from any political or social interests. The ensuing lassitude verged on degeneracy. The worst impact was on the children. The instant the Russians marched in, all schools, all educational institutions, were shut down; and for two whole years, tens of thousands of children had no training, no instruction. A tiny few were taught at home, but most received neither guidance nor supervision; they were tossed into the street with all its terrible influences. It was only recently that the authorities had permitted the opening of primary schools—but no Jewish ones.

Moreover, the Jewish population suffered at the hands of the cruel and savage Russian military, whose atrocities added a particular confusion and despair to a shattered and devastated existence.

Since the start of the Russian occupation, tens of thousands of Jews had been shipped to Russia—to the provinces of Nizhny Novgorod and Penza and to Siberia. The deportations were totally random. In some places, the authorities carried off only hostages, in others able-bodied men. In many towns, they expelled entire Jewish populations. And the expulsions were usually so hurried and ruthless that the victims could take nothing along. There is no describing the hardships they suffered en route or the deaths resulting from hunger, feebleness, and disease. Upon arriving somewhere, they were greeted warmly and humanely by the Christian population. Jewish relief committees were set up everywhere, providing food and clothes and finding jobs, so that most of the homeless settled in nicely and had an income. Some four thousand in Penza were helped by the American consul in Moscow. From funds collected in the United States, he apportioned ten rubles per person each month.

At the turn of 1916, the authorities ordered the repatriation of all Galician deportees except for hostages. The homeless were utterly delighted—but then they experienced a bitter disappointment. Upon returning after great effort and agony, they were not allowed into their hometowns. In some spots, the excuse was that battles were being fought in the area. Elsewhere, the authorities claimed that the shtetls were totally destroyed, and that the returnees couldn't be lodged anywhere because their homes were occupied by the military. And so the tens of thousands of repatriates were scattered in towns and townlets that were not their homes. However, since the Russians never calculated how many refugees a place could absorb, they would transfer thousands to a tiny shtetl. Thus Skolat, which already had some 1,000 local Jews, received 4,000 more from Podvolotshisk and Husiatyn. And the rest of the homeless were dispersed in the same way. The 5,000 inhabitants of Snyatin were sent to Czortkow and Yagelnitse, 4,000 from Husiatyn to Skolat and Kopetshinyets; 1,500 from Skala to Borshtshov and Ozyerani; 5,000 from Podvolotshisk to Tarnopol and Skolat. The Jewish population of Zaleszcziki was resettled in Kheroskov, the Jewish population of Atinye in Grzimalov, and so forth. Furthermore, 2,500 from the villages were scattered throughout the region.

These people were in a dreadful predicament. However bad the circumstances of the local Galician Jews, each nevertheless had his own nook and was in his own surroundings. But when the homeless—famished, impoverished, and wretched after their miserable odysseys and without the slightest household comforts—arrived in a spot where the existing plight was disastrous enough, their situation became truly abominable.

They were a terrible burden on poor Jewish communities that couldn't even help, much less support, their own paupers. Still, powerless as they were, the local Jews had to care for the newcomers. At the very least, they couldn't let them remain out in the open; they had to provide some sort of refuge. This aggravated the housing crisis, which was already bad enough because so many homes had been wiped out in all towns and the largest buildings had been requisitioned by the military. The homeless were squeezed into the existing spaces, four or five families to a minuscule room. Every last synagogue and study house was occupied, every last barn and stable. The crowding and the famine encouraged epidemics. During the first six months, before assistance could be marshaled, over five thousand of the thirty-five thousand returnees died of starvation and all kinds of sicknesses!

Among the social relief agencies, the Zemstvo Alliance was the first and the most solid in responding to the plight of the Galician Jews. Back in 1915, the alliance had already begun organizing help for the inhabitants of the occupied territory. The alliance had established food centers where homeless Christians and Jews had each received a pound of bread per adult and half a pound per child every day, along with a ladle of soup or dry barley. The huge number of recipients can be gleaned from the fact that 107,000 rubles were spent every month on the Jews alone. Aside from these free soup kitchens, the Zemstvo Alliance set up cooperative stores that sold food at cost—that is, half to one third of the going market prices.

The alliance also did a great deal in organizing medical aid for the local populace by installing numerous hospitals and outpatient clinics and consistently fighting the epidemics, especially typhus.

Moreover, the Zemstvo Alliance set up foster homes for both Christians and Jews in six places. These six homes had a total of more than 1,000 Jewish children (325 in Tarnopol, 208 in Ozyerani, 200 in Skolat, 125 in Czortkow, 115 in Grzimalov, and about 100 in Borshtshov). The Christian population had a very positive attitude toward Jewish children. In several places the alliance organized help for women.

At the start of 1916, when the Kiev relief committee had initiated systematic help for the Galician Jews, it focused on those needs that the Zemstvo Alliance could not cover. The committee donated more food (white bread, milk, eggs, and, once a week, meat) for old people, children, the chronically ill, and convalescents. Beyond that, it supplied fuel, homes, and shoe repair to rabbis, kosher slaughterers, and other religious personnel. It also provided assistance to heders and medical treatment in places left out by the Zemstvo Alliance. Priority was given to the homeless. Local paupers were helped only in exceptional cases, which amounted to just one tenth of the entire budget.

In early spring 1916, the Zemstvo Alliance started curtailing its aid to the homeless. It began a registry in order to determine the number of employable people, who would then be dropped from the welfare list. More than half the names were struck off. In Tarnopol, for example, of the two thousand recipients at the soup kitchens, only six hundred children were left. Little by little the soup kitchens were shut down in Grzimalov, Trembovle, Bodzonov, Kheroskov, Kopetshinyets, Ozyerani, Borshtshov, Koralov, Melnitse. They remained only in Tarnopol, Zbarz, Czortkow, Skolat, Yagelnitse, Kolomyja, and Stanislavov. And even in these places, the budget kept growing tighter, so that a single day's bread ration was doled out only every two or three days and eventually once a week, supposedly because of the bread shortage.

The co-op stores were in even worse shape. Practically none gave

Jews access to the administration, which consisted of local Poles and Ruthenians. They behaved very badly toward Jews, compelling them to avoid the shops altogether. In some, the Christians either refused to hand over any food to Jews or allotted special days for them or special times (two hours a week in Tarnopol). In Czortkow, the Zemstvo Alliance's co-op had a sign: "As ordered by the authorities, we are not allowed to sell any goods to Jews." The excuse was that Jews didn't need cheap food and were using it for commercial purposes.

In many places, the alliance liquidated the hospitals and outpatient clinics, where Jews received free medical treatment.

All this made it necessary for Kiev's relief committee to widen its scope. The "employable" whom the alliance had excluded needed as much help as the unemployable because none of them could find any sort of job. The forced labor inflicted on thousands of Jews entailed an official salary, but not a single kopek was ever paid to a Jewish laborer. The relief committee had to feed not only the able-bodied homeless but also a large portion of the needy locals, especially the professionals, who were no better off than the homeless. Consequently, the committee's Galician budget climbed month by month, surpassing fifty thousand rubles by the end of the year.

3

After Lwow, Tarnopol is the largest city in eastern Galicia, and it has one of the oldest Jewish communities. It is rich in historic monuments and memories, with names prominent both in Orthodox circles and in the Enlightenment period. The stone synagogue is one of the most ancient and most beautiful in Galicia.

Tarnopol had barely suffered from the battles when the Russian army marched in. No charred neighborhoods or devastated houses. When I arrived, the city seemed calm yet bustling. The streets were crowded with pedestrians, all the stores were open, and the market was doing a lively business. But upon closer inspection, I noted that most of the people in the streets, the market, and the railroad station were military personnel, medics, nurses, and plain Russian civilians. The only language heard all around was Russian. Few local civilians were visible. And there were almost no members of the bourgeoisie or the intelligentsia—people sporting middle-class, often rich and elegant apparel. The rare professionals wore old, threadbare clothing. They were sad, hushed, cautious, unsure of themselves, their faces tired and despondent, their eyes bleak and dreamy.

Nearly all the shop signs were in Russian—a Russian bristling with horrible mistakes. At every step of the way, a sign announced: "Russian store" or "Russian establishment." And inside there were indeed Russians, with typical features and typical shirts: merchants from Kaluga, Tula, Moscow, and other Russian cities, doing business here with the help of the administration. But although these shops, big or little, were open, they had few customers. There was no jewelry boutique anywhere. Nor a single shop with luxury articles. In other stores, the shelves were empty, and the windows exhibited forlorn and dusty pieces of linen and vials of perfume, leftovers from the past. At the market, the main commodities were food and the most basic necessities: rolls, lard, and cigarettes.

The same neglect that filled the shops was also apparent in the streets and houses. The streets were muddy and clogged with filth, the houses squalid, falling apart. In two or three places there were large, uncompleted buildings whose construction had been halted by the war.

As darkness set in, the civilians started vanishing, and by nine they were all gone because of the curfew. The streets were now the exclusive turf of the military.

It took me only one day to grasp the essential mood of Tarnopol. This big, cultured European city was strangled, emaciated, as if stricken with a fatal disease and dying, slowly and helplessly. I saw the same thing later on in other cultured cities throughout the occupied zone.

The first thing I did in Tarnopol was contact the local relief committee. As in other places, the members were selected at random, with no sanction of any kind from the population. Arriving in a new place, the deputy from the Kiev committee would always seek out the more prominent, better-known men who were left, former community leaders. He would invite them and the rabbi (if he was still in town) to discuss the local situation. Then they would set up a committee, which would later be confirmed in Kiev. Most of the wealthy and professional contingent had fled with the Austrians, and many of the remaining people had been taken hostage. Nevertheless, the large towns (including Tarnopol, Czortkow, and Czernowitz) still had a few intelligent activists who could join the relief committees and organize the work.

Things were far worse in the smaller towns, which had always had few educated people interested in community affairs. Everyone needed help, and, for all their goodwill, the few conscripts were incapable of running a committee. This caused friction. Yet I never heard anyone in the villages voice the least suspicion; no one ever accused any committee of wrongdoing.

The Tarnopol committee included several respectable, prominent men such as Professor Rozenboym, Yitsik Nakht, and Mr. Tauber, an Orthodox Jew and wealthy merchant, who became committee chairman. Assisted by his son, he worked very hard in this capacity.

The committee's estimate for December exceeded twenty thousand rubles—nearly half the total budget for the whole of Galicia. And the first thing the members told me was that this was not enough; they needed a much larger sum. This was unfair. I pointed out that Tarnopol had rich Jews, who could help the poor, so that it should not devour the entire Galician budget.

Mr. Tauber replied:

> There are few people left here with any kind of assets or earnings—and they give more than they can to the needy locals, whom no one else is aiding. The Zemstvo Alliance and the Kiev committee are helping only the homeless, of whom there are 10,000 in Tarnopol. They fled here from all the shtetls and villages. We've got homeless people from places that were retaken by the Austrians and especially returnees from Russia who are not allowed back into their hometowns. We've got about 1,000 families from Rohotin and about 600 from Podvolotshisk. All told, we've got homeless people from 122 different places. Initially, the Zemstvo Alliance helped 5,300 people. It handed out one pound of bread per adult and half a pound per child, three pieces of sugar for two days, and some barley and beans. Then, when they registered the "employable" men (who can't find any

kind of employment anywhere), there were only 3,500 recipients left—1,700 of them homeless. From May 20 until the end of July, the alliance provided cash instead of food: eighteen kopeks per head, which added up to 20,700 rubles a month. The population was happy with this arrangement, but the governor prohibited the distribution of cash, and so the alliance went back to handing out food.

Now our committee also has to support the "employable," and the poor are getting more numerous by the month. People who gave charity six months ago are now forced to ask for help themselves. All avenues are exhausted. We've got landowners, millionaires with huge accounts in Austrian banks, estates and houses in the occupied areas—and they're starving to death. We have to set up a loan institution for them. And there are other needs: shoes, clothes, fuel, homes.

He was right, of course. Softening the plight required ten times more than the Kiev committee had allocated. But the province was as needy as Tarnopol, perhaps more so, and the question remained: Why did Tarnopol require half the overall budget?

We went to the committee headquarters, which had a six-man staff. As a result, the office was in ideal running order, and the books were kept meticulously. But I couldn't find the signatures of the welfare recipients. I also thought that the monthly overhead of nine hundred rubles was too high. However, Mr. Tauber explained that the committee employees were professionals who needed aid, which they would have gotten if not for their salaries.

The committee's main outlay was for improved rations for the sick, the old, and children: white bread, eggs, sometimes meat. The members had determined that it was more convenient to provide money than food. Instead of having to line up for hours on end, the recipients could get enough cash for two weeks. But the Kiev committee disagreed. And I too found it irrational, since the recipients wouldn't necessarily purchase better food.

I spent a few hours witnessing the food distribution. I looked at these ill-clad, barefoot, emaciated homeless, these shadows of human beings, and I listened to their pleas and complaints. Nearly everyone asked for something: one more glass of milk, one more egg, and they would cite their illnesses, their feebleness, their ordeals.

Next I went off into the city, stopping at a few homes, where four or five families were squeezed into a single tiny room. Again I saw the scrawny, haggard refugees; I listened to their sighs, to their tales of woe. All this made me realize that the Galician situation had deteriorated during the year and a half since my last visit.

And the tragedy was even worse for children. The schools had been closed throughout these eighteen months of occupation, and the children had grown wild. Barefoot, tattered, emaciated, with green little faces and gaping, feverish eyes, they scurried around, lost, unsupervised, contaminated by the most poisonous filth of the street.

Homelsky told me, "I personally saw a twelve-year-old boy offer his ten-year-old sister to the officers!"

And other children worked as guides, leading the soldiers to the brothels.

With immense effort, the Jews managed to talk the authorities into letting them "pray" with the children. Under this pretext, they founded small elementary religious schools known as "prayer houses." Eight hundred children were registered in these schools, but no more than eighty showed up. The rest had no clothes or were so deeply entangled in street life that no one could force them to attend school.

The Zemstvo Alliance set up a foster home for girls—350. Most of them had been prostitutes.

I saw several older Jews with long earlocks cleaning the street. They were half-naked despite the freezing weather.

"We're in dire need of clothing, especially shoes, for the forced laborers and also for the schoolchildren," said the committee member who was accompanying me. "They used to grab 500 or 600 people a day for forced labor, but it was summer, and so it wasn't that bad. Now it's only 100, 120—but their plight is horrible. They're freezing to death."

The tragedy was even greater because Kiev had collected clothing for these unfortunates: twenty-five bales worth two hundred thousand rubles. It would take four boxcars to ship them to Galicia; the clothing had been waiting at a granary in Proskurov for three months, but the authorities still couldn't get hold of the boxcars. Several days after my arrival in Tarnopol,

I was notified that the storehouse had caught fire, and several bales of blankets had been consumed. It wasn't till a month later that Tarnopol received the surviving clothes.

I could spend only a few days here. My itinerary would be taking me to Skolat, Grzimalov, Kheroskov, Kopetshinyets, Probuzhne, Suchostow, and Czortkow. After that, I would be heading for Czernowitz and other points in Bukovina.

4

For the past two and a half years, Tarnopol Province and part of Czortkow Province as far as Tlusti had been in Russian hands. The Austrians had retreated almost without a fight, which was why the towns and villages had remained intact. I traveled from Tarnopol to Czortkow and all the way to Tlusti—a total of ninety miles—without seeing a destroyed city or even a burned village. However, the farms, mostly Jewish, had been looted and wrecked.

Driving along the highway, I found occasional evidence of war: trenches, barbed wire, fallen telegraph poles. It was as if an army had marched through years ago and the area had remained deserted and unchanged. The telegraph poles were bent over or on the ground, their torn wires dangling like threads from a ragged garment, trembling, swaying, humming in the wind. And the holes in the highway had never been repaired.

My driver, a man from the countryside, told me that most of the fields had not been sown. Battles had been fought nearby, and who could tell what the next day might bring? Nobody cared to waste the seed. Furthermore, the sprouts had been eaten up by mice in nine districts and had survived in only three.

"Are you people Unitarians?" I asked him.

"Yes, we were Unitarians," he answered with a sigh.

"What do you mean 'were'? Did they force you to become Orthodox?"

After pausing awhile, he replied diplomatically, "We received orders, and we obeyed." He then added: "It was bad shutting down all our schools. The children don't know about God, about the Father."

"What was the attitude toward Jews?" I asked.

"Jews? All the bunks were in their hands." (Later on, I realized he meant banks.) He didn't say another word.

We had breakfast at a tavern. The whole place consisted of a single large room, where we found the owner, his wife, and their five children all warming themselves around a small iron stove. A short distance away stood an elderly Jew with a hungry, dejected face, stretching his frozen hands toward the heat. I asked him who he was. A transient. He had been a *melamed,* a religious teacher, but now there was no one to teach. No one could afford a *melamed.* I gave him a ruble. He gaped at me, and his eyes filled with tears.

Next I asked the tavern owner how the Russian soldiers were behaving toward him and other Jews. Did they loot, did they beat people?

"No, the soldiers don't do us any harm." Then he added: "The Russian troops are better than the Austrians. The Russians understand that a Jew has to live on something, and they give him a chance to earn a kopek."

I reached Skolat late at night. The only inn had a vacant room, but it was as cold as outdoors.

I awoke at the first glimmer of day. When I stuck my head out from under the two furs, I saw an elderly Jewish woman standing by the stove. Noticing I was awake, she gestured reassuringly and said: "Sleep, sleep! I'll wait!"

I was surprised. "What do you want?"

"I have to talk to you. I'm sure that later on all sorts of people will be coming to you from the town—and you won't have any time. So I'll wait till you get up. I live here, in the inn."

Obviously, word had gotten out as to who I was, and the woman had come with her request at the crack of dawn. Even though she had given me permission to go back to sleep, she kept talking. She was a refugee from Volotshisk, a middle-class woman, who had lived in high style. Now she and her children were "dry clumps of mud." The innkeeper's wife was a relative of hers and had given them a nook, for which she and her children had to perform all sorts of hard labor. On top of that, they had to anticipate her every wish, smile when she spoke, never grimace. During this year and a half, they had suffered terribly from cold and hunger. Her two grown daughters, such lovely girls, hadn't had shoes for an entire year. Then the relief committee had doled out eighteen rubles for footwear. But what can you get for eighteen rubles? And aside from shoes, they needed clothes. My visitor knew that I had brought along a quantity of blankets, and she asked for blankets for herself and her children.

She spoke quickly, nervously, blurting out sharp comments like "God plays with us like a child with a doll." She kept switching between tears and laughter. When she told me about her daughters, tears came pouring out; but then she would burst out laughing when she mentioned God: "God Almighty—hahaha!" It was as if she were talking about some bizarre entity that had nothing to do with what was happening all around.

Before she could leave, another woman walked in. She was well dressed and had a gold watch (which, she later said, was the only vestige of her former wealth). She was accompanied by a young man, a member of the local relief committee. The woman had a different kind of request. Her only son, a wonderful boy, had completed five classes at the gymnasium, but for the past two years he had been idle. What would become of him? She had asked the committee to hire a tutor who would prepare him for the university.

The man broke in: "Your son can earn money giving private lessons."

"Lessons?" The mother was offended. "With his family background my son is not the sort to give lessons!"

But seeing that I was unmoved by her son's need for a tutor, she made a second request: "I don't want to be an educated person anymore!" she declared categorically. "I'd rather get bread and milk."

I wasn't surprised by the opposition of "educated" and "bread and milk." I knew that the welfare recipients were divided into two groups: the "intelligentsia" was given cash, while simpler people were given food. It took a long time to find food, and because of the shortage, cash was not very useful.

I promised to transmit her request and said that I wanted to get into my clothes. But she had one more request—regarding the abandoned bride. Perhaps I knew about her.

I did know about her. Homelsky had briefed me. The girl, twenty-seven or twenty-eight, had been deserted by her fiancé. They had found a boy, an artisan, who was willing to marry her. But he wanted a dowry of three hundred rubles—not a kopek less. They had collected fifty rubles in town, the girl had some fifty rubles in savings, Homelsky had assigned fifty rubles from the committee, donated fifty himself, and persuaded me to add fifty more. This was no ordinary match; it would be the first wedding here in two and a half years—a major event.

My visitor was related to the girl. She explained that aside from the dowry they needed money for a bridal gown and some linen, and the groom insisted on getting boots; he refused to go barefoot under the wedding canopy. I promised to think about it, and I was finally able to climb out from under the furs and wash and dress.

Now the town rabbi came to say hello. He entered quietly with a sanctimonious smile, buttered me up a little, brought me a Talmudic tract, and with an air of mystery he stated that he couldn't manage on the thirty-two rubles a month he got from the committee. It was too little for a family of six, and he wanted an increase.

The rabbi was followed by a short Jew with nasty, piercing eyes. He slunk in cautiously, closed the door, peered around, and began murmuring agitatedly. He had come to open my eyes, to inform me that all the help we were giving the population was useless. In fact, it was detrimental. The only people who really needed it were the widows and the orphans. For them, one thousand rubles a month was enough. The other fifteen thousand was good money after bad.

"I'm not saying, God forbid, that the committee should keep the money themselves," he whispered. "But, if you catch my drift, a greasy pot makes greasy hands. . . . They all get their bit."

"What should be done?" I asked him.

"What?" He flared up. "Don't hand out any money! You've turned us all into beggars. It would be better if you got the authorities to let us return to our homes in Podvolotshisk. Back there, we'll stand on our own two feet and become our old selves again."

The man got on my nerves with his darting eyes, his muttering, his creepy movements. But I thought there was a lot to what he said, and I invited him to return that evening and acquaint me with the situation. As he left, he asked me to tell nobody about his visit. Otherwise he feared the soldiers would kill him.

Next came committee members. But although the committee was made up of local residents and refugees, only the destitute showed up. Homelsky had already told me that there was bad blood between the two groups. From their first words I saw that the homeless people despised the others. Podvolotshisk, where most of the refugees were from, had always been a place of "better people," while Skolat had always been a "town of beggars." But now their fortunes had been reversed, and the refugees from Podvolotshisk were dependent on the favor of Skolat. The townsfolk here were furious because the Kiev committee was giving most of its help to the homeless and only a few hundred rubles to the locals. At the same time, they were doing everything in their power to prevent the refugees from being sent home. And no wonder! Every month a sum of over two thousand rubles flowed into town just to pay the rents for the refugees. And they were also good for business.

The local Jews numbered some 3,000, including 1,053 paupers. Among the paupers, 534 had suffered because of the war and were entitled to welfare, which they got from the Zemstvo Alliance. There were also 1,893 homeless, chiefly from Volotshisk, and 1,718 were being assisted. The estimate for January was 16,209 rubles: 14,400 for the homeless, 900 for the local needy, and 900 for the Jews in the surrounding villages.

The budget was to be discussed at today's committee meeting, which Homelsky would attend. Both the locals and the homeless pinned great hopes on my intercession.

Since Homelsky wasn't expected before evening, I made use of the time to go and watch the committee's distribution of charity, view the homeless shelters, and get a look at the town. The biggest building, and the only one distinguishing the town, is the large brick synagogue. Its first stone was supposedly laid by Rabbi Leyvik Yitskhik of Berditshev.

According to legend, upon nearing the synagogue, he got down on all fours, crawled inside, and clambered over the benches to the Holy Ark. When asked why he had come in like that, he replied, "Such great and holy men have walked across the floor, and I am not worthy of setting foot where they have stood."

Now refugees were walking across that floor. They were crowded into every nook and cranny with their packs, crates, and beds, like a panicky mob in a depot.

Near the synagogue there was a sort of almshouse, to which the old, the crippled, the blind had been sent.

I stopped an old man who looked about ninety. "Where are you from, Granddad?"

"I'm from Horlitse."

"Why were you expelled?"

"What do you mean why? Can't you see I'm a spy?! Ha!" He laughed good-naturedly, beamed at me like a man who's told a good joke, and tenderly ran his fingers over my arm.

I toured a series of homeless shelters. There were three, four, and more families per room. They huddled, squeezed in. The rooms were cold. The children of several families were all in one bed, covered with a comforter. A dozen little faces were peeping out, greenish, emaciated, with sad little eyes. The biggest impact was made on me by a large room with a riddled and collapsed wall. The holes were stopped up with ragged clothes. The other walls were coated with frozen dew. A few sick people and a woman who had given birth were lying there.

Later on, her husband, a tailor, came to me and demanded a double ration of wood and a larger allowance of milk. I agreed and also gave him three rubles. What struck me was that, unlike the others, he demanded rather than pleaded. His wife was his, the newborn was also his, but was he the only person with a responsibility toward them? Didn't others also have an obligation toward the baby and the mother? The father articulated it all so clearly you felt his demands were not personal.

That evening, at the committee meeting, Mr. Homelsky read aloud the welfare estimate, which assigned only nine hundred rubles for the needy. The local representatives stood up and voiced their objections.

"We have a list of 534 paupers who have suffered in the war: soldiers' wives, people ruined by pogroms, families of deportees. We deserve a third, at least a fourth, of the allocated sum—that is, about four thousand rubles."

Homelsky replied: "The Kiev committee has granted help only for the homeless. In Russia we've got millions of poor, including people hurt by the war and confined to their homes, and there is no possible way the committee can help them. That's the job of the local Jewish communities."

"How can you compare the Jewish communities in Russia to our communities?"

Homelsky blew up. "Stop talking nonsense! You don't think I understand the situation in Skolat? I know a lot of people have gotten rich. The town has earned a lot of money, and it's capable of supporting its own poor. The nine hundred rubles I've budgeted may be unnecessary too."

"Who told you our town has gotten rich?" yelled one of the locals. "That's a Podvolotshisk fantasy! Everything looks big in their eyes!"

"You know what?" Homelsky offered a compromise. "We'll assign you another one thousand rubles, but only if your community can match it."

"We can't get anything else out of our town. It's already provided beyond its means. You've got to give us at least another two thousand rubles."

"Not on your life!" Homelsky dug in his heels.

"In that case, we don't need anything! We'll make a complaint!" shouted one of the members, a butcher. "Don't think you're the only one holding the purse strings! There are people above you! They'll force you to hand over what we're owed!"

"Who's going to force us?" I asked him.

"You'll see who—don't worry!"

"You might as well put your cards on the table," one of the homeless representatives broke in. "You've gone to the district supervisor and complained about the Kiev committee."

"Well, so you know," the butcher responded softly.

I couldn't contain myself any longer: "I cannot negotiate with people who involve the authorities in our affairs and denounce us. I'm going to report this to the Kiev committee and demand that it pass a resolution." And with that, we left the meeting.

We pondered the situation. Naturally, we could have taught the people a lesson; we could have terminated the local committee's activities. But where would that get us, and, mainly, whom would we really hurt? So, furious as I was, I suggested that Homelsky compromise and increase the subsidy. Besides, I felt the complaints were partly justified.

Given the estimate of 16,000 rubles, the allocation of 900 for local paupers was really too small. We agreed to add 2,000 rubles for the locals.

5

The next morning, a soldier brought me a note from Count Aleksei Alekseievich Zhukovski, the district supervisor, who wanted to see me about an important matter. I later found out that he was a member of the Petrograd aristocracy but had come down in the world, apparently for some unpleasant reason.

He received me very courteously and expressed his great satisfaction that the Kiev committee was aiding the homeless. He then went on: "Unfortunately, the local committees are unsuccessful. The Skolat committee is not very objective; it leans more to one side than the other. The paupers from Podvolotshisk are getting almost twenty times more than the locals."

6

My next stop was Khorostkov, a large town with over 350 Jewish families. A few had left with the arrival of the Russians. But they had been replaced by more than 1,000 refugees, particularly from Husiatyn. At the start of the year, the Zemstvo Alliance had helped 1,506 people: 976 homeless and 530 locals. In June it reduced aid, especially to locals, down to some 1,200 (907 homeless plus 293 locals). The Kiev committee had handed out 43,038 rubles. Last month's budget alone had amounted to over 7,000 rubles, including some 800 for the locals. Here, too, there had been requests for more aid for the latter.

I went to one member's home and met with the committee. We

discussed all the needs of the indigents. The clothing shortage was the biggest problem. Entire families remained indoors for lack of warm clothes, and no shoes were to be had. The committee had received a few dozen pairs but was holding them back pending a larger shipment. Why? If only these twenty or twenty-five pairs were distributed, the people who got none would tear the members to shreds. Furthermore, the town was afflicted with epidemics of typhoid and scarlet fever, but no medical help was available.

During the meeting, an elderly woman burst in, came over to me, and began in a bold, rattling tone: "I'm a granddaughter of Rabbi Zusye of Anipolye and a great-granddaughter of Rabbi Leyvik Yitskhik of Berditshev, and on my mother's side I'm a descendant of the Baal-Shem-Tov. Our family includes seventeen rebbes, and I'm third cousins with the great rabbi of Brody!"

Having poured out her entire lineage, she stood there, eyeing me sharply to gauge how shaken I was.

"What can I do for you?"

What indeed could I do for her? Well, if you're descended from so many notables, naturally you deserve a special support. When I replied that we didn't go by illustrious ancestry, she glared at me for a while, then shrugged in supreme protest and walked out.

That evening, after completing our work, we were enjoying a glass of tea when an old man showed up: the town cantor, a lank, scraggy man with soft, young, sparkling eyes. He was here to request aid. The amount he asked for was so minuscule and so equitable that I instantly agreed. I asked whether he knew any Hasidic stories. Now he livened up and enthusiastically launched into tale after tale. And what a storyteller he was! Filled with rapture, teeming with marvelous details like a true poet. Each tale he recounted was a work of art! I felt sad that I couldn't write them down word for word. Characteristically, all his stories were about the Messiah. Later on, I concluded that elderly Jews throughout Galicia were deeply interested in the Messiah. I can recall only one of the cantor's stories:

> When Rabbi Yisroel of Rezhin was in prison, his Hasids and his relatives moved heaven and earth for his release. And when he

was set free, the joy was inconceivable. They had banquets; they danced and sang. But one of his Hasids, Motele, who had always been devoted heart and soul to the rebbe, neither danced nor sang. He sat there gloomily, refusing to speak to anyone.

People urged him: "Please! It's a wonderful celebration. The rebbe is out of prison, and you're not happy, you're mournful. Why?"

"I faithfully believed that our rebbe was the Messiah, and I told myself: 'Let the blister burst! Let it burst!' But the blister hasn't burst. The Messiah hasn't come. The rebbe was set free, and now we're right back where we started. So how can I be happy?"

While the cantor was speaking, I suddenly heard a quiet, doleful violin emitting an ancient and deeply plaintive melody. In the doorway I saw a famished, tattered, embittered Jew in his fifties, playing an old, poor violin. And both were weeping, both were shedding silent, heartrending tears. Both were wordlessly asking for help. The musician was a refugee from Podvolotshisk. After losing all his worldly possessions, he had gone into exile with his only solace, his instrument. Then his violin had been stolen. Returning to Penza, he had nothing to do. There were no weddings, no celebrations. Who needed a klezmer? But he had heard that a "committee officer" had come. So he had dug up a violin somewhere to welcome me with. And now his gentle strains told me about his harsh plight, about his misery and anguish. It was very touching to hear his violin weeping, to see the hungry man's tears.

During my prewar ethnographic research, I had noticed that so many folk songs and folktales are full of grief and lament: "So they began to weep and wail," "Woe and sorrow," and so on. And Russian folk songs likewise say that "he shed a torrent of tears," "bathed in tears." I had always seen this as mere grandiloquence. But now, in Galicia, I realized that it is true to life. I saw people "shedding torrents of tears." There are moments when tears come streaming on their own, almost unnoticed, as surrogates for words. They flow as easily as words; they keep pouring when words have lost all strength and there is no one to talk to.

When the musician stopped, and I asked him to sit down with us, the cantor recalled a legend about a melody:

A Jew came to consult with the rebbe of Rezhin. So the rebbe
crooned "Elijah the Prophet" set to a non-Jewish tune and asked
his visitor to memorize it. The visitor didn't understand the reason why, but he obeyed the rebbe and learned the melody by
heart. Fifteen years later, while traveling at night, the man had to
pass through a forest haunted by demons. Walking along, he
suddenly saw that he was accompanied by a short Gentile with a
pipe. The Jew was terrified. The Gentile asked him where he was
going, and the Jew replied, "To the next town." The Gentile then
said, "I'm going there too." Then the Gentile took the Jew's arm
and said, "Sing something for me." The Jew was even more terrified. But he remembered "Elijah the Prophet" with the non-
Jewish melody, which he had been taught by the rebbe of
Rezhin, and he began to sing it. And he kept singing until they
reached the town, and there the Gentile vanished.

7

In Khorostkov I met two Jews, Rabbi Frenkel of Husiatyn and Mr. Lipo
Shvager. They jointly owned a large bookstore specializing in old Jewish
books, rare items, and manuscripts. This was Galicia's biggest outlet for
old Jewish religious tomes. It had been utterly wiped out by the pogrom
and the fire. They had managed to save only a few manuscripts and old
books. I took some of them back to Petrograd for safekeeping at the
museum.

Lipo Shvager, who was closely related to the rabbi of Kopetshinyets,
told me a wondrous tale, a mystical, symbolic legend. In fact, it has
already entered the cycle of Hasidic lore about miracles:

At the start of the war, the rebbe, accompanied by his entire family, went to a spa in Hamburg. Lipo Shvager also happened to be
there. When the Russians began occupying Galicia, the rebbe
summoned him and said: "I have to tell you that I own two letters: one personally written by the Baal-Shem-Tov and the other
signed by him. They might, God forbid, be destroyed in the war.

So please go to Kopetshinyets immediately and save these letters.
If you're not able to come back here, store them in a safe place.
You ought to know that your trip will be very perilous. You
could be shot, or someone might kill you because of a rumor—
heaven help us! But these dangers should not keep you from performing your sacred mission and saving those letters."

Shvager instantly agreed to go, and he asked, "But, Rebbe,
what about your property, the gold and silver and the precious
objects in your court?"

Indeed, the rebbe's property was said to be worth several million Austrian crowns.

"All that stuff is expendable," he calmly replied. "But the
Baal-Shem-Tov's letters must be saved."

Shvager left, and he reached Kopetshinyets several hours
before the Russians. Needless to say, there was no question of his
returning to Hamburg. But he did have time to hide the letters in
a metal case, which he buried six feet deep in the rebbe's basement wall. He also buried some of the rebbe's gold and silver
there. During the next three of four months, he had no access to
that cellar. Meanwhile, he narrowly escaped death several times.
Once he was even arrested on suspicion of espionage. Finally,
when he was able to go back to the basement, he couldn't find a
single one of the expensive articles he had buried there. Everything had been dug up and carried off. And the wall where he
had concealed the case containing the letters had likewise been
dug open. The case was gone.

You can imagine the effect this had on Shvager. He almost
died of shock. A few days later, however, while digging farther
into the wall, he suddenly found the case. It was undamaged, untouched. But when he opened it, he was amazed to discover that
all the script had vanished from the letter written by the Baal-
Shem-Tov. The paper was blank.

Frankly, I didn't put much stock in Shvager's tale. It was one of the
usual legends that emerge during such tumultuous times. So I asked to
see the letters. He said they were at the inner sanctum in Kopetshinyets
and refused to show them to me. But when I met him there a few weeks
later, I urged and prodded him, and he yielded, though very reluctantly.
He brought the letters to the synagogue. They were wrapped in several

sheets of paper. With great reverence he unfolded the letters without touching them directly. I saw two small sheets of ancient paper, both of them dated "5513" [1753]. One was covered on both sides with a dense and tiny handwriting, which, according to Shvager, belonged to Gershen of Kitev [the Baal-Shem-Tov's secretary]. (The text had already been printed.) At the very edge of the other side, there was a barely perceptible signature in long, sharp, single letters: "Yisroel Baal-Shem." The second sheet, half decayed and with faint spots left by moisture or tears, was completely blank, with no trace of writing.

Shvager, gazing at both letters with dreamy, mystical eyes, said: "I was told that the script vanished because of the dampness and that it can be chemically restored. . . . But we Hasids have a different view. . . . A very different view."

Peering at the letter, from which the script had "flown away," I recalled the shard of the Ten Commandments that I had found at the profaned and shattered synagogue in Dembits. All that was left on the fragment were the words *kill* and *commit adultery.*

The two symbolic episodes fused into the phrase "Shattered tablets and flying letters." [When Moses returned with the tablets of the Decalogue, he was so horrified at the sight of the Jews worshiping the Golden Calf that he broke the Ten Commandments to bits; hence the image of the shattered tablets. When the Romans, destroying the Temple, set the Scrolls of the Law on fire, the letters of the holy script supposedly flew to heaven from the burned parchment. Today the Hebrew idiom, literally "letters flying away," means "unfulfilled promises."] These two symbols, "shattered tablets" and "flying letters," summed up the life of the Galician Jews.

During my first tour of Galicia, I had virtually followed the trail blazed by the combat. I had wandered through places still warm from fires; I had seen the fresh signs of pogroms. The fear of death lurked in every corner. Every town, every house, every article spoke of dramatic events, and there was even more tragedy in the people, who had survived recent mortal terror and were shocked and nearly crazy with despair. I found people who were virtually "shattered tablets," with blood pouring from every "break." The cataclysm had been purely external, coming with the war. Hundreds and thousands of lives were cut short, fortunes destroyed, great cultural treasures wiped out. But the storm had not yet reached the depths of the soul, not yet annihilated human dignity. A rich or decent man might have suddenly been reduced to poverty and hunger and, most tragic of all, had too much pride to hold out his hand. Many such victims preferred starvation to charity. The catastrophe striking the ruined, bloody, and degraded populace was huge, almost epic. But in its vast scope, in its acuteness, there was a severe beauty that transformed these human sorrows and sufferings into an epic tragedy.

Now, while traveling through the "intact" towns and townlets, I no longer encountered the earlier sublime and beautiful drama. Tragedy was commonplace. The heroes of the national tragedy had become professional beggars. They had forgotten the past, they were afraid to look into the future, and they lived with the petty mendicant concerns of the present day, anxious about a piece of bread, a heap of barley. People had grown accustomed to constant hunger, to rags, to lining up for hours at the food centers. They roamed about, neglected, silent, despondent, indifferent to their dreadful situation. The few remaining members of the intelligentsia had likewise gotten used to their isolation from any sort of culture, social life, spiritual and intellectual pleasure. And all these living corpses trudged past me not as shattered tablets but as tablets from which the letters had been erased. These people had lost the supreme sanctity of human dignity.

8

From Kherostkov I went to the shtetl of Kopetshinyets, where I likewise conversed with the police chief about the Jewish relief committee. He invited me to his office, where I also found an elderly Pole, whom he introduced as mayor of the town.

In questioning me about the Kiev committee, the police chief said: "Your local group doesn't appear to be doing its job properly. There seems to be a conflict of interest."

"What makes you think so? Do you have any evidence?"

Instead of responding, he stated in a markedly distrustful tone, "I'd advise you to scrutinize the committee's books thoroughly."

"I have scrutinized them, and I've found them to be in order."

He smirked, and so did the mayor. "You know, books can be doctored so that everything looks right, but there's more there than meets the eye."

"Please tell me your suspicions loud and clear," I exclaimed. "The committee members struck me as decent people. They work long hours and without pay. . . ."

"Without pay . . . ," the police chief echoed sarcastically and exchanged mysterious glances with the mayor.

I repeated my request.

"I can't tell you anything about the committee as a whole, but I have my doubts about the chairman, Mr. Nakht."

"Why?"

"Let the mayor explain."

And explain he did. Among its various forms of help, the committee, obtaining wood at cost from the authorities, sold it at one third the free market price. Mr. Nakht was in charge of distributing the wood, and he supposedly refused to hand it over to the poor. So they bought it at the municipal warehouses for a lot more money. When asked why they didn't get it from the committee, they unanimously replied, "Nakht won't give it to us."

Frankly, I didn't lend much credence to their accusations. Listening to the police chief and watching his gestures, I sensed an ulterior motive that had little to do with the interests of the Jewish population. And I knew that the mayor didn't just happen to be there. Upon checking into the matter, I learned that he owned a wood business, which had dipped greatly because of the committee; and so, with the police chief's help, he was trying to discredit Mr. Nakht in my eyes since he was the committee's most important worker.

The budget for Kopetshinyets was 8,607 rubles, but the committee appealed for another 2,000 specifically for footwear. Kiev had already granted the shtetl a total of 37,790 rubles for the entire period.

Most of the refugees here were from Husiatyn. They had all prepared to return home, but the situation was complicated. There was a lot of fighting and divisiveness.

Husiatyn had suffered terrible destruction—unusual even for Galicia. Located on the old Russian-Austrian border, Husiatyn was divided into Russian and Austrian towns by the Zbrutsh River. The Russian part was poor and neglected, far from the railroad, and with no trace of culture. Austrian Husiatyn, by contrast, was a rich, flourishing commercial center with all sorts of cultural institutions and establishments, with fine houses, electric lighting, sewers, with elementary and middle schools and eleven banks. The population was almost entirely Jewish—one thousand families. And this was the home of the famous rabbi of Husiatyn. The old Husiatyn synagogue was one of the loveliest and most splendid in Galicia. When I saw it in ruins, without doors or windows, its regal magnificence nonetheless stood out against its surroundings.

At the outbreak of hostilities, the Austrians crossed the border and took Russian Husiatyn. The next day, after a battle near Paradek (some ten miles away), the Austrians fell back. Next, a Russian regiment occupied Russian, then Austrian Husiatyn. A pogrom occurred immediately. The soldiers looted stores, offices, banks, and private homes. As usual, peasants came from the surrounding villages and began making off with whole wagonloads of Jewish property. Anything they couldn't carry, they tore, wrecked, and shattered. Still not satisfied, they set the whole town ablaze. They went from house to house, from apartment to apartment, pouring kerosene over the remaining items and igniting them. And whatever the first regiment had had no time to wipe out was destroyed by the succeeding ones. Within days the town was reduced to ruins and ashes. Of the more than seven hundred houses, only twenty-three were left standing. The old synagogue and the rebbe's court with its large study house were saved by Jewish troops, who said that if the synagogue and the court were set on fire, they would torch the church and the Christian homes. These same Jewish soldiers then brought the surviving Torah scrolls across to Russian Husiatyn.

Some four hundred wealthier families had managed to leave and go farther into Austria. During the pogrom and the fire, the other six hundred families had fled to the surrounding villages and forests and stayed there. The overall damage was estimated at thirty million rubles. Two lunatics were killed, a boy and girl. The synagogue's old beadle, whom the soldiers had driven into the river with their whips, had caught cold and died.

The condition of the Jews was terrible. When the chaos died down and the runaways gradually straggled back, they had nowhere to live and nothing to live on. But then help came unexpectedly from Yevetsky, the police captain in Russian Husiatyn. First, by aggressively investigating the Christian townsfolk, he tracked down many of the plundered goods and restored them to their owners. He also imprisoned the thieves—one of them a Kiev Jew, who had bought stolen property. Furthermore, he formed a relief committee and collected money from the surrounding landowners. He invited ten Jews to join the committee, which included the rabbis and most prominent residents of both Husiatyns. The committee handed out a pound of bread a day to every needy Jew, plus potatoes, low-priced wood, and four and a half kopeks in cash. For the Sabbath, the committee distributed beans and challah. In four or five months, the committee aided a total of some fifteen hundred people. It received six hundred rubles from Petrograd's committee, three hundred from Kiev's, and about one thousand from other Jewish institutions. The rest of the money was gathered from the Christians.

After hearing about the committee, nearly all the inhabitants returned and moved into the basements and ruins. Forty or fifty ragged, barefoot people squeezed into a single room. The crowding, the hunger, the poverty triggered epidemics of typhus and other illnesses. Then an edict was issued, strictly prohibiting any contact between the two Husiatyns. Both the committee and the private contributors stopped assisting the unfortunates. Begging and pleading were heard from the other side of the river, but no one could offer a helping hand. Brave young Jews who smuggled bread across paid dearly for their courage: several were wounded or arrested.

Then an order was issued: the entire Jewish population of Austrian Husiatyn, some fifteen hundred people, would have to leave town by noon the next day. No exemptions were granted; everyone was expelled—even a blind hospital patient was kicked out over the protests of the Christian administrators.

The displaced Jews settled in Kopetshinyets for the next year and a half. Despite support from the Zemstvo Alliance and the Kiev committee, they suffered the worst destitution. During that period, Husiatyn was ruined even more. Everything left behind in the Jewish homes was looted, and the few standing houses were occupied by Gentiles.

Several months ago, an unconfirmed notification claimed that Jews deported from Husiatyn were allowed to go back. No sooner had several dozen families shown up than a new expulsion was ordered. Nevertheless, other families sneaked in. By now, some one hundred were back. They squatted in cellars and suffered at the hands of the Gentiles, who had captured all the commerce and didn't want the Jews around. Yet all the refugees from Husiatyn, young and old, were intent on returning. They waved off charity; all they wanted was to go home. Two hundred fifty households—one thousand people all told—were ready to return, and they were planning to settle in peasant homes.

As soon as I reached Kopetshinyets, the rabbi of Husiatyn likewise arrived as a delegate for the Jews of that shtetl. He asked me to set up a relief committee with funds from Kiev. The rabbi asserted that his townsfolk had the right to no less help and perhaps more than other homeless in other towns. If they had come home without assistance and at the risk of their lives, they should be given the chance to get back on their feet.

The rabbi's arguments seemed genuine. But the committee opposed his demand, and Mr. Homelsky sided with the members. They explained that several hundred Jews who had gone back to Husiatyn needed no aid. They were the ones with some kind of wherewithal. Given the tiny number of Jews left in the town, they were earning quite a nice income because of the strong military presence. If a relief committee were organized there, not only would it create beggars, but all the Husiatyn refugees in Kopetshinyets, whom it was already hard to hold back, would throng into their hometown. Since there was nowhere for them to live, and it was winter, epidemics would break out. For all these reasons, I was advised to steer clear of Husiatyn.

It also turned out that the prewar rabbi of Husiatyn was Rabbi Frenkel, who was in Kopetshinyets with the refugees. The new rabbi, who had now come from Husiatyn, had seized Frenkel's post, and many of the Husiatyn Jews were quite upset. They viewed the rabbi's efforts to set up a committee as self-serving—a way of consolidating his position. On the other hand, those in favor of a Husiatyn committee had the following explanation for the resistance shown by the Kopetshinyets committee. First of all, they blamed it on an intrigue by Rabbi Frenkel, who wanted to prevent the new rabbi from gaining a solid foothold in Husiatyn. And second, they alleged that the Kopetshinyets residents wanted to keep the refugees there because of the rent and the other income they received.

Several days later, I was in Probuzhne, a shtetl on the road to Husiatyn. The local committee, especially the chairman, an intelligent lawyer named Dr. Rozenboym, strongly urged me to visit Husiatyn. I listed the objections to founding a committee there, but the members disagreed. Finally, Dr. Rozenboym said in a mournful tone: "Our committee, a group of professionals, has done a lot for the revival of Husiatyn. And don't think our motives are altruistic. Not at all. We simply had nothing to do and were going crazy with idleness. So we got more and more involved in the work, more and more enthusiastic, and we figured we'd accomplish something. But now your attitude toward Husiatyn has dampened our enthusiasm."

I began to waver. Perhaps I should go and organize a committee there after all. But Mr. Homelsky, who was more familiar with the circumstances than I, was categorically opposed—and I relied on him.

Earlier, Probuzhne had housed over 600 refugees, of whom 140 had now returned to Skolat. The remaining 460 (130 families) were from nineteen different places, chiefly Zaleshtshik and Husiatyn. The Zemstvo Alliance had supported 200 of these homeless. Going by the estimate of the Kiev committee, I left 2,000 rubles here. For that entire period, Kiev had given Probuzhne a total of 14,405 rubles, plus something extra for Passover.

Before going to Probuzhne, I stopped in Suchostow, a small shtetl that was getting 400 rubles a month. The committee chairman, a naive and artless man, was scorned by the local rabbi's widow and daughters, with whom I was staying. However, his description of the shortages, especially the lack of wood, was so forthright that I couldn't refuse giving him an increase of 200 rubles.

Suchostow has one of the oldest wooden synagogues—splendid for its primitive architecture. The Vienna Archaeological Society became interested in this synagogue and took steps to preserve it as a rare historic landmark. It was, of course, very dear and sacred to the local Jews, who made it the subject of the usual legends that are told about old synagogues everywhere: it never burned, it had been discovered fully built in the ground, and so forth.

I stepped inside. Not only were the building and everything in it destroyed, including all the holy books, but the place had simply been turned into a toilet. I had seen such desecration before, but I was surprised by something else. The soldiers who had wrecked and dirtied the synagogue had left long ago, and Jews were allowed free access; but no one had thought of cleaning up, of gathering the stray pages of the holy books. However, when I promised to give the Jews a few rubles to clean up the synagogue, a couple of people expressed interest.

I then went on to Czortkow. As we approached it, the drayman pointed to the rebbe's devastated court and began telling wondrous stories:

"Can you imagine the things that went on here? The whole world came to visit. And the way he lived! Like an emperor! A band was always playing! . . . And when he left, he told all his servants to stay on, and he promised to keep paying their wages. He's been away for two and a half years already, but they're still receiving their salaries."

"What about the local population? Are there a lot of poor Jews? Are they being helped?'

"We've got enough paupers. But they're being helped. The Zemstvo Alliance is helping everyone."

"What about a Jewish committee? Does it provide enough aid?"

"What committee? I don't know. I haven't heard anything about that."

9

Compared with other places, Czortkow, a large and lovely town with several thousand Jewish inhabitants, had suffered little in the war since no battles had been fought here. But during September 1915, when the

Russians pulled out, Czortkow had been in a state of anarchy for an entire week with pogroms and looting.

At the start of hostilities, a large segment of the Jewish population had left with the Austrians. But then homeless Jews from nearby towns and townlets had sought refuge in this bigger center. The first pogrom in Husiatyn drove some 120 families here. Finding jobs, they remained. And when nearly all the five thousand Jews of Husiatyn were expelled within hours, they poured into Czortkow. The response to the disaster was generous. Within days, the locals had set up free soup kitchens.

I slept in the local druggist's home after spending the evening with several intelligent young men, who had devoted a lot of time to helping the indigents.

One of them told me: "You can't imagine the mood here during these two and a half years. These years were blotted out of our lives. It was one long period of waiting, of chasing news and rumors. It always seemed as if the Austrians were about to come back and the war would be over. We had no energy, no courage to do any sort of work."

Another young man went on:

We've been going crazy doing nothing. My father started memorizing Goethe and Schiller. We began learning Russian, reading *Kievskaya Misl* every day. There are probably few people in Russia who know as much about domestic Russian issues as we do. We cover everything—every session of the Duma, every one of Vladimir Purishkevitsh's speeches, and it all gives us reason for endless debate.

We've been studying the Russians, and despite the suffering they've inflicted, we like the Russian character. For all his crudeness, the Russian is filled with idealism and humanity. The Ruthenian and the German can't hold a candle to him. Here's an example: A few weeks ago I saw a scene from my window. It was raining. The street was covered with deep, swampy mud. A military transport rolled by. The soldiers were sitting in their wagons, soaked and exhausted. An old Jewish woman was trudging along, muddy and ragged. One of the soldiers noticed her, stopped his wagon, and offered her a ride. Our Austrian soldiers would never do a thing like that.

I visited the rabbi, Hirsh Rapaport, who had been described to me as very learned and brilliant. I found him absorbed in a holy book. After a hearty welcome, he listened to me closely, nodding in sad silence. A few times, he tried to speak but plainly couldn't find the right words. When I said a few comforting things, he eyed me with bitter reproach and lowered his head. But as I was about to leave, he removed a volume from a closet and showed me a passage which said that the sufferings portending the Messiah would begin in the year 5674 (1914) and that the Messiah would come in 5684 (1924). Next he pulled out *Pirkey d'Rabbi Eliezer,* a book of biblical commentary, and showed me a passage listing the signs that would herald the arrival of the Messiah. He paid special heed to one: "And the ink and the pen will vanish."

In Czortkow, I heard about a man who had taken an oath of silence fifteen years ago and not spoken a word since. He had been a rich merchant, whose stock included gunpowder. One day he had a fight with his wife and had yelled at her, "Go to blazes!" A few hours later, she had gone down to the basement with a candle, which she had inadvertently set down on the powder keg. The powder exploded, killing her and their two children. The traumatized merchant believed that his curse was responsible for the disaster and had gone to the rabbi to ask for atonement. After hearing him out, the rebbe said, "If a man has such a tongue, he should hold it." From then on, the man never spoke another word. He stayed in Czortkow, moving to a tiny room by the rabbi's synagogue, sitting there perpetually engrossed in the holy texts. His room contained only a small table and two chairs. There was no bed. In those fifteen years, he had never lain down. He would doze at the table for a couple of hours. As for food, he lived on whatever was brought by charitable people—so long as they didn't forget. Only old acquaintances knew the man's real name. The townsfolk called him "Shoysek"—Hebrew for "the silent man."

The silent man received me warmly and asked me in sign language what I wanted.

"I'd like to know how you feel about what's happening in the world," I replied.

He scrutinized me with his clear, childlike eyes and burst into sudden laughter. Taking a holy book from the table, he opened it, turned to a folded page, and somewhat triumphantly indicated a passage. I looked at it. The passage spoke about the coming of the Messiah.

In the most dreadful despair, when the Jews lost hope of salvation, they were drawn with passionate faith to the ancient channel of national deliverance and revival—the Messiah.

I left Czortkow in the afternoon. It was a lovely winter day. The sun was shining, pouring radiance on the downy, silvery snow, which lay everywhere, rich and weightless. The world was dominated by two colors, white and black, and each stroke was as sharp as if etched in steel. The view was broad and opulent as if nature were spreading a silvery white cloth in preparation for a banquet.

My driver, a boy from Podvolotshisk, was enchanted by the sun. He stood in the sleigh, driving the horses harder and harder and singing loudly and wildly—a medley of cantorial chants and Gentile ditties.

All at once, a hare popped up far away. It stood on its hind legs, its ears alert and its little body quivering with strenuous attention. Suddenly, it took fright and whizzed off. A while later, another creature, a larger one with a bushy tail, showed up in the distance. I couldn't tell what it was.

"A wolf!" my driver shouted, interrupting his song.

As we drew closer, I saw that it was a fox. It moved in our direction, stealthily, never once shifting its smart, heedful little eyes from us.

"Oh, too bad we don't have a rifle!" said my driver. "He'd make a lovely stole!"

But I wasn't sorry that we had no rifle. I gazed lovingly at the little fox, at the snow, at the sun-kissed expanse, and my heart sang that I was alive, that I was present in this glorious moment, and I felt a deep rapport with the boundless, incomprehensible world.

I spent only a few hours in Yagelnitse, visiting a Jewish girls' home, which had twenty-five children between the ages of five and twelve. They were gaunt, despondent. The administrator and instructor, a local woman, told me there was room for lots more children, but the shortage of clothes and shoes prevented many from reaching the home. It was impossible to set up any kind of systematic schooling because there were no textbooks, no stationery. So the teacher was limited to telling the children stories and teaching them songs, which they memorized.

Quiet and apathetic, they sat around a big table, and the teacher cued them to sing. They intoned a mournful Jewish song about military recruits:

> *Better to study Torah with Rashi*
> *Than to eat the army's kasha,*
> *Better never to be born*
> *Than wear the emperor's uniform.*

I was surprised. "Where did they learn that?"

"There was a Jewish soldier here; he was billeted in a Jewish home. He taught the song to the children, and it spread all over the shtetl. Now all the children know it by heart."

How interesting that a Jewish soldier had brought an antimilitary song to this occupied country.

I visited the food center established by the Association of Towns. The center, I had been told, refused to distribute bread to Jews. The manager explained that he had received no food for weeks now and had nothing to hand out. A cartoon he had drawn hung on the wall. It showed a throng of people driven by famine personified in a skeleton clutching a whip. They were mobbing a door with a sign that said "Food Center of the Association of Towns." The door sported a huge padlock.

The manager gave me the cartoon as a souvenir.

10

Yagelnitse is the southernmost part of the area of Galicia held nonstop by the Russians until their final pullout, so the town was barely damaged. Outside Yagelnitse, the sight was very different. At every step, there were trenches, barbed wire, pits left by shells, burned villages—and ruins, endless ruins.

And the farther you traveled, the greater the devastation: towns burned, smashed, wiped off the face of the earth. Upon seeing them, you instantly knew that these places hadn't simply gone up in flames. A cruel and bloody storm of annihilation had blasted through—a hurricane of insanity. It was as if the ripped, shattered, mutilated skeletons of houses constituted in themselves the very spirit of the war, which, sweeping through in all its blind ferocity, had petrified into a stone carcass.

Tlusti, a shtetl several dozen miles from Yagelnitse, was a shambles. Of its 560 houses, barely 32 had survived—and were half wrecked at that. Squeezed into them were 143 of the more than 2,000 families (over 5,000 people) that had once lived here.

The Russians first marched in at the start of the war, during the month of Elul 5674, autumn 1914. Only sixty or seventy Jewish families took off with the Austrians. The town had not suffered from any battle, but the combination of pogroms, forced labor, confiscations, and isolation from the rest of the world produced a terrible famine. That summer, at the end of Tammuz, mid-July, a cholera epidemic broke out. Within six or seven weeks, it claimed three hundred lives, including the rabbi's. The terrified inhabitants began fleeing to wherever they could. More than one hundred families defied the severe prohibition against leaving the town. One year later, around Rosh Hashanah, in September 1915, the Russians pulled out, but not before torching the shtetl. The Austrians showed up, spent no more than a week here, and retreated once again. They were joined by almost the entire Jewish population. Perhaps ten families remained.

Upon returning, the Russians again set fire to the town, and they also tore down some fifty houses for wood.

One week after the reappearance of the Russians, two hundred Jewish families passed through. They were being deported from Ustyetsky to Zbarz. Fifty or sixty stayed here, settling in the empty homes. Next came some thirty or forty families expelled from the surrounding villages. At the same time, around fifty families who had fled the cholera epidemic also came back. Thus, more than half the residents were newcomers; they had no work of any sort and were starving.

That evening, upon reaching Tlusti, I went to a local committee member, and we had our meeting at his home. The session dragged on until midnight because of a conflict. The committee asked for an increase in the wood supply, but Homelsky had told me not to approve any such thing. When the meeting was adjourned, I realized I needed a place to stay. There was a terrible frost; the wind was blasting, which made traveling at night dangerous. My drayman, who was already asleep, would hardly have agreed to drive in this weather. But in this cramped home, there was absolutely no space for me. The committee chairman, who was said to be wealthy, offered to put me up—and I accepted. But when we arrived at his home, I saw that he and the other six members of his family were all living in a single, tiny room. My host and his wife whispered together, and then she began preparing the sole couch for me.

"Where will you sleep?" I asked.

"Don't worry, don't worry," my host assured me. "Everything's been arranged."

When I insisted, he told me he was sending his wife and three daughters to stay with neighbors, while he, his son, and his old father would sleep here on the floor. This was very unpleasant for me, but there was nothing I could do. So I spent the night.

The instant I lay down, I felt a strong, icy draft from the window near the couch. When I got up and checked, I found that the window frame was much smaller than the opening, leaving wide gaps on top and on one side. Obviously the wrong size of frame had been installed. I stuffed my pillow into the gaps, but it barely filled them. When I awoke at dawn, my tongue was dry and there was a horribly bitter taste in my mouth. I saw that the walls and the ceiling were coated with thick mildew. That awful taste remained in my mouth for several days. And that was how the rich people were living.

Before my departure, I tried to pay the lady of the house for putting me up. She wouldn't hear of it. However, her elderly father-in-law, greedily ogling the rubles in my hand, yelled at her: "Take it, take it! If someone offers—take! Take!"

Tlusti has its holy relics. Supposedly, it was the birthplace of the Baal-Shem-Tov.* In any case, this was where his mother had lived and where

---

*Rabbi Yisroel Baal-Shem-Tov (1698–1760) was the founder of Hasidism.

he had spent his youth. At the cemetery, the locals point out his mother's grave. And in town, they show you the former site of the Baal-Shem-Tov's *mikvah,* his ritual bathhouse. Since his mother was a midwife, he was at first named Yisroel the Midwife's Son.

The people here told me a lot of stories about the Baal-Shem-Tov. A man named Hersh had attacked the Baal-Shem-Tov, who then said, "He will remember me." Hersh and his descendants were cursed for ten generations. His family is still hounded by misfortune, and no rabbi can help them.

Once, on the eve of Passover, some Gentiles placed a dead child in the Baal-Shem-Tov's home in order to invoke a blood libel. Upon finding the body, the Baal-Shem-Tov dressed it in Jewish clothes, including a cap, and put the corpse at his table. It sat there as if alive. The Baal-Shem-Tov then cried, "Bastard, rock!" And the dead child began rocking back and forth over the Haggadah. Meanwhile townspeople and soldiers surrounded the house. When they broke in, they searched but found nothing. It never occurred to them that the boy at the table rocking over the Haggadah was the dead child. After they left, the Baal-Shem-Tov buried him in the yard.

I was told other stories—how the Baal-Shem-Tov set the Struzh River on fire—but I've forgotten them.

II

I crossed the border into Bukovina.

The farther south I went, the lovelier and more vivid the scenery. The shtetls and villages were nestled in valleys ringed by mountains. Many of the views recalled Swiss landscapes. From afar, tall trees rose from orchards, church steeples towered (the churches were intact everywhere), and the spires of town halls pierced the sky. But when I came closer, I found a cemetery, charred ruins that looked like unburied corpses. It was horrifying. When I met someone, I could read the entire tragedy of the area in his gaze. And behind a calm appearance I sensed the bitterness and rage of a powerless victim. Russian soldiers wandering the ruins expressed amazement that human beings, his brothers, could have left behind this wasteland. Without necessarily understanding, they were ashamed of these atrocities. I too felt ashamed. . . .

I arrived in Zaleshtshik, a large town of eight thousand people (90 percent Jews) and one thousand houses.

Many months had gone by since the invasions and the fires and the pogroms, but their traces were still fresh. All kinds of icons, which had shielded the Gentiles against injury, were still hanging on their doors and in their windows. Tattered pages from sacred Jewish books were scattered in the streets. Mountains of ripped volumes and Torah scrolls lay in the shattered synagogues and study houses. In one synagogue alone, the Russians had torn up thirty-five Torah scrolls.

The streets were empty. Here and there, in a torched house that still had its walls, stood a small table with bread and cigarettes—and next to it an old Jewish man or woman, blue from the cold. All their customers were soldiers.

I saw that the windows of these ruined houses were stuffed with rags or boarded up. In these unheated kennels were human beings, whole families, starving, usually sick because all kinds of epidemics were raging. . . . I met families with one member in America, a second in the Austrian army, a third somewhere in Vienna or Budapest, the fourth in exile in Siberia, and the rest—here. And no one had news of the rest of his family.

If people came back and found that their house had gone up in smoke, they settled in another home with walls and roofs. They roamed the town, finding a door here, a window there. After the Jews had been expelled, the town had collected their belongings—clothes, pillows, featherbeds—and hidden them. Now everyone went to the town hall and picked out whatever he needed without worrying about the owners. It was like a commune.

I visited an ice-cold study house. In one tiny, heated room, an approximate quorum of poor Jews was sitting by the stove. One man, about seventy-five years old, was the rabbi of a nearby shtetl. Sick and weak, he was shivering despite his threadbare fur coat and the warmth of the stove.

I asked a few questions.

"What's there to say?" he responded indifferently. "Maybe it's supposed to be this way. You have to resign yourself to anything and everything."

After a pause he began to speak in a kind of recitative way, as if intoning the Book of Lamentations: "I was the rabbi of my shtetl for forty years, but now it's been destroyed. I had my own home, but it went up in flames. I had two sons, but they were taken away. Who knows if they're still alive? And then the holy books. . . . All of them burned. What am I without the holy books? It's like being without a hand . . . without a heart."

Lowering his head, he added: "I was working on a treatise for thirty years—I poured my heart and soul into it. And it got burned too.

"Well, but then again," he said more cheerily, "the Holy One, Blessed Be He, is worse off than us. We each have our worries, but He's got all the Jewish worries on his shoulders."

I handed him a cigarette.

"Oh, look! A cigarette! What reason do I have to worry?" He lit up.

In Snyatin I found the same situation as in Zaleshtshik. The same destruction, icons outside the Gentile homes, and the pages of holy books near the Jewish homes. The same charred ruins, with the same fitted doors from other houses, the same shattered windows stuffed with rags. However, a few dozen shops were open in the marketplace.

The cold, the famine, the crowded conditions had triggered epidemics of typhus, smallpox, dysentery. At the hospital I found seventy-two typhus cases. There must have been the same number out in the town.

There was no relief committee in Snyatin or Zaleshtshik. Fyodor Fedorovich Trepov, the governor-general, refused to allow any such organization in the province of Bukovina. He claimed that the Jews were wealthy enough to get along without help. So the Jews had to operate illegally, with Homelsky appointing a committee. . . .

Much to my surprise, I found an inn in Snyatin. True, the inn had only a one guest room, with a dirt floor. But the room was big and had four windows as well as a bed with bedding and clean linen. There was also a kitchen, where the innkeeper's wife was working with her five small children. The room she gave me was always ready for guests, especially officers.

I struck up a conversation with the wife, a prematurely aged woman of twenty-eight. She had been pregnant with her fifth child when her husband had reported for duty in the Austrian army. When she was on the verge of giving birth, the population had been expelled. She had been given a hand wagon. After putting in the two smaller children, she had harnessed herself to the wagon and started out with everyone else. The two older children, five and six years of age, walked behind. It had taken a whole week to cover the thirty miles to Czortkow. They had been weak with thirst, hunger, and exhaustion. In Czortkow she had given birth lying on hay in a stable. During her confinement, she had fallen ill with typhus. Her joints had been inflamed.

Meanwhile the Austrians had retaken Snyatin. Her husband had gotten a pass to see his family. When he arrived, no one could tell him what had become of them. The locals told him that the Russian army had driven all the Jews to the bridge and blown it up. Every last one, they said, had been killed or drowned. Hearing this, the husband wanted to kill himself but was talked out of it. The neighbors said he stayed in his home for days at a time, lamenting and banging his head against the wall.

Meanwhile, the wife recovered and went to work to feed her children, who, miraculously, hadn't died of starvation. When the Jews were allowed back into Snyatin, she had been one of the first to come, after learning that her cottage was intact. She had managed to set herself up, more or less, earning money by baking bread and renting out the room. She had remarkable energy and vitality. But her husband, still with the Austrian army, did not yet know that his family was alive.

I noticed the same energy in others. I spent three days watching the deportees begin their lives anew, and I was both astonished and delighted by what I saw. Only two months had passed since they had come home, and despite the terrible conditions, the cold, the hunger, and the epidemics, the town was coming back to life. Some fifty shops had opened; the peasants were bringing grain and purchasing wares that the storekeepers had managed to unearth. Nearly all the craftsmen had set up workshops and were hard at work. The synagogue had been repaired. A rabbi and a ritual slaughterer were in place, and setting up religious schools. They were sure that within six months, the town would be flourishing, assuming there was no more bloodshed.

While the woman was telling me her story, her eldest boy came in. He was skin and bones, his arms like rails, his face without a drop of color. But his little eyes were bright and alert.

"Were you at school?" I asked him.

"Of course. I began studying Talmud the day before the Russians came."

"And now?"

"I've forgotten everything."

"Do you remember what happened here when they drove you out?"

"Certainly. A Cossack with a fur hat ran in and yelled, 'All you Jews, clear out!' I'm scared of Cossacks." He curled up in the chair to demonstrate his fear. A vague smile appeared on his thin, pale lips.

Snyatin had its own memories of the Baal-Shem-Tov. It was said that he had taught at a *kheder*. One year he had been unable to obtain an *etrog* for the Succot festival. He was very worried. On the eve of Succot, a Gentile horseman entered the town on a panting, sweat-drenched horse. "Where is Moyshe-Srulik?" the rider demanded. The Baal-Shem-Tov came out of his house. The rider handed him an *etrog* and vanished.

12

I left Snyatin in a wagon driven by an elderly Jew from a small Galician shtetl. He had a pair of good horses and earned a decent living. Earlier, however, after the Russians had pulled in, he had gone through a lot. He described a typical event of that period: soldiers had seized his very last horse. He spoke with good-natured irony, as if talking about a long-past misfortune. But his story had a profound impact on me, revealing the most important feature of the Russians, the most important reason for their defeats.

> Before the war, I had an income from a pair of horses and two small wagons. When the Russians came, they grabbed one of my horses and a wagon. So I made do with a single horse. One day,

while I was driving through town, I was stopped by some Russian soldiers. They unhitched my horse and went off with it. There I was, with my wagon, stranded in the middle of the countryside. I wept bitterly. Some more soldiers walked by. They asked me why I was crying, and I told them. So they said, "Your horse was probably taken to police headquarters, two miles from here. Go over and appeal to the commander—he's a colonel. He'll return your horse."

So I followed their advice and went to police headquarters. When I arrived, I looked—and it was true. A lot of horses were standing around, and I recognized mine among them. I even pulled up some grass and fed it to him. Then I went to the commander. I found him drinking tea at an outdoor table—an elderly man with a fine and decent appearance. I bowed and told him about how I was robbed. So he said, "Go to the horses and tell the soldiers I've authorized you to take back your horse." I went over. But the soldiers laughed and began beating me. I went back to the commander and told him what had happened. So he called to his orderly and said, "Ivan, accompany him to the horses, and if you find his horse, tell the men that I order them to return it." But by the time we got there, the soldiers had hidden my horse. I searched, but I couldn't find it. We went back to the commander, and Ivan told him that my horse wasn't there.

"Damn it," yelled the colonel, "you're trying to put one over on me. Ivan, get some rope and hang him up by his feet from the tree—for five minutes. That'll teach him."

Ivan didn't hesitate. He bound my feet together, slung the rope over a thick branch, and began hoisting me up. I was already upside down. But then a young man, a student or an officer, came out of the house, saw me dangling, and said to the commander, "What are you doing? Don't you find it awful torturing a man like that?"

The commander shouted, "Ivan, let him down." So Ivan untied me. I stood there in my torment, with tears pouring from my eyes.

The commander yelled, "Why are you crying?"

"Why shouldn't I cry? You seized my only horse, you beat me, you strung me up—and on top of it I'm famished. I haven't eaten all day."

"You haven't eaten?" cried the commander. "Ivan, take him to the kitchen, give him some bread and a glass of tea—let him eat."

Ivan took me to the kitchen, gave me a glass of tea, three lumps of sugar, and a large chunk of bread. I ate. When I finished my tea, Ivan gave me a refill with three more lumps of sugar. But then the commander walked in, saw me, and yelled, "Look at the Jew making himself at home! Get out of here!" And he gave me a powerful blow. I scurried away, terrified out of my wits, and broke into a run. Then I heard Ivan behind me: "Stop. Come back. The commandant wants you."

So I doubled back. The commander was standing by the kitchen door, holding three rubles. "Take something for your horse. And remember, we Russians might beat people, but we let no one cry and we give them money."

I took the three rubles, thanked him, and headed toward my wagon. But I hadn't gone one hundred feet before Ivan caught up with me. "The commander has ordered me to take back the three rubles and slap you three times." I forked over the money, but he didn't slap me; he felt sorry for me.

I returned to my wagon. A short time later, Ivan brought me a horse—not my own, a different horse, a worse one: "Here, the commander sent this to you for your horse."

I've often noted that Galician Jews, tormented and ruined by the Russian army, nevertheless enthuse about the Russian character. They always have a story about a soldier or an officer who displayed a poignant idealism and humanity. The following letter was written by a Russian soldier to his parents:

We were in the fortress town of Osovets. It was around eleven A.M. on the festival of Hoshanah Rabah. Suddenly we heard Romantov, a major general, calling, "Jews, step forward!" All two hundred Jewish soldiers obeyed. Romantov launched into a speech:

Jewish children:
Do you know what day this is for the Jews? This is the day on which your prayers are answered. Pray to your God, God of

Israel, God of Abraham, Isaac, and Jacob. The God who brought you out of bondage in Egypt and led you across the Red Sea is a great and merciful God. He spreads out His arms and gathers in the prayers of His beloved nation. After all, our Jesus Christ is also descended from you Jews. Pray, my children, as best you can. If you have to read from a prayer book, then do so. If you can recite from memory, then fine. Perhaps your prayers will move God to help us.

Every Jew prayed. Then we got back in formation.

I. M. Perpikar

Then there was the letter the Proskurov relief committee received from a priest in Satano, which had expelled its Jews. He wrote about the local Christian relief committee:

So long as our committee was operating, everything was in order. The houses were sealed, property was closely guarded, and there was no looting. But with the arrival of the transport company, our guards refused to serve, and when the committee saw how powerless it was, it had to halt its activities. By now, half the Jewish homes have been pillaged and cleaned out. The Proskurov committee must therefore take any possible measures to protect the poor and meager belongings that have survived. The members should also organize an investigation into who perpetrated the thefts and sold the loot in the marketplace—it won't be hard to work out. Nor would it hurt to touch on the question of why the local authorities did nothing to stop the plundering. . . . Take steps as quickly as feasible—otherwise, within three or four weeks, there won't even be a muddy rug left in any Jewish house.

Respectfully,
Father W. Wolosewicz
Member of the Committee
8 August (1915)

And here is a letter from a Russian ensign to a six-year-old girl with whose family he was briefly billeted:

> A testament to Niute from a man about to go into combat. My dear, sweet Niute, when you're all grown up, love your nation, which suffers so much. Don't turn your back on it, and take pride in being a Jew.
>
> After spending several days with your parents, who showed so much loving hospitality to us Christians, even though we oppress you, I realized that your people treat all persons like brothers, no matter what their faith. We all have one God, to whom we pray and who will lead you Jews on a radiant path.
>
> You, Niute, are lucky that your life is beginning at a time when, amid the booming of cannon and the storm of rifles, we are sacrificing our lives for a grand goal, and our blood is joining all nations together in a single family. When the Great War is over, do not forget those men who, in the cold trenches, encountered the birth of Jesus Christ, who told us to love all our neighbors.
>
> Ensign Nikolai Maslenikov

But the Russian also inflicted atrocities: In a Russian-occupied shtetl near Wolkowisk, the soldiers drove the Jews into the marketplace and ordered them to strip naked. The men and women were ordered to dance with one another and then ride on pigs. Finally, one tenth of the naked Jews were shot and killed. Soldiers forced a son to hang his own father. And in the town of Nazardin, they dug up a young Jew who had been buried a day earlier, and they strung up the corpse in his prayer shawl.

As for the Germans, they were cruel as well. In Blonye, a shtetl near Warsaw, I heard that when the Germans marched in, they came upon a farm several miles from town, a barrack with 192 cholera patients. The retreating Russians had been unable to take them along. The Germans were scared the disease might spread, so they put straw around the barrack and ignited it. All 192 patients burned to death.

I don't know what's worse: torching a barrack filled with sick people or making people strip naked, ride on pigs, and gunning them down. The barrack fire, no matter how inhumane, at least had a specific goal. With the Germans, you knew who you were dealing with. You knew that when it came to a necessary objective, they wouldn't stop at the worst cruelty. By the same token, you could be certain that if you didn't get in their way, they wouldn't lay a finger on you. But with Russians, you were never sure of your life, of your dignity. The Russians were never guided by sound logic or practical considerations.

In a dreadful crisis that demanded all our mental and physical strength, I saw the Russian soldiers indulge in wild nonsense and bestial games. I never doubted that Russia would lose the war. But in fact it was even worse. The savagery affected everyone, from the Cossack to the czar. What were the expulsions of Jews from whole areas if not capricious games, madness with no political or military justification? The result was the collapse of the Russian Empire.

13

Czernowitz, the capital of the tiny province of Bukovina, is practically the only place that was spared the storm, an oasis in the wasteland. From a distance of a few miles, I could see a big European city with large churches, brick buildings, and palaces.

Riding through the wide, bustling streets, I saw large boutiques filled with all sorts of elegant articles, the rich edifices, the hotels with their good, clean rooms, the posters announcing soirees, concerts, spectacles, and other entertainments. I felt spirited away to a different world. And yet I experienced a strange and horrible sensation: I caught myself longing for the burned, mutilated homes and stores. My eyes looked for them. And the houses with windows, the open boutiques, the calm streets—all this everyday life struck me as abnormal.

Later on, I learned that veterans of battle, who have seen corpses, maimed bodies, and rivers of blood, yearn for those things. Ordinary life seems pale to them without the cannon, without the shrieks. . . .

I met the representatives of the Jewish population, the leaders who had hung on in Czernowitz, weathering all the torments of the Russian occupation. They had formed a committee that included Marek Fish (a rich storekeeper), Yirmiye Sikopant (the head of the orphanage), Dovid Shekhner, Shimen Sas, Hersh Rimer, and Leo Hershman.

Their attitude to welfare was very different. "We're very glad that so far we haven't gotten any help from Kiev," said Mr. Fish. "We haven't turned into beggars."

He told me the city required no help. True, the richer Jews had left; those who remained had been ruined by the war, the expropriations, and the lootings. Nevertheless, they were able to maintain the poor, even the homeless, of whom some five hundred were needy. The committee had managed to gather thirty thousand crowns locally. When the Jewish hospital had run out of funds and was about to close, they had succeeded in collecting sixty-five hundred crowns within an hour.

The other committee members expressed a different opinion. They believed they couldn't get along with no outside assistance. The city was growing poorer and poorer, and those who could donate refused. Had the committee been officially approved, it could have levied contributions. Money was especially needed for Passover. But the governor-general flatly opposed the formation of any Jewish relief committee. The members could only hope that I, as a representative of the Kiev committee, might get him to change his mind. In Kiev, H. D. Margolin had given me a recommendation to Trepov's aide, Colonel Krilov, who might help me in this matter.

Turning down any direct benefits from Kiev, the Czernowitz leaders asked me to get the Kiev committee to lend them money for the wives of reservists. The Austrian government had given these women booklets according to which they were to receive a monthly compensation. Now, under the Russians, they could get nothing. But the assets were secure, and the government would pay everything once peace was concluded. So the committee had decided to set up a fund, using the reservist booklets as collateral for loans amounting to 50 percent of the sums due. The plan was to amass several tens of thousands of crowns in Czernowitz and receive matching loans from the Kiev committee under the auspices of the local Jewish administration.

Mr. Sikopant called for a meeting of some ten or twelve wealthy householders, who guaranteed twenty thousand crowns. I promised to ask the Kiev committee for a matching sum. (Unfortunately, I failed, for when I returned to Kiev, the committee's finances were so shaky that it couldn't increase its budget by the requested amount.)

I had to see the governor-general not only about permission to start a Jewish relief committee but about other matters, too. Passover was only a month away, and we were wondering about matzohs for the indigent and for the frontline Jewish troops. Together with Mr. Homelsky, we drew up a budget, a very skimpy one. At least fifty thousand rubles was needed. Throughout the occupied territory, the Russians had strictly prohibited the transport of flour from one place to another, so that many towns and hamlets might be unable to bake matzohs. The Grzimalov committee began obtaining Passover flour more cheaply for the town and nearby places. Tarnopol was also supplied. And some merchants there actually took it upon themselves to provide Passover flour for all Galicia and Bukovina if allowed by the governor-general. We calculated that 350 to 400 sacks were required.

I would have to ask Trepov to authorize the shipment of the flour, grant Passover furloughs in the closest shtetls to the Jewish soldiers near the front, and allow us to send matzohs to those at the front lines. First, I met with Colonel Krilov. Margolin's recommendation impressed him deeply. The colonel said he was an ardent friend of the Jews and would try to get Trepov to okay my requests. But, with a sigh, he confided that we would have a hard time because Trepov was angry at the local Jews for their animosity toward the Russians. Nevertheless, he advised me to make the attempt. A few days later, Krilov told me that the governor-general was willing to see me.

Trepov's reception was very cold. He stood there without even extending his hand and told me to be brief. When I started to talk about relief committees, he impatiently broke in: "I was already petitioned to allow them, and I categorically refused. If the inhabitants in a defeated country are very hostile to us, I can't permit them to have their organizations."

"Such committees," I responded, "are authorized throughout Galicia."

"I'm not concerned with what goes on in Galicia. And I consider their approval a clear case of negligence."

"They've been operating for more than a year, and the local authorities are very satisfied with their activities, which they find useful."

"That may be so there, but conditions are different here."

"I must tell you," I went on, "that this issue is important not only for the local population but for the army as well. In places where no committees exist and the inhabitants don't have even the most basic food, epidemics of cholera and typhus erupt and then spread into the army."

"For God's sake!" he screamed. "Why are you telling me about the plight of the population? I don't know about Galicia, but here in Bukovina the Jews are rich and up to their ears in gold. They don't need any help. The few paupers who require aid can he taken care of privately without committees and organizations."

Convinced there was nothing I could do, I moved on to my requests for flour transports and Passover furloughs. But Trepov replied that these issues were not within his jurisdiction; I should go to the head of the military staff in Kamenyets-Podolsk.

Before leaving, I brought up the matter again. I told the governor-general that his refusal put the Kiev committee in a desperate predicament. The committee was authorized, recognized as a useful institution, and received government subsidies. Without a relief committee in Bukovina, the Kiev committee could not conduct its normal work.

My argument had a slight effect.

"Submit a detailed report," he answered, "and I'll take it under advisement."

On my way out, Krilov came over and whispered, "Have the Kiev committee send him a written petition signed by Margolin and Brodsky. He knows them personally. I'll help you."

Because of this and also because I had to appeal to army headquarters in Kamenyets, I had to get back to Kiev. After drawing up an account of my activities during the several months of my travels, a plan for further work, and an estimate for Passover, I prepared to leave. But first I visited the devastated town of Sadagora near Czernowitz.

14

For years now, Sadagora has been the seat of a Hasidic dynasty that traces its ancestry back to Ber of Mezeritsh, the greatest disciple of the Baal-Shem-Tov. The Mezeritsher's grandson, Sholem-Shakhne of Pogrebishts, who founded the Sadagora dynasty, was a great cabalist with an extraordinary personality. He dressed in European style and led a grand, aristocratic life like the great Poles of his day. His son, the renowned Yisroel of Rezhin, who first settled in Sadagora, surpassed his father in both greatness and conduct. Tradition, which ascribes a whole slew of miracles to the Rezhiner, assures us that he contained the soul of the Baal-Shem-Tov. His court was like an emperor's. A band of twenty-four musicians played during every meal, and his carriage was drawn by six horses. His son and his grandson continued his luxurious ways, and the court of Sadagora was famed as the richest and noblest of the Hasidic courts.

The war, which ravaged so many Jewish treasures, also devastated this court with its unique style and its great material and spiritual antiquities, which had been handed down through generations.

Before the war, the town of Sadagora had had some ten thousand inhabitants, three-quarters of them Jewish. In September 1914, when the Russians first took Sadagora, a terrible pogrom was launched. All the Jewish homes and businesses were pillaged, and many Jews were killed or wounded.

Leyb Retter, the wealthy and venerated chairman of the local Jewish administration and also a mayoral assistant, was killed along with three others when they tried to protect their wives and daughters from rape. Aside from one hundred Jewish women whom the local pharmacist hid in his cellar for three days and nights without food or water, every last woman, young or old, was violated. At a nearby estate belonging to Aleykim Gastanter, an officer carried away the owner's two daughters, and Vaysenberg's daughter was also taken away. Supposedly, they were returned a couple of days later.

The Russians left Sadagora within a short time. When they returned, in December of that same year, nearly all the Jews fled, generally to Czernowitz. Their properties were looted by the peasants from the surrounding countryside. The few remaining Jews had to endure great slander and torment.

An interesting case was the defamation and arrest of two Jews, Yitsik Shmatnik and Shmuel Zagrebelsky (a Russian subject). It seems that a telephone was found in a granary at the rebbe's court, where they were living. Later on, it turned out that when the first Russian division pulled in, a telephone linked up with Czernowitz had been discovered in the rebbe's home. So the troops had torn out the wires and thrown the apparatus into the granary. After a time, when a second division marched in and found the apparatus, they accused Shmatnik and Zagrebelsky of transmitting military secrets to the Austrians in Czernowitz. The two Jews were put on trial, and this was the verdict:

· MAY 16, 1915 ·

The Court-Martial declares the defendants not guilty of conspiring with one another and then, at the end of April of the year 1915, during the time of the Russian-Austrian War, in the town of Sadagora, where Russian military was stationed, of using a telephone found in their place of residence and connected to Czernowitz, where Austrian military was stationed, and communicating all sorts of the latest information about the number and location of the Russian military—because the charges have not been proved.

We therefore . . . rule as follows;

The court hereby acquits the defendants, Yitsik Shmatnik and Shmuel Zagrebelsky, of the above charges.

But although exculpated, the two Jews were deported to Russia anyway: Zagrebelsky to prison in Kiev and Shmatnik to Siberia.

I drove to Sadagora in a military car together with Dr. Ratni, a Jewish army surgeon at a Czernowitz hospital. I was also taking along a Sadagora Jew, a *melamed,* who had been in Czernowitz all this time, too scared to head back to Sadagora—terrified of the soldiers and the Gentiles there.

He offered to sell me some rare old holy books he had concealed in Sadagora. He knew that his cottage at the edge of town had not gone up in flames, and he was certain his tomes were still in one piece.

"I hid them so well," he boasted, "that the devil himself couldn't find them."

And indeed his home was still standing, but without doors or windows. Inside, we found straw and horse droppings.

The *melamed* gaped like a lunatic at his cottage. He barely recognized it.

"Where are your books stowed?" I asked him.

"In the attic," he replied in a dull voice.

We got hold of a ladder and climbed up to the attic. So much for the books! Even the chimney bricks had been torn off.

The man stood in the attic, demoralized, staring at the corner where he had hidden his books. He had covered them with bricks, confident that no one would find them. Utterly surprised and with his head hanging, he rode back toward Czernowitz.

I myself went to the Hasidic rebbe's court, which was located on the outskirts of town.

Two red medieval castles in Moorish style were flanked by ingeniously ornamented circular towers with battlements and enormous portals. Of the two castles, which were identical in size and architecture, one was the rebbe's home, the other the synagogue.

The walls of both buildings were still whole, but the interiors had been thoroughly looted, wrecked, and soiled. Now both structures housed a military typhus hospital.

I shuddered when I saw the rebbe's house: gutted rooms, broken walls thickly coated with mud and spit. In the largest room, the walls were lined with cots, on which sick Romanian soldiers, newly arrived from the front, were sitting or lying. Dark, haggard, gloomy shadows in wet, muddy, tattered overcoats, half barefoot, squeezed together, trembling with fever, moaning. In the next room, orderlies were bandaging wounds and trimming the hair of typhus patients. The third room contained a bath; it had a heated cauldron. Amid dense steam and a suffocating stench, a few dozen naked soldiers were shuffling about, sick and emaciated.

In the first room, the senior physician, motioning toward the Romanian troops, said to me: "How do you like our heroes, our brave allies? Ha! They thought that waging war is as simple as playing in a Romanian band." Then, more softly, as if murmuring a secret, he added: "Do you know what the czar said about Romanians? 'Romania isn't a nation, it's a profession.' Ha! Brilliant."

When we stepped outside, the physician halted, and, pointing toward a wall, he said, "Do you see these palaces? Marvelous architecture, real castles! . . . They belonged to a very great Jewish rabbi, a kind of archduke, whom the Jews idolize. He was incredibly rich, he had hundreds of millions, and he transferred everything to Austria in time. This house is a historic building. This was the site of the famous Beilis trial, which agitated the entire world."

I was astonished. "What do you mean this was the site of the Beilis trial?"

"Here, here!" he responded, smiling like a man who is in on a secret. "I know it for certain!"

"What are you talking about? The trial took place in Kiev."

"Kiev!" He scornfully waved it off. "That was for show! Puppets were dancing in Kiev, and the strings were being pulled here. This is where the real trial took place."

"How could that be?"

"The greatest Jewish rabbis convened here with the richest bankers in the world, and the entire trial took place right here. It was presided over by the local archimandrite. They worked out all the details and fixed the huge sum of money that it would cost. From here, all the directives and orders were transmitted to Kiev. And whatever was determined here was enacted there."

He told everything with such deep conviction that I had no doubt: the old, educated Russian intellectual earnestly believed in that wild fantasy.

He pointed to the other castle. "That's the second building. It used to be a synagogue. We set up a hospital there. It's got all of eighty cots."

I entered the large and very lofty synagogue. There I instantly noticed the rows of cots with sick and dying men lying there in military overcoats. The air was heavy and stank. The sick were all gaping at us—with pitiful eyes pleading for help. In other cots, the eyes were cold, hard, and serious—and already hopeless, self-absorbed. A whole gamut of looks!

I peered around. Torn, naked, filthy walls, with a few traditional pictures left here and there: lions and leopards, musical instruments. An expensive but broken chandelier hung from the ceiling.

Then my eyes alighted on the eastern wall—and what I saw made me tremble. The rich ornamentation of the Holy Ark with the Tablets of the Law above it was untouched. But at the center, on the empty Holy Ark, a Christian icon had been inserted. *Desecration.* The word flashed through my mind. And this jolted me more than any pogrom. An ancient emotion stirred in my heart, an echo of the Destruction of the Temple. I stood there, unable to avert my eyes from that bizarre image. I felt that a dreadful profaning had occurred here, a degrading of both religions. The savage hand of a brutal soldier had violated both God and man. . . .

The doctor was telling me something, but I wasn't listening.

Upon returning to Czernowitz, I met a Hasidic Jew from Sadagora. I told him what I had seen in the rebbe's synagogue. He wasn't surprised. His embittered face remained cold and stony.

"It scarcely matters compared with what happened to the rebbe's grave." He sighed softly.

"What happened?"

"You don't know? The army destroyed the entire cemetery. They smashed all the headstones—as well as the small temple on Yisroel of Rezhin's grave, which they dug up, and they made off with his bones. Someone had told them that Jews bury money in graves, so they hunted for it."

I recalled a story about the Rezhiner:

> Because of a defamation, the rebbe, as we know, was arrested for supposedly ordering or allowing the murder of two Jewish informers. But even though he was ultimately released, the Russians continued to persecute him. He fled to Austria, and the Russian government tried to extradite him. With great efforts and with the help of Prince Metternich, he persuaded the Austrian government not to send him back.
>
> This was the basis of the legend about a great struggle between the rebbe and Nicholas I. It was said that the czar nurtured a fierce personal enmity toward the Rezhiner and

persecuted him. The government ministers were amazed and once asked Nicholas: "Why are you persecuting the Rezhiner? Is it suitable for a great monarch like yourself to devote his life to chasing a despicable Jew?"

Nicholas jumped up and angrily shouted: "What do you mean 'a despicable Jew'? I spend my life twisting the world one way, and he twists it the other way. And I can't get the better of him!"

The rebbe used to say: "I was born on the same day as he was, but three hours later—and I can't get at him. If I'd been born just fifteen minutes earlier, I could defeat him."

And he would not reveal himself as a tsadik and mount his Hasidic throne so long as Nicholas was czar: "It's him or me!"

There was a tumult in all the heavenly palaces, and it was decided that Nicholas should be dethroned. But then the czar's guardian angel spoke up: "What's going on here? There's no law and no judge—this is anarchy! If both men wanted to mount the imperial throne, we could discuss which should yield to the other. But Nicholas—long may he live—is already emperor. So how can he be deposed?"

The celestial tribunal ruled that Nicholas should remain in power and that the Rezhiner should submit and reveal himself. But to make it up to him, the tribunal allowed him to go through all the palaces and take whatever he liked. And when he walked through the Palace of Music, he took along the most beautiful melody.

Nicholas I has long since died and decayed, but the war between him and his antagonist is still raging. He has stretched out his dead hand through three generations of emperors. He has destroyed the Rezhiner's court, profaned his synagogue, and flung his bones from his grave.

Pogroms were launched repeatedly throughout the area of Sadagora. The Jews of the shtetl of Bashkautsk were driven out naked for several miles. Characteristically, in a few places, such as Vaslutsk, the Ruthenian peasants openly robbed Jews, threatening to slaughter them. And as soon as the Russians marched in, all these thieves became Russophiles and started pulling their weight at the town hall. On the other hand, the Jews fled to the nearby shtetl of Czernowki and hid out in the surrounding forests for eight or ten weeks. Here, the Ruthenians secretly brought them food, shielded them, and never gave them away. When the Russian troops found one of these Jews, Shmuel Sender, they instantly chopped him to bits. And in Vaslutsk they shot and killed a boy named Aaron Rat.

15

I spent only a few days in Kiev—mostly haggling with the relief committee, which had received no money from St. Petersburg in a long time. Up to its ears in debt, it didn't know where to obtain the large funds that Homelsky and I requested. The February budget had already reached 120,000 rubles. Early debts had not been paid, and a minimum of 50,000 rubles was imperative for Passover. A total of some 200,000 was needed. Homelsky was so enervated by all the dickering that he flatly refused to do any more work until the committee forked over the entire amount. With a great deal of effort, we succeeded in calming him down, and the committee managed to hand over some money for current expenses.

I reported on my activities during the past two months and submitted a plan to reorganize the relief work and make it more efficient by focusing entirely on reviving the shtetls to which the Jews were returning. Assistance could be cut back in places like Satanov and stopped altogether in, say, Sokal and Kudrentsy, where a few inhabitants had come back and set themselves up with no outside help—and so on. As for populations that hadn't been expelled, I suggested putting the local Jewish administrations in charge of relief, on condition that they cover half the expenditures. This was possible in most shtetls, so that Kiev's overall budget would shrink by 5,000 to 10,000 rubles a month.

The committee accepted my proposal. I was given all the necessary documents for petitioning army headquarters in Kamenyets about Passover as well as the committee's personal request to the governor-general of Czernowitz to allow Jewish relief committees in Bukovina.

On the train to Czernowitz, I ran into the doctor attached to Demidov's medical division, Kozhenevksy, whom I've already talked about. I asked him about the division's activities.

"It's stationed in Volotshisk, but it's got a lot of new people."

"Where are the others?"

"They joined the army: Tatarnikov, Count Bobrinksi, and others."

"Why?"

"You know that nearly all the young men working for us were aristocrats. Their goal was not to avoid military service but to devote all their energy to the cause. And I must say, they behaved like idealists, like penitents. They worked like dogs. They slept on the ground; they did the hardest and crudest drudgery; they ate from the same cauldron as the troops and with the same wooden spoons, which they kept in their boots—just like the rank and file. It was a kind of populism, which took hold of a large segment of the aristocratic intelligentsia, and it's fused with a deep patriotism. Do you know Count Bobrinski's mother? She had two sons. One was killed at the start of the war; the other, who worked for us, died in combat a couple of months ago. She didn't shed a single tear. She said, 'It's not too great a sacrifice for Russia.' Our young men saw troops and officers going out to battle, getting killed or wounded, while they themselves were exempt. And so they couldn't just remain in our medical division; they had to join the active army. Count Bobrinski has already been killed, and I think there was someone else. . . ."

In Czernowitz, Krilov, who promised to help, submitted the Kiev committee's request to the governor-general. I expected an answer within a week.

On Purim, I went to synagogue to hear the reading of the Book of Esther. At the mention of Haman's name, the children traditionally make noise, say, by clapping; but when these children tried to clap, though very softly, their frightened parents hastily shushed them.

"Why didn't they let the children make noise?" I asked somebody afterward.

"Someone might object," he stammered. "Try and prove that they meant the ancient Haman and not the present one."

I left for Kamenyets, intending to stay two or three days, but it took me a week to cover that great distance because there were no direct passenger trains from Czernowitz.

Kamenyets had been the headquarters of the supreme commander in chief, Nikolay Nikolayevitsh. (I may be wrong; it may have been Commander Ivanov.) Drunkenness and licentiousness were commonplace, and money was squandered like water. The shopkeepers and other businessmen grew rich. However, the inhabitants suffered greatly from the arbitrary and unbridled conduct of the staff officers. But when Brusilov set up his headquarters here, everything changed. His staff was ruled by rigorous discipline, diligence, and thrift. The Russians' behavior toward the population, including the Jews, was correct in every way. On several occasions, Brusilov demonstrated sympathy toward Jews. In particular, he stopped the persecutions. He even attended a benefit evening for the Jewish war victims. On the whole, he was loved and esteemed.

I didn't get to see Brusilov himself. He was either sick or busy and couldn't come to headquarters. I was received by the staff administrator, an old general, who listened very closely and cordially to my requests regarding Passover:

"Everything that can possibly be done," he replied, "will be done so that the troops can celebrate Passover appropriately. But I don't know how to implement it."

"We ought to check how it was done last year," said his adjutant.

"Very true," the general agreed. "General I. must know what to do." He rang up General I. and gave me a document to present to him.

But General I. didn't know what to do, and so he sent me, together with another document, to another general, who, in turn, sent me to a colonel. I spent two days going from one office to the next, until finally I was told that there was no way of knowing what had been done last year, because the staff had taken along its archives. So I went back to the staff administrator, who promised to discuss the matter with Brusilov. The next day, the administrator told me that the general had granted all my requests:

1. He authorized the transportation of four hundred sacks of flour to various points in Galicia and Bukovina.
2. Jewish soldiers in rear divisions would be furloughed for Passover and allowed to go to the nearest town.
3. And we would be permitted to send matzohs to the frontline soldiers.

The general promised that he would immediately ascertain the number of Jews in the army, determine the places to which they could go for Passover, and set up the shipments of matzohs to the troops at the front.

While visiting the headquarters and other military institutions, I noticed a great deal of agitation. But I didn't learn the reason until later. It was February 28, 1917. The revolution had broken out in Petrograd. Apparently, the staff had received some pertinent information or known about it beforehand. But no one in Kamenyets had the faintest inkling.

I left Kamenyets on February 28 and reached Czernowitz on March 1. A direct freight line had just started shuttling between these two towns, and I spent two days riding in boxcars or on locomotives. I saw no newspapers, nor could I get any news from Petrograd. But the conversations taking place in my presence were highly symptomatic. At one point, I shared a heated freight car with soldiers, railroaders. When they took off their overcoats and remained in shirts belted with ropes, they became ordinary farmers with big beards and careworn but energetic faces, talking only about farm matters: about soil, about seed, about shortages. No one was interested in the war. But when they turned to political issues, they were so full of hatred and anger toward the government, so publicly scornful of the emperor ("What does he know?"), so quick to label all the ministers and generals thieves and butchers. I was amazed.

"The only decent guy is Kerensky," a soldier exclaimed. "He tells all of them off, and openly at that. He's not scared."

The night of February 28, I was waiting for a train in a cold and tiny room at a small station. Around dawn, I was joined by a young telegraph employee. He was quite drunk, and he railed at the government, on and on. I didn't respond. He then yelled heatedly: "It's their turn now. He's settling accounts. He's whipping the hell out of them!"

"Who?" I asked drowsily.

"Who? Kerensky! Listen to what he told them."

And he drunkenly repeated a speech I had read in a newspaper several days earlier. However, the speech wasn't by Kerensky; it was by Rittik, the representative of the agriculture ministry. And I said so to the young man.

"Rittik? Who's Rittik? It's Kerensky! He's the only one who can talk like that. . . . They're out to get him—they're sharpening their teeth; they want to arrest him. Not on your life! They won't succeed! It won't be allowed."

And on and on he went with his drunken babbling, which he himself didn't understand. But here, in the most out-of-the-way corner, his prattling reflected the mood of this historic moment.

16

It was late at night when I arrived in Czernowitz. The next day, March 1, I bought a newspaper, *Kievskaya Misl,* from the day before. There was nothing from Petrograd; only a brief item that no performances had taken place in the theaters.

I headed to the governor-general's office to obtain a response to my petition for relief committees. In the room I waited in, one of Trepov's adjutants was sitting and writing. Yesterday's army newspaper lay on the table. I picked it up and learned that Nicholas had dissolved the Duma.

Out loud, I said, "The Duma's been dissolved?"

The adjutant looked up from his work, glanced at me in surprise, and said, "That's old news!"

"What do you mean old?"

The paper had come out only yesterday.

The adjutant said, "A new cabinet's been formed; it's headed by Milyukov."

I was dumbfounded. "Headed by Milyukov? What do you mean?"

"A revolution has broken out in Petrograd."

The adjutant spoke calmly, but there was a touch of satisfaction in his tone.

Instead of waiting for the governor-general, I dashed off to see Dr. Ratni. There, I found sheer turmoil. I was told that the czar had been overthrown in Petrograd and the wildest rumors were circulating. It was said that four thousand people had been killed, and that Nicholas had abdicated. But nothing concrete was known.

The day wore on in feverish expectation. The next morning, at the crack of dawn, a long line started forming at the newsstand. But the new *Kievskaya Misl* dashed our hopes. It didn't contain a single telegram, a single word about Petrograd and the events taking place there. It was as if the city had vanished from the face of the earth.

To make up for it, we received bulletins containing lots of details about the upheaval. One bulletin said that Purishkevitsh had been named a minister—even head of the cabinet. Another bulletin said that Kerensky had been appointed to the cabinet. That last statement surprised everyone all the more.

Out in the street, I saw an army doctor whom I had once met in a hospital. Far in the distance, he began waving a document at me. He ran up, shook my hand, and exclaimed, "Mazel tov! Mazel tov! Just look!" And he showed me the document.

"What's that?"

"This is what Russia has been awaiting for three centuries! Nicholas has stepped down! He's renounced the throne!"

The document contained Nicholas's abdication text . . .

"Where'd you get this?"

"At headquarters. It's just been printed. They're keeping it a secret for now. But tomorrow they're going to announce it officially!"

However, the official declaration wasn't made by headquarters until a day later, when the newspapers confirmed that the revolution had taken place.

There were different rumors about Brusilov's reactions. Supposedly, upon receiving the wire from the new government, he stated, "I will do my duty toward the fatherland." A cautious response that anyone could interpret as he wished. According to later gossip, the coup had taken place with the compliance of the commanders, who, led by Ruzsky and Brusilov, had formed a secret alliance with the Constitutional Democrats.

However, it wasn't until March 4 that the *Kievskaya Misl* ran the first news of the revolution. Nicholas had given up the throne.

In the descriptions of the events in St. Petersburg, the phrase "Workers Councils" appeared with a large space between these two nouns, as if something had been omitted. I couldn't figure it out, but then I subsequently learned that either the writers hadn't had the courage, or the censor, still at his desk, had crossed out a few words. The phrase should have read: "Workers and Soldiers Councils." However, the frontline rank and file were to be kept in the dark.

Nothing was perceptible in the streets. The troops and the officers acted normally. When I approached a group of soldiers, I heard their comments:

"Everyone says that a ukase has been issued."

"Wait and see!"

"You can wait and wait!"

"What ukase are you talking about?" I asked.

"They say the government's issued a ukase granting soldiers a monthly pay of fifty rubles."

"Ha! Fifty rubles!" a skeptic retorted. "There isn't that much money in the whole treasury!"

Among Jews, the news triggered great interest, agitation, but no joy. They were terrified. First of all, they didn't believe that the revolution had succeeded. Who could tell what was going on in Russia? The next day might bring the news that the revolutionaries had all been hanged or shot and that Nicholas had retaken the throne. Second, the Jewish population feared that a revolution would make Russia stronger so that it would go on fighting the war—and absolutely no one wanted that. The sole concern of everybody here, Jew and Gentile, was whether the revolution would bring a speedy end to the war. Almost every Jew I met asked me: "Well? What's happening? Are we going to have peace now?"

I didn't know what to answer. I was certain that the revolution would spark a round of patriotism and drag out the war. But I didn't want to say that. Why make everyone worry?

The revolution brought so many changes in the overall Russian situation that attitudes began to change with regard to the occupied territories. We could now organize relief activities that we could never have dreamed of. Our top priorities were removing all specifically anti-Jewish restraints, ending the looting and murder, punishing the perpetrators, and, insofar as possible, giving restitution to the victims. In addition, deportees should be allowed to come home. We also had the task of reorganizing our activities on a democratic basis, putting the new communities in charge and convening assemblies. But the most important goal was to replace Trepov's administration.

For all these reasons, I had to leave for Petrograd immediately, hoping to implement everything without too much effort. My demands for the Galician Jews were consistent with the most elementary principles of justice and the members of the new government were almost like my family: Milyukov, Kerensky, and even Lvov were my good friends, people with whom I could easily discuss all these issues.

Aside from going to Petrograd to help the Galician Jews, I wanted to be at the center of this tremendous historical moment. But then something got in the way. I had agreed to take Passover money to several towns, no one else was available. Homelsky, who had other things to take care of, was away. If I went straight to Petrograd, I would be leaving some destitute towns without Passover assistance. As I yearned for Petrograd, I forced myself to stay on.

My itinerary would lead me to Seret, Sutshove, Raduts, and Gora-Humara—towns scattered across Bukovina, all the way to the Romanian border. There were no direct rail links. I had to make do with freight trains, wagons, and, where feasible, trucks. Moving as fast as possible, I made the trip in four or five days.

During that time, I was constantly thrown together with troops and officers, all of them in a holiday mood. People greeted one another joyfully, expressing their highest hopes, particularly with regard to the revolution's effect on the war. The officers voiced their delight openly; the rank and file were more restrained, more reticent, but listened to the swirling conversations with great interest. No one mentioned the czar. These people had an instinctive fear of his very name and would not dare utter a word against him.

I still met officers who knew nothing about the upheaval or had heard only vague rumors, so it became my job to tell them. I had taken along a newspaper, and people grabbed it out of my hand and read it aloud to other passengers.

On the train from Seret to Sutshove there were troops and officers as well as Cossacks. I read the description of events out loud. Everyone paid close and grave attention, as if listening to a prayer.

"The army has won a great victory," one officer stated.

"We were fighting two enemies," another one said. "Now we've defeated one."

"The army is breathing a sigh of relief."

Next to me sat a lieutenant colonel, who kept voicing his enthusiasm, especially about the speeches given by Rodzianko and Milyukov: "What men! What minds! They foresaw it all! They took care of everything!"

"They prepared the way!"

"You know," someone else interjected, "Purishkevitsh was here a month ago. When he was asked how things were in Petrograd, he said, 'Fine, thank God.' 'What's the news?' we asked. 'News?' he responded enigmatically. 'News? There may be news in February.' No one understood. But now we see that they knew and were ready for everything."

Even the news that all the Jewish lawyers had been promoted to barristers brought cries of satisfaction. "Fine. Everything will be in line with truth and justice. All the mommy's boys are going to lose their clout—no more nepotism for those little boys! So much for them!"

"Now they'll take the police out of the army."

A Cossack came over and quietly asked, "Is it true that they've kicked Kaiser Wilhelm in the backside?"

In general, the Cossacks were the most exuberant; they even dared to refer to the czar by name, dropping the title "His Majesty." On the other hand, among themselves, the officers talked about ridding themselves of the Cossacks and putting an end to their brutality.

People laughed when they heard about how cabinet ministers had hidden on the rooftops.

I gave my newspaper to an officer. He didn't know how to thank me. "I'm taking it to the front; I'll guard it like a sacred treasure. In Czernowitz they were charging sixty rubles a copy, yet still they were all sold out."

17

The four towns I toured during those few days were fairly small. Before the war they had each had eight to twelve thousand inhabitants, more than half Jewish. The wealthier Jews and the intelligentsia had left with the Austrians. The Russians had occupied the towns several times and carried out pogroms. On the whole, Seret, Sutshove, and Raduts had sustained little damage. But in Gora-Humara, I found terrible devastation.

The town, right by the Romanian border, lies in a very lovely mountain area reminiscent of Switzerland. Upon approaching, I heard a loud booming of cannon. I arrived very late and spent the night in an empty, muddy room that bore a sign: "Officers' Quarters." At dawn, I tracked down the kosher butcher, who, I had been told, was extremely prominent and who indeed made a very good impression on me. I found him and his entire family in a tiny room. The other rooms were occupied by soldiers. All in all, I felt the nearness of the front.

The butcher told me that at first the Russians had been calm. But then several days later, something awful happened. The Russians sent out reconnoiterers, whom the Austrians captured and killed. Supposedly, they had inflicted dreadful tortures, slicing off their tongues and gouging out their eyes. When the Russians found the mutilated corpses, they were furious. To retaliate, General Keller, who had taken Gora-Humara, ordered that it be burned to a crisp even though the peaceful citizens had in no way been involved with those atrocities. One morning, all the inhabitants were booted out of their homes and not allowed to take anything along. Cossacks then went from house to house, setting fire to each one. Practically the entire town went up in flames, including four synagogues with all their holy books.

Like the three other towns, Gora-Humara had several hundred needy Jewish refugees. In all these places I left 1,000 to 1,500 rubles for Passover plus 500 rubles for matzohs for the Jewish soldiers. According to the butcher, there were several thousand frontline Jewish soldiers asking for matzohs. I promised to transmit as much cash as necessary for the shipment.

The butcher also complained that the Zemstvo Alliance had commandeered the Jewish bathhouse, which had cost one hundred thousand Austrian crowns. Not only were the Jews deprived of their bathhouse, but it had been the only institution contributing money to the needy. (Subsequently, the community administration sent me an official petition to the alliance in regard to that matter.)

Leaving Gora-Humara, I heard stories about the relations between the Russian and the Romanian military. Initially, the latter had treated the Russians as friends. But gradually things had deteriorated, and now there were clashes. War erupted over every bale of hay, every bit of corn flour. A couple of days ago, a Russian division and a Romanian division had actually fought a battle over several wagons of hay—with casualties on both sides.

I was riding in a boxcar for horses. There were eight horses accompanied by soldiers. For the entire trip they argued about who was better off, infantry or cavalry.

"What's wrong with you people?" a trooper heatedly snapped. "You finish your training and you go strolling with the ladies or turn in, but we have to take care of our horses and everything else until four in the morning. We dig around in dung with our bare hands, and when we go to church we stink to high heaven."

The soldier he was talking to burst out laughing. "You certainly have a hard life! At the last station there was this fat gendarme. His whole job consists of walking out to the train—and he even complained about how hard it was! Ha!"

Late at night, a lieutenant colonel boarded the train. The soldiers stopped talking and laughing. The newcomer looked around. Spotting my officer's uniform, he cautiously moved toward me and asked in a soft, distraught voice: "Do you know what's happened in Petrograd? Do you have any details? I've just spent two weeks in an isolated farmhouse, and all I've heard are vague rumors."

I told him. The soldiers listened even though they already knew about the events. The lieutenant colonel was deeply surprised. He tsked and tsked and cried out in astonishment.

A Cossack who had come into our car exclaimed, "What are the Jews going to say now? This'll put an end to their machinations."

I broke in sharply. "It's time people stopped making such statements. There are no Jews now; all people are citizens with equal rights in a free Russia."

Needless to say, the officer agreed with me. "This isn't the right time to deal with them. Once we establish a new order, we can take care of the Jews."

A warning.

I assumed that during my few days of traveling, God only knew what changes had occurred in Czernowitz, that the torrent of revolution had swept this far. But I was wrong. Nonetheless, the papers ran staggering news every day. The revolutionary mood in Russia was intensifying by the hour, and yet here in Czernowitz it was as if nothing were happening. At a general assembly of the Zemstvo Alliance and the Association of Towns, revolutionary speeches were given and the members voted to send a welcoming telegram to Petrograd. A feverish excitement had taken hold of the military and the barracks and was, no doubt, at boiling point. But on the outside everything was normal. All the officials, with Trepov in the lead, were still in place. The bureaucratic machinery was the same as before. Whatever was happening in Russia seemed disconnected from this region.

Naturally, I had very little interest in the issue of authorization for Jewish welfare committees. Besides, I was certain that Trepov would allow them. But I went to see him about the permits anyway, just to gauge his mood. The atmosphere in his office was unchanged. The officials sat there working calmly, responding tersely to the servile petitioners. They let me wait for a long time. Then Trepov's adjutant came out and said in a cold, dry voice, "The governor-general finds it impossible to approve your request for authorization of relief committees in Czernowitz and the rest of Bukovina."

I was taken aback. I had been bitten by a dying snake that wanted us to feel its power for at least one more day.

Krilov came out shortly. Embarrassed, unable to look me in the eye, he stammered, "Just imagine! The governor-general refused to sanction the committees. . . . I just don't understand him—at a time like this . . ."

I couldn't help laughing. "Don't worry. We'll manage without his permission."

"Of course, of course. . . . A time like this . . ."

The Jewish leaders in Czernowitz had little faith in the Russian revolution. At the meeting I called that night, I informed them of my future plans and suggested that the local Jewish administration should petition the new Russian regime about the Bukovina Jews and their complete lack of rights. But nearly everyone disagreed.

"We don't know and don't understand what's going on in your Russia! Who can say what'll happen a few days from now? What if everything is suddenly restored? That's why we'd rather avoid coming out with anything for now so that they won't give us any grief later on."

The next day, when I made the same proposal at a similar gathering in Tarnopol, the response was the same, and the following reason was added: "Don't forget that we're Austrian subjects and we're loyal to our fatherland and our government. We can't send any sort of petitions about our rights to the enemy government, no matter how liberal and revolutionary it may be."

I concurred, and I dropped the matter. In Tarnopol, I witnessed the first street demonstration by soldiers, who carried red flags and sang the "Marseillaise." Next, speeches were given by orators standing on a wagon in the square. They were too far away for me to hear them, but I could see them yelling, twisting, gesticulating, and straining every nerve. And every phrase provoked a roar of applause.

18

I reached Kiev on March 11. There I handed in my accounts and any remaining funds. I also submitted my plan for further assistance in Galicia and Bukovina. First, the committee should convene delegates from the local aid groups, elected by the communities, all of whom would then decide on future activities. I also drew up a report for the provisional government about the Jewish situation in the occupied territories, calling for necessary reforms.

During my two days in Kiev, I attended two meetings. One was called by the Socialist-Revolutionaries, and I expected to hear the same fulsome demagogic claptrap as in 1905. But this time, the mood was very different—it was sober and earnest. The speakers warned against empty phrases and demanded that we commit twice as much strength to the work ahead of us. I recall one remark: "The prodigal son has come home as a victor with a laurel wreath. He has found his house adorned with flowers on the outside, but inside he has discovered an unburied corpse.

This corpse is the war. We have to finish the war. And until then we must not speak of holidays, of celebrations."

A poignant scene took place. The chairman proposed that they honor the memory of the fallen warriors, but rather than standing up, all the people in the room fell to their knees and sang "An Everlasting Memorial."

The second gathering, a typical one, was organized by political prisoners who had returned from prison or Siberia. Some had been away for ten or twelve years. They were pale, emaciated, poorly clad, with thick beards, intelligent faces, feverishly sparkling eyes. Their voices were loud but not bold, and their movements were uncertain and shaky. They looked like the dead arisen from their graves.

The meeting had been called by the political Red Cross for the purpose of establishing help for the prisoners who had nothing to eat and nowhere to sleep. But not a word was said about that all evening. The politicals gave solemn speeches about the dreadful situation of their criminal comrades and demanded that they too be given amnesties. At the very least, their sentences should be reviewed because over half the prisoners were innocent. Several highly anxious women talked about the dreadful plight and inhuman work of the prison matrons and demanded that the government improve their conditions. At the very end, the president of the Red Cross touched on the actual reason for the gathering and indicated that several people here had no place to spend the night.

I was profoundly moved by the idealism of the young martyrs, but they sounded so impractical and helpless in their speeches that I was terrified not only for them but for the country they now ruled.

On March 13 , I was in Petrograd. At this point, I don't wish to dwell on the events I witnessed during that stormy period. I only want to mention that what surprised me most was the general mood of the city. Two weeks had passed since the upheaval, and the atmosphere was still mellow, celebratory, fraternal. In the streets, in the trolleys, in the lines outside shops, indeed everywhere, there was not a single shout, a single curse. People addressed each other tenderly as "comrade," and at the outdoor meetings taking place day and night, you heard praises for the revolution and all sorts of idealistic demands.

Nevertheless, you sensed that something fearful was imminent, that the revolution had no solid foundation, that the government had no power, and that the army was starting to disintegrate. Order No. 1, sent to the army by the Workers' and Soldiers' Council and flouting all military discipline, caused horrible turmoil in both military and civilian circles. The council itself then got scared and rescinded the order, but it was too late. There were already two regimes, the provisional government and the Workers' and Soldiers' Council, and each ignored the other.

Since my report on Galicia and Bukovina dealt with foreign nationals, I had to approach Foreign Minister Milyukov. Besides, I was better acquainted with him than with any other cabinet member. He received me on March 15, and I submitted the following text:

Citizen Minister!

May it please you to focus your attention on the terrible situation of the populace in those sectors of Galicia and Bukovina that are occupied by the Russian military. Dozens of towns and townlets have been completely or almost completely burned down and destroyed. Thousands of peaceful civilians have been killed by fire and sword, by hunger and poverty. All economic and cultural life has been devastated. However, the population has endured all these calamities with a certain amount of patience, treating them as unfortunate consequences of the horrible war.

But aside from the sufferings and difficulties caused by the war, one segment of the population has been and still is subjected to extraordinary persecutions that are linked solely to the nationality of these inhabitants.

As we know, the Jews in Austria have the same rights as any other citizens of that country. But when the region was occupied by the Russian military, the local Jews, as has now been determined, proved loyal to the Russian occupation authorities, contrary to all defamation, and never provided them with any reason for special persecutions. Nonetheless, from the very first day of the occupation, the local Jews were deprived of not only all equal rights but also the most elementary human rights, so that they were virtually outlaws.

Jews everywhere have been expelled from municipal governments, law courts, and other institutions where they still remained. Jewish community administrations, which dealt with cultural and charitable matters, have been shut down. Jewish landowners, leaseholders, businessmen, and artisans have been driven from the villages; the properties of the landowners have been requisitioned or laid waste. In dozens of towns and townlets, every last [Jewish] inhabitant has been booted out, sometimes within hours, and sent to Russia. In some places, rich and educated Jews have been taken hostage and usually deported to Siberia with not even the semblance of a trial or inquiry.

At the same time the occupation authorities have ruined and keep ruining the Jews and keep looting their property. Hundreds, indeed thousands, of stores and homes are being confiscated or simply pillaged. The thefts, the lootings, the graft perpetrated by the administration, from the topmost to the lowest ranks, have ballooned to such vast proportions that the infamy cries to high heaven, and the authorities that carry out these plunderings are joined by the town governments, which were chosen by the basest elements of the population.

Furthermore, the administrations, especially the bottom echelons, treat Jews with immeasurable cruelty. Jews are cursed at, insulted, and often beaten. Nowhere do the authorities respect the Jewish faith. Quite the contrary; they make every effort to desecrate what Jews hold sacred. On the Sabbath and on holy days the Jews are forced to clean the streets, dig trenches, sit in stores; and with few exceptions, Jewish houses of worship have been destroyed or turned into hospitals, barracks, and even stables and toilets. The Torah scrolls have been ripped up everywhere and their parchment bindings made into sacks, drums, shoes, and so forth. And the holy books in all synagogues have been torn up and burned.

Given all these things, may I, in the name of human rights and international law, appeal to you, Citizen Minister, to restore the rights to the Jews in the occupied territories. That is:

1. [May I ask you to] order the return of Jewish officials to their positions in municipal governments, courts of law, and other institutions, from which they have been expelled because they are Jews.
2. Allow the Jews to reinstate community administrations for cultural and charitable activities.
3. Allow the Jews to reopen their elementary and middle schools because during these two and a half years the lack of

schooling has been very destructive to the younger generation.

4. Allow Jews to go back to their villages, townlets, and towns, from which they were driven, and to regain at least some of their homes, which were commandeered for military purposes and for use as hospitals.

5. Release the hostages and allow them to go home.

6. Have a separate trial for each deported Jew and repatriate the innocent ones.

7. Stop the confiscations of property and merchandise belonging to Jews still in Austria and rigorously investigate the earlier requisitions and robberies.

8. Exempt the Jews from forced labor and commerce on the Sabbath and on holy days if no exception is necessary.

9. Restore the synagogues to the Jews, and together with that we request that the Holy Synod ask the military not to touch the Jewish schools and synagogues, the Torah scrolls, or any sacred articles and holy books, just like sacred Christian objects.

10. Give the Jews back the bathhouses, which, aside from their hygienic importance, also have a religious significance.

11. All Jews whose homes, businesses, merchandise, or property were wrecked, not through the events of the war, and all landowners whose inventories have been requisitioned or wrecked, should be given a certain amount of [financial] support to rebuild their homes, their stores, or resume their farming.

I hope that the provisional government, which has introduced human and civil rights in the renewed Russia, will turn its attention to the unbearable conditions of the peaceful inhabitants in the occupied areas of Galicia and Bukovina and will restore to these civilians the rights they were robbed of by the servants of the old regime.

Please be assured, Citizen Minister, of my deepest feelings of respect, devotion, and enthusiasm for your heroic deeds.

Milyukov received me in the foreign ministry. He was friendly and down-to-earth, as in earlier times. Delivering my written report, I told him about the Jewish situation in Galicia. He listened carefully, promised to convey my report to the cabinet and to help meet my demands. It turned out that the minister wasn't even clear about what kind of administration had been set up in the occupied territory.

"Is that a military administration?" he asked me.

"No, a civilian one. There's a governor-general."

"What's his name?"

"Trepov, the son of the famous Trepov. He's a fierce reactionary. And so far he's behaving as if nothing's happened."

Milyukov was shocked. "What are you talking about? I didn't realize. There's so much work to be done. . . . We've had no time to think about that region. Besides, I was sure that everything there was in the hands of the military. . . . Needless to say, we have to get rid of Trepov immediately. But I don't know whom to replace him with."

"If you'll permit me, I can suggest a suitable candidate."

"By all means, please do."

"Prince P. T. Dolgorukov. He spent a long time in Galicia, he's acquainted with the local conditions, and the inhabitants have the fondest memories of him."

"Right! That's very true! He's the most suitable man for the position. I'm just not certain that he'll accept. He's going to be here in a day or two, and I'll offer him the job."

I stood up to leave, but the minister held me back. "Stay a bit. I want to ask you something. You've been to Galicia, you've traveled quite a distance to get here, and you've met a lot of people. What's your impression of the overall situation?"

"May I be very frank?"

"That's what I'm asking for. I'm very interested in hearing what an outsider has to say."

"This is my impression. The revolution has aroused joy and enthusiasm everywhere—both among civilians and in the military. The enemies of the revolution are hidden and silent. But they haven't disappeared. They're strong, and they're waiting. A defeated enemy usually throws himself at the victor's feet purely in order to trip him up."

"Right!"

"Well, and I have to say that one doesn't sense a strong government presence in the country. At this very serious juncture the government should be strong and decisive, terrify its enemies and offer potent support to its friends. But this isn't happening. One has the impression that there's no order in this country, that all doors are open and everyone can do as he wishes."

Milyukov sat there for a while, silent, lost in thought. Then he leaned toward me, put his hand on my knees, and in deep and intimate sadness he said: "You think we don't understand? We understand and feel it very clearly. I assure you: We'd have a strong government if we really had the reins in our hands for just two hours. But we've never had the de facto power for even two hours."

The next day I met with M. Vinaver and told him about my audience with the minister. He thought that my report on Galicia should also be submitted to Prince Lvov, the head of the cabinet. On March 19, Vinaver did so. On March 20, I delivered my report at the Petrograd relief committee and proposed that we organize a meeting in Galicia and Bukovina. The committee agreed with my ideas.

To get the government to initiate the reforms in Galicia more quickly, Deputy Fridman, who ran the Jewish Press Bureau, sent a copy of my report to every newspaper. It was printed in all Jewish newspapers, two Russian ones in Petrograd, *Dielo Naroda* and *Dien*, and many provincial ones.

But neither the press nor our personal appeals moved the government. The ministers kept expressing their complete willingness to take all necessary steps but maintained, "We can't do everything at once." Moreover, they said that everything would be implemented by the administrator of Galicia and Bukovina, who would be designated any day now to replace Trepov.

Two weeks after I submitted my report, the newspapers announced that Prince Dolgorukov had been appointed governor-general of Galicia and Bukovina. At this point, I was in Moscow, and when I telephoned the prince's quarters, I was told he had left for Galicia.

But imagine my surprise a few days later when I found out that the post was to be held not by Dolgorukov but by A. Doroshenko, chairman of the Kiev division of the Zemstvo Alliance. Eventually, I learned that the prince had actually been named, but that he had been bitterly opposed by Kiev's parliament, the Rada, which had formed under the leadership of Professor Grushevsky. When Milyukov had been in Kiev, the Rada representatives had banged their fists on the table and ominously shouted that they would not brook a Muscovite administrator for Ukrainian Galicia. They demanded a Ukrainian, suggested Doroshenko, and the government buckled so as not to provoke the Rada.

I also approached the justice minister—first Kerensky, then Pereverzev, his representative—about sending a commission to Galicia to investigate all the acts perpetrated against the Jews by the military and civilian authorities. The commission should include lawyers of the various ethnic groups in that region: a Jew, a Pole, a Ruthenian. The ministers accepted my idea but kept putting off the decision from day to day. At last, Pereverzev officially endorsed the commission and even agreed to include two Jews, one Pole, one Ruthenian, and one Russian. In accordance with my proposal, they invited the Jewish attorneys Shaul Ginzburg (former editor of *Friend*) and Arnold Zaydenman (a Zionist leader). But their departure kept getting delayed, and just as everything was ready and they were about to leave, a catastrophe erupted. The Austrians broke through the Russian front, and the Russians pulled out of Galicia and Bukovina.

While appealing to the government, I had also sent the newspapers my open letter to the Holiest Synod about the atrocities committed by the Christ-loving military against the synagogues and Torah scrolls. I demanded that the synod order the military to behave respectfully toward what the Jews hold sacred. At the same time, I gave Dr. Aizenshtat, Petrograd's government rabbi, all the items (sacks, drum skins, shoes, and so forth) made from the scroll parchments. I wanted him to show them personally to the Petrograd metropolitan. Dr. Aizenshtat did so, and the synod, according to the rabbi, issued such an appeal to the military. I never saw the appeal and know nothing about its text.

19

The events taking place in Petrograd were so important and stupendous that as I was drawn into them, I had to terminate my mission in Galicia. I knew that the welfare campaign was in good hands: Homelsky supplied Passover matzohs to all the towns and to the Jewish soldiers and Dr. Lander resumed his work there. Moreover, since Doroshenko—a decent man and an ardent socialist—had been appointed commissar of Galicia and Bukovina, the Jewish situation was bound to improve tremendously.

In mid-April, a conference of the relief committees of the Kiev region took place. Dr. Lander's speech about the Jewish situation in Galicia and Bukovina made a profound impression. A motion was passed to call a meeting of the representatives of the Kiev relief committees and the representatives of the Jewish administrations in those provinces. The purpose of this get-together was to thoroughly rework the entire welfare effort.

Top priority was given to regulating the economic life of the Jewish communities that had returned to their homes: Zhvanets, Tarnarude, Husiatyn, Satano, Zbarz, and so on. It was also decided that the relief committees in both Russia and Galicia should be reorganized, so that the members would be elected, with no less than one third representing the homeless. The committees themselves would now function not in individual but in collective terms: cooperatives, help through jobs, et cetera.

The group further resolved: to petition the government to increase the assistance for Jewish war victims and to repatriate the Galician Jews, who, although completely innocent of any crimes, had been deported to Siberia and to many towns in European Russia.

The delegates also voted to send me the following telegram: "The Kiev District Conference of representatives of relief committees for the homeless, having listened to the report given by Comrade P. Lander about the welfare activities benefiting the Jewish population of Galicia, ardently greets you, dear S. A., as a self-sacrificing worker striving to ease the situation of our Galician brethren. The conference sends you its fervent wishes that you may continue your self-sacrificing work for our people for many more years."

As soon as Doroshenko became commissar of Galicia and Bukovina, the Kiev front committee in the All-Russian Zemstvo Alliance created a special commission headed by F. Linitshenko. Its goal: to decide whether to establish a civilian administration in Galicia and what steps were to be taken in rebuilding the ruined communities. The commission invited representatives of the Jewish and Ukrainian relief committees.

I don't quite recall whether I happened to be in Kiev or was specifically summoned there, but the committee designated me and H. B. Veynshlboym (its secretary) as its delegates to that commission.

At the first session, acting on behalf of the Kiev committee, I greeted Mr. Doroshenko as free Russia's first representative in Galicia, a man in whom Jews could place their trust, confident that he would terminate the disenfranchisement of Jews and the violence inflicted on them. I called not only for the elimination of all kinds of barriers but also for the reestablishment of the Jewish administrations with autonomous authority in cultural and charitable activities and with the right to participate in the municipal governments. Next I focused on the specific ways in which the Jewish situation differed from the overall state of affairs in Galicia. Because of those features, I went on, the commissar's Galician administration should include an official representative of the Jewish population, a man to deal with Jewish matters.

Doroshenko reacted warmly, saying he not only accepted my proposal but also planned to introduce such representatives in the administrations of the commissars of Tarnopol and Czernowitz. He then asked me and Veynshlboym to suggest a suitable candidate.

There were only two possible men for the job, Dr. Lander and Mr. Homelsky. But since Dr. Lander was older and more experienced, and since he had been working in Galicia all this time, and as a military physician to boot, we considered him the more suitable nominee. We recommended him but pointed out that he was in military service, that he had an official position, and that his appointment to the Galician administration would require approval by his superiors. Since it was up to Brusilov, Doroshenko asked him to release Lander from his current duties and assign him to the Galician commissariat. That was how the participants of that session put Lander in charge of Jewish affairs in Galicia. We saw it as a giant leap forward.

At that same meeting, Veynshlboym raised the question of repatriating the innocent Galician Jews. The government had stated that it had no objections and was willing to grant permission, but the local authorities were creating difficulties. Just the other day, a group of deportees, traveling at government expense, had arrived from Siberia. But they had been stopped here in Kiev, and the Tatyana committee refused to issue the required travel permits. The reason: "We should not allow homeless people" (read: "Jews") "to get to the front." Nor was this an isolated episode.

Veynshlboym's protest was seconded by the representative from the Association of Towns. The commission passed a resolution to clarify the matter and remove any obstacles impeding the homeless. But this was of little help. Despite all government promises, the tens of thousands of expelled and deported Galician Jews were not permitted to return to their homes.

On April 25, Linitshenko, the commission's chairman, painted a nightmarish picture of the food crisis in occupied Galicia, and he categorically opposed a mass return of the deported and the homeless at this moment since it could lead to mass starvation. However, once the food crisis, which they were now dealing with, was overcome, they would be able to implement a systematic repatriation of the deportees and the homeless. Until then, they would have to block it. At the same time, the Department for the Homeless dispatched the following circular to all the relief organizations:

> According to information that we have received, there is a strong push among the homeless to immediately return to their homes or to a frontline area. Given the current events in Russia, their desire to get as close as possible to their homes is understandable; nevertheless, the Department for the Homeless considers it its duty to announce that because of the shortages of food, housing, and all the necessities of life, the frontline military authorities are urgently demanding that all measures be taken to halt the return of the homeless. Their uncontrolled return is certain to bring mass diseases and create terrible living conditions for both the

repatriates and the local population, since under such circumstances it would be impossible to organize a relief committee.

Considering the tremendous significance of this question for the welfare of the homeless and for maintaining the necessary order and medical care in the rear of the Russian army, the department is urgently asking all national and social relief organizations to explain to the homeless the full dangers of returning to the places destroyed by the war and devoid of even the most basic provisions. Furthermore, these organizations should take all possible measures to stop the unchecked influx of the homeless to the front. They should likewise point out to the homeless that according to orders from the military authorities, the railroads are not permitted to accept the homeless or carry them to the combat region.

The special commission, together with the representatives of the national relief organizations, worked out a project for the civil organization of occupied Galicia. It would include the establishment of local self-government.

Contrary to the former system of oppression and despotism, the order of the new Russian state requires:

1. The establishment of local self-government in both villages and towns.
2. Complete freedom for the population both in setting up the old forms of self-government and in rebuilding them on new foundations; in this way the population can avoid any pressure, which goes against the principles of international law.
3. Participation in the revival of social organizations such as cooperatives, loan societies, ethnic and charitable committees. Establishment of law courts on the basis of local laws and restoration of the autonomous rights formerly enjoyed by the Jewish community administrations.
4. These revived social organizations must gradually take over the relief activities currently implemented by the Zemstvo Alliance and the Association of Towns.

The project was approved by the government, but before it could be carried out in the occupied territories, the Russians vanished from them. Almost a month passed before Brusilov's staff gave official authorization for putting Dr. Lander in charge of Jewish matters for the commissar of Galicia. He held that position for some two months. As he told me afterward, he endured a lot of fear and difficulty until the Russian retreat.

From the very first moment of his tenure, he kept running into the adamant resistance of the military, which was growing more and more reactionary, evincing more and more antisemitism. Doroshenko behaved very decently toward Lander and agreed with his suggestions. Unhappily, the commissar's de facto power was very limited. People simply disobeyed him, ignored his directives, and even did the opposite of what he demanded. The Jewish representative heard complaints and laments from many towns and hamlets about all sorts of arbitrary actions, lootings, military pogroms. But there was nothing he could do. The screams and protests about plunderings and unlawful requisitions in Stanislavov even reached Fridman, the former Duma deputy. He officially asked Doroshenko about it and received a very unsatisfactory answer. Throughout that period, Dr. Lander kept dashing from place to place, trying to shield the Jews, which left him no time for organizational work.

The real hell began for him with the pullout of the disintegrated and demoralized Russian army, which launched a series of terrible pogroms. Lander himself was caught in the Tarnopol pogrom and barely escaped with his life. Nevertheless, he managed to save Czernowitz from a pogrom that had been organized and was about to erupt.

20

Some months later, Tarnopol was the site of a conference. Representatives of the Kiev committee got together with delegates from Jewish community administrations and relief committees in Galicia. To my great regret, I was unable to attend. Nor did I subsequently glean any precise information about the meeting—about its makeup, its activities, its resolutions. All I knew was that the participants had been in high spirits and labored intensively on a whole system of plans for reorganizing welfare on both an efficient and democratic foundation.

I received the following wire:

THE FIRST CONFERENCE OF THE REPRESENTATIVES OF THE JEWISH
POPULATIONS IN GALICIA AND BUKOVINA, CONVENING IN TARNOPOL,
GREETS YOU AS THE PREMIER REPRESENTATIVE OF RUSSIAN JEWRY IN
GALICIA, THE PREMIER DEFENDER OF OUR BRETHREN IN THESE DIFFI-
CULT TIMES. YOU WERE THE FIRST TO ESTABLISH A CLOSE TIE BETWEEN
THE RUSSIAN JEWS AND THE GALICIAN JEWS, AND YOU ONCE AGAIN
CONFIRMED THE WORLDWIDE UNITY OF THE JEWISH PEOPLE. FOR THE
MORAL SUPPORT THAT YOU BROUGHT US, WE SEND YOU OUR HEART-
FELT GREETINGS AND OUR MOST FERVENT WISHES.

THE EXECUTIVE COMMITTEE OF THE CONFERENCE:
GRINBERG, VAYNFELD, AND KRUP

This deeply poignant telegram was the last word that I received from
our Galician comrades.

There was only one more time that I acted on behalf of Galician Jews.
On July 21, at the preliminary meeting (which I did manage to attend), I
suggested that the conference should include representatives of the Jewish deportees in Russia and of the sixty thousand Jews in the occupied
areas of Galicia and Bukovina.

By now, the second half of my motion was unnecessary. Nearly the
entire Russian military had already left those sectors. In its panicky
retreat, it had soaked the region in Jewish blood.

The Russian occupation of Galicia, inaugurated by the grim power of
czarist autocracy, had commenced with bloody pogroms in Brody and
Lwow. And now, in the storm of revolution, it had reached its finale,
when the collapsing and degenerate Russian army wrought dreadful
havoc in Kalushts and Tarnopol. But I would rather not dwell on the
horrible and bestial pogroms that raged in Kalushts and Tarnopol. . . .

That was the end of the horrifying epic, the three years of Russian rule
in the occupied territory, the bloody destruction of major Jewish centers
in Poland, Galicia, and Bukovina.

Shvat 5680 / February 1920

Index

About the Author

S. ANSKY (1863–1920), writer, politician, and folklorist, is perhaps best known for his classic play, *The Dybbuk.* Born Shloyme Zanvel Rappaport in Vitebsk, within Russia's Pale of Settlement, Ansky was a vocal and visible Russian and Yiddish journalist as well as a powerful force in socialist politics, even serving in the Russian Duma prior to the Bolshevik revolution. His greatest contribution, however, was the archive he built of Russian-Jewish folklore—songs, stories, and superstitions—collected during his many ethnographic expeditions in the Pale of Settlement.